# the GREAT SOUTHERN FOOD Festival ★★★ Cookbook

*Celebrating Everything from Peaches to Peanuts, Onions to Okra*

## MINDY B. HENDERSON

THOMAS NELSON
*Since 1798*

NASHVILLE  DALLAS  MEXICO CITY  RIO DE JANEIRO  BEIJING

Published in Nashville, Tennessee, by Thomas Nelson. Thomas Nelson is a registered trademark of Thomas Nelson, Inc.

Thomas Nelson, Inc. titles may be purchased in bulk for educational, business, fund-raising, or sales promotional use. For information, please e-mail SpecialMarkets@ThomasNelson.com.

Page design by Walter Petrie

**Library of Congress Cataloging-in-Publication Data**

Henderson, Mindy B., 1960–
  The great Southern food festival cookbook : celebrating everything from peaches to peanuts, onions to okra / Mindy Henderson, Bryan Curtis.
    p. cm.
  Includes index.
  ISBN 978-1-4016-0361-8
  1. Cookery, American—Southern style.  2. Festivals—Southern States.  I. Curtis, Bryan, 1960–
II. Title.
TX715.2.S68H46 2008
641.5975—dc22                                                          2008005114

Printed in the United States of America

08 09 10 11 12  QW  5 4 3 2 1

# Contents

## August                                                                145

## September                                                             167

## October                                                               209

## November     267

# Acknowledgments

Thank you to my friend for life, Bryan Curtis, for helping me collect information and recipes for this book. Another fun adventure for us to add to our list, Bryan!

Thank you also to my mom, Carolyn Jenkins Booth, who instilled in me, through her great cooking, the love of good Southern food. Thanks, Mom!

# Introduction

Hospitality—the friendly reception of guests or strangers—defines the South. Whether having company over for dinner, taking food to someone who feels under the weather, or maybe just easing someone's day with a smile or a wave of the hand, Southerners are famous for their hospitality. But in many places across the South, Southern hospitality gets done up really big once a year when Southerners host a festival that might bring thousands or sometimes hundreds of thousands of people to town for a visit.

While you will find all kinds of festivals around the South honoring everything from music to mules, it is the food festival that really helps define a town and its people. These festivals in many cases started as a way to honor local farmers, and that's one reason many still exist today. But the festivals do so much more; they put a spotlight on an entire community—city government, local cooks, high school bands, and local artists, just to name a few.

As you read through the pages of this book, you will see plenty of chances to eat good food at any of the 75 Southern food festivals included here. But if you stop at the food, you'll miss not only every kind of beauty pageant you can imagine, but also such delightful traditions as toilet seat horseshoes, hog calling, cow chip bingo, greased pole climbing, Elvis impersonators, parades, eating contests, and even outhouse races. Southern food festivals reveal the very personality of the town and of the people who throw these huge parties.

As I gathered the material for this book, I had the good fortune to talk with many of the people involved in the planning of these Southern food festivals. All of them share one vital characteristic: pride in their community and the festival they help put on. And they were all very excited to know that readers of this book who might never have heard about the Irmo Okra Strut or the RC and Moon Pie Festival will now know a little more about them—and even better—might make a trip there some time soon.

I hope as you read through this book that you will come to better understand the South—a place where knowing how to fry chicken is honored and where hospitality never goes out of style.

**AUTHOR'S NOTE:** At the time of the publication of this book, all the information provided about each festival was correct. Before planning a trip to one of these wonderful events, please consult the festival Web site or the local chamber of commerce for updated information.

# January

# Florida Citrus Festival

**WHERE:** Winter Haven, Florida

**WHEN:** Third Thursday in January through the following Sunday (an 11-day festival)

The Florida Citrus Festival began in 1924 and draws an estimated 150,000 people each year to its various events. This festival, a part of the Polk County Fair, combines traditional fair events such as livestock shows, midway rides, and every kind of food you can imagine with activities specific to the citrus festival, including four different beauty pageants, karaoke competitions, a battle of the bands, a citrus cooking competition, and one of the festival highlights—the grapefruit packing contest.

For more information, please visit *www.citrusfestival.com*.

## DID YOU KNOW?

Almost all of the flowers on a citrus tree fall off. Less than 1 percent remain and become fruit.

## Southern Lemon Pound Cake

*Cake:*

3   cups all-purpose flour

1/8 teaspoon salt

1/2 teaspoon baking powder

1/2 cup vegetable shortening

1   cup (2 sticks) butter, softened

3   cups sugar

5   eggs

1   tablespoon lemon flavoring

1   cup milk

*Frosting:*

1   pound confectioners' sugar

1   (8-ounce) package cream cheese, softened

2   tablespoons lemon juice, at room temperature

■  For the cake, preheat the oven to 325 degrees. In a medium bowl, sift the flour, baking powder, and salt together. In a separate large bowl, mix the shortening, butter, and sugar together until light and fluffy. Add one egg at a time, beating for 1 minute after each addition. Add the lemon flavoring and beat for 30 seconds. Add portions of the dry ingredients alternately with the milk, and beat until completely mixed. Pour the mixture into a greased and floured 10-inch Bundt or tube pan, and bake for 80 minutes. Remove from the oven and cool.

■  For the frosting, sift the confectioner's sugar into a medium bowl. Mix in the cream cheese. Add the lemon juice, 1/2 teaspoon at a time, until the frosting reaches spreading consistency. Spread the frosting on the cooled cake.

**MAKES 12 SERVINGS**

## Florida Citrusade

6    lemons, divided

6    oranges, divided

4    limes

3    quarts water

1 1/2 cups sugar

■  Combine the juice from 5 of the lemons, 5 of the oranges, and the limes in 1-gallon pitcher. Thinly slice the remaining 1 lemon and the remaining 1 orange and set aside. Add the water and sugar to the pitcher and mix well. Chill thoroughly and refrigerate until ready to serve. Pour into glasses over ice and serve with the orange and lemon slices.

**MAKES ABOUT 1 GALLON**

## Orange Pecan Pound Cake

1    cup vegetable shortening

3    cups sugar

6    eggs

3    cups all-purpose flour

1/4    teaspoon baking soda

1/4    teaspoon salt

1    (8-ounce) container sour cream

1 1/2    tablespoons orange extract

1    cup chopped pecans
     Confectioners' sugar (optional)

■ Preheat the oven to 325 degrees. Grease and flour a 10-inch Bundt or tube pan. Cream the shortening in the bowl of a mixer. Gradually add the sugar, beating well at medium speed. Add the eggs one at a time, beating well after each addition.

■ Combine the flour, baking soda, and salt in a small bowl. Add to the creamed mixture alternately with the sour cream, beginning and ending with the flour mixture. Mix just until blended after each addition. Stir in the orange extract and chopped pecans.

■ Pour into the prepared pan. Bake for 90 minutes or until a toothpick inserted in the center of the cake comes out clean. Allow the cake to cool in the pan for 10 to 15 minutes.

Remove the cake from the pan and let cool completely. Cover the cake with sifted confectioners' sugar, if desired.

**MAKES 12 SERVINGS**

## Key Lime Cookies

2    cups all-purpose flour

1    teaspoon baking powder

1/4    teaspoon salt

1/2    cup (1 stick) butter, softened

1 1/4    cups sugar

1    egg plus 1 egg yolk

5    tablespoons fresh key lime juice

2    teaspoons grated lime rind
     Confectioners' sugar

■ Preheat the oven to 350 degrees. In a medium bowl combine the flour, baking powder and salt; set aside. In a large mixing bowl, cream the butter and sugar until fluffy. Add the egg and egg yolk, beating until light and creamy. Add the lime juice and lime rind and beat until well mixed. Stir in the flour mixture until just mixed. The dough will be soft. Form the dough into 1/2-inch balls and place on a cookie sheet. If the dough is too soft to handle it can be refrigerated until firm enough to gently shape into balls. Bake until lightly browned, about 10 to

12 minutes. Transfer the cookies to a wire rack. While still warm, sift confectioners' sugar over the cookies. Cool completely.

**MAKES ABOUT 24 COOKIES**

# Fresh Grapefruit Cake

*Cake:*

2/3    cup butter, softened

1 3/4   cups sugar

2     eggs

3     cups sifted cake flour

1/2   teaspoon salt

2 1/2   teaspoons baking powder

1/2   cup grapefruit juice

3/4   cup milk

1     teaspoon grated grapefruit rind

1 1/2   teaspoons vanilla extract

*Grapefruit Frosting:*

1 1/2   cups sugar

2     egg whites

1     tablespoon light corn syrup

1/8   teaspoon salt

1/3   cup grapefruit juice

1     tablespoon grated grapefruit rind

2     teaspoons vanilla

■ For the cake, preheat the oven to 350 degrees. Grease and flour two 9-inch round cake pans. Cream the butter in the bowl of a mixer. Gradually add the sugar, beating well. Add the eggs, one at a time, beating well after each addition.

■ In a separate bowl combine the flour, salt, and baking powder. Add to the creamed mixture, alternating with the grapefruit juice, beginning and ending with the flour mixture. Mix just until blended after each addition. Gradually add the milk. Stir in the grapefruit rind and vanilla; mix well.

■ Pour the batter into the prepared cake pans. Bake for 25 minutes. Cool in the pans for 10 minutes. Remove the cakes from the pans and let cool completely on a wire rack.

■ For the frosting, combine the sugar, egg whites, corn syrup, salt, and grapefruit juice in the top of a double boiler. Beat at low speed with an electric mixer for 30 seconds or just until mixed. Place over boiling water, beating constantly at high speed for 7 minutes or until stiff peaks are formed. Remove from the heat. Add the grapefruit rind and vanilla. Return to the heat for 1 to 2 minutes or until the frosting is thick enough to spread. Spread the frosting between each layer and on the top and side of the cake.

**MAKES 12 SERVINGS**

## Orange Walnut French Toast

| 1 | loaf Italian bread, cut into 1-inch-thick slices |
|---|---|
| 4 | eggs |
| 2/3 | cup orange juice |
| 1/2 | cup milk |
| 1/4 | cup sugar |
| 1/4 | teaspoon nutmeg |
| 1 | teaspoon vanilla extract |
| 1/4 | cup (1/2 stick) butter, melted |
| 1/2 | cup chopped walnuts |

■ Place the bread slices in a single layer in a 2-quart casserole dish. Beat the eggs in a large bowl. Add the orange juice, milk, sugar, nutmeg, and vanilla and mix together with a whisk. Pour the mixture over the bread. Cover and refrigerate overnight, turning the bread slices one time before preparing the next morning.

■ When ready to cook, preheat the oven to 400 degrees. Pour the melted butter onto a baking pan and spread evenly. Arrange the soaked bread slices in a single layer in the pan. Sprinkle evenly with the nuts. Bake for 20 to 25 minutes or until golden brown.

**MAKES 3 TO 4 SERVINGS**

### DID YOU KNOW?
Navel oranges are so named because of the belly-button-shaped bump on the bottom. The larger the navel, the sweeter the orange.

# February

# Chocolate Lovers Festival

**WHERE:** Fairfax, Virginia

**WHEN:** The first weekend of February (Saturday and Sunday)

Sure, you'll find things like a kids' play area, bake sales, arts and crafts, and open houses at Fairfax's historic buildings—stuff you find at other festivals all across the South. But the Chocolate Lovers Festival is really about one thing: Chocolate. Here you can join the thousands who come to taste the wares of hundreds of chocolate vendors and visit the Chocolate Challenge, an art contest where the medium is chocolate—and we are talking about sculptures and cakes. There's also a pancake breakfast—but at the Chocolate Lovers Festival, the pancakes are, of course, chocolate chip.

For more information, please visit *www.chocolatefestival.net*.

## DID YOU KNOW?

The first European to discover chocolate is believed to be Christopher Columbus. Upon returning from his fourth voyage to the New World in 1502, one of the treasures he presented to the Spanish court was cocoa beans.

# Triple Chocolate Pound Cake

1   (18.25-ounce) package double chocolate or chocolate fudge cake mix
1   (3-ounce) package instant chocolate pudding mix
4   eggs
1   cup sour cream
4   ounces cream cheese, softened
1/2   cup oil
1/2   cup water
11/2   cups semisweet chocolate chips

■ Preheat the oven to 350 degrees. Grease and flour a 12-cup fluted tube pan or a 10-inch tube pan using some of the cake mix for dusting.

■ In a large mixing bowl combine the cake mix, pudding mix, eggs, sour cream, cream cheese, oil, and water and beat on low speed with an electric mixer just to moisten, scraping the side of the bowl frequently. Beat on medium speed for 2 minutes. Stir in the chocolate chips. Pour into the prepared pan. Bake for 50 minutes, or until a toothpick inserted near the center comes out clean. Let cool 10 minutes and then loosen the cake from the side of the pan with a spatula or knife. Gently remove the cake and cool completely on a wire rack.

**MAKES 12 SERVINGS**

# Toffee Bars

*Bars:*

1   cup (2 sticks) butter or margarine, melted
1   cup firmly packed brown sugar
2   cups all-purpose flour
1/2   teaspoon baking soda
1   egg yolk, lightly beaten
1/2   teaspoon vanilla extract

*Topping:*

11/2   cups confectioners' sugar
2   tablespoons cocoa
3   tablespoons butter, softened
1   egg white
1   teaspoon vanilla extract

■ For the bars, preheat the oven to 350 degrees. In a large bowl combine the melted butter and brown sugar. Blend in the flour, baking soda, egg yolk, and vanilla. Spread the batter into an ungreased 13 x 10-inch jelly-roll pan. Bake for 10 to 12 minutes.

■ For the topping, combine the confectioners' sugar, cocoa, butter, egg white, and vanilla in a large bowl. Spread over the warm toffee bars. Cool and cut into 11/2-inch square bars.

**MAKES 35 BARS**

# Brownie Pudding

2    teaspoons instant coffee powder or granules

2    tablespoons hot water

1    cup all-purpose flour

1/2    cup sugar

2    teaspoons baking powder

1/4    teaspoon salt

3/4    cup unsweetened cocoa, divided

1/2    cup milk

1/4    cup (1/2 stick) butter or margarine, melted

1    teaspoon vanilla extract

13/4    cups boiling water

1/2    cup firmly packed light brown sugar
     Vanilla ice cream (optional)

■ Preheat the oven to 350 degrees. In a cup dissolve the instant coffee in the 2 tablespoons hot water and set aside. In a medium bowl combine the flour, sugar, baking powder, salt, and 1/2 cup of the cocoa. In a 2-cup glass measuring cup combine the milk, melted butter, vanilla, and dissolved instant coffee. With a spoon, stir the liquid mixture into the dry mixture just until blended. Pour the batter into an ungreased 8 x 8-inch glass baking dish.

■ In a small bowl, combine the brown sugar and the remaining 1/4 cup cocoa. Sprinkle over the batter. Carefully pour the 13/4 cups boiling water over the brownie mixture. Do not stir. Bake for 30 minutes. This dessert will separate into cake and pudding layers. Cool in the pan on a wire rack for 10 minutes and serve hot with vanilla ice cream, if desired.

**MAKES 8 SERVINGS**

# Chocolate Almond Bark

1    tablespoon olive oil

2    cups almonds
     Salt to taste

24    ounces chocolate chips

■ Preheat the oven to 350 degrees. Pour the olive oil into a jelly-roll pan. Add the almonds and stir to coat. Sprinkle the almonds with salt. Roast for 30 minutes. Cool.

■ Melt the chocolate chips in a microwave-safe bowl in the microwave or in a double boiler. Stir in the roasted almonds. Line a baking sheet with waxed paper. Spread the almond mixture over the waxed paper and refrigerate. When hardened, break into pieces.

**MAKES 24 PIECES**

## White Chocolate Party Mix

1   (10-ounce) package miniature pretzels
5   cups Cheerios cereal
5   cups Corn Chex cereal
2   cups peanuts
1   pound M&M's
2   (12-ounce) packages white chocolate morsels
3   tablespoons oil

■ In a large bowl, combine the pretzels, Cheerios, Corn Chex, peanuts, and M&M's; set aside. In a microwave-safe bowl combine the white chocolate chips and oil and cook on medium heat for 2 minutes, stirring once. Microwave on high for 10 seconds longer. Stir until smooth. Pour the melted chocolate over the cereal mixture, mixing well. Spread onto three waxed paper–lined cookie sheets. Cool, and then break apart. Store in an airtight container.

**MAKES 24 SERVINGS**

## Cookie Brittle

1     cup (2 sticks) butter, softened
1½   teaspoons vanilla extract
1     teaspoon salt
1     cup sugar
2     cups all-purpose flour, sifted
1     (6-ounce) package chocolate chips
1     cup pecans, chopped

■ Preheat the oven to 375 degrees. Combine the butter, vanilla, and salt in a large mixing bowl and beat well. Gradually beat in the sugar. Add the flour. Fold in the chocolate chips and pecans. Press the batter evenly into an ungreased 16 x 11-inch pan. Bake for 25 minutes or until brown. Cool, and then break into irregular pieces.

**MAKES 24 SERVINGS**

> ### DID YOU KNOW?
> Because chocolate was considered to be a great delicacy, the French monarch Louis XIV created the court position of Royal Chocolate Maker to the King.

# Delray Beach Garlic Festival

**WHERE:** Delray Beach, Florida

**WHEN:** Second weekend in February (Friday through Sunday)

Each year Mr. Garlic, the official mascot of the Delray Beach Garlic Festival, welcomes more than 30,000 people to this Florida beach community to enjoy live music from nationally known entertainers, arts and crafts, and a children's area with rides and games. But the main draws to this festival are demonstrations and competitions from some of the region's best cooks, all competing for the coveted title of "Garlic Chef."

For more information, please visit *www.dbgarlicfest.com*.

## DID YOU KNOW?

The strong flavor of garlic is caused by a chemical reaction that happens when garlic cells are broken; the flavor is the strongest right after the garlic is cut. Smoked garlic is sweet and nutty rather than pungent because this chemical reaction cannot occur after garlic is cooked.

# Potato-Crusted Diver Sea Scallops

● ● ● ● ● ● ● ● ● ● ● ● ● ● ● ● ● ● ● ● ● ● ● ● ●

*Potato Crust:*

Vegetable oil for frying

1 large potato, shredded

2 tablespoons minced garlic

1/2 cup minced shallots

1/2 cup flour

1 egg

Salt and pepper to taste

*Sauce:*

1/4 cup white wine

1/4 cup heavy cream

1 cup (2 sticks) butter, cut into pieces

2 tablespoons roasted garlic

*Scallops:*

5 (U-10) scallops

Salt and pepper to taste

1/2 cup plus 1 tablespoon olive oil, divided

2 tablespoons roasted garlic

1 pound spinach

Garlic chives for garnish

■ For the potato crust, in a skillet heat the vegetable oil to 300 degrees. Cook the potato in the oil until soft, about 2 minutes. Set aside to cool. When the potato is cool, in a large bowl combine the potato, garlic, shallots, flour, egg, and salt and pepper to taste. Refrigerate.

■ For the sauce, in a small saucepan over high heat reduce the wine until almost dry. Add the cream and reduce by half. Whisk in the butter one piece at a time. Stir in the roasted garlic. Keep the sauce warm over low heat.

■ For the scallops, preheat the oven to 375 degrees. Season the scallops with salt and pepper. Coat the top and the side of each scallop with the potato crust mixture. Heat 1/2 cup of the olive oil in an ovenproof skillet over medium-high heat. Add the scallops, potato crust-side-down, and cook until golden brown. Turn the scallops over and transfer to the oven. Bake for approximately 5 minutes. In a separate pan coated with the remaining 1 tablespoon of olive oil, sauté the garlic. Add the spinach and cook until the spinach is wilted.

■ To serve, place the spinach in the middle of each plate. Place the scallops on top of the spinach and spoon the sauce around the plate. Garnish with garlic chives.

**MAKES 5 APPETIZER-SIZE SERVINGS OR 2 DINNER SERVINGS**

## Poached Halibut with Snow Peas

1    garlic bulb

2    cups olive oil

4    sprigs thyme

2    tablespoons salt

4    (7-ounce) halibut steaks

     Salt and pepper to taste

2    elephant garlic cloves, peeled

1 1/2  cups milk, divided

1    cup vegetable oil

3/4   cup heavy cream

4    garlic cloves, peeled

2    cups blanched snow peas

16   blanched pearl onions

■ Slice the garlic bulb in half horizontally. Combine the garlic, olive oil, thyme, and salt in a medium bowl. In a large sauté pan, heat the infused oil until warm, about 150 degrees. Season the halibut with salt and pepper. Add to the oil and cook for about 7 to 9 minutes.

■ Slice the elephant garlic with a mandolin. Combine the elephant garlic and 1/2 cup of the milk in a small saucepan over medium-high heat. Bring to a boil. Strain and repeat 2 more times, using the remaining 1 cup milk. Rinse the elephant garlic. Heat the vegetable oil to 300 degrees in a saucepan. Add the elephant garlic and cook until light brown and crispy, about 5 minutes; set aside. In a separate saucepan bring the heavy cream and 4 garlic cloves to a boil. Strain, reserving the cream.

■ To serve, sauté the snow peas and pearl onions in a pan. Arrange on the bottom of each plate and top with the fish. Using an immersion blender, foam the garlic cream. Spoon the cream on top of the fish and place the elephant garlic chips on top of and around the fish.

**MAKES 4 SERVINGS**

## Roasted Duck with Garlic, Oranges, and Grand Marnier

2    quarts plus 1/2 cup fresh orange juice, divided

1    quart plus 2 tablespoons soy sauce, divided

10   garlic cloves, peeled

2    whole ducks

5    cups chicken broth

1    cup quick grits

1/4   cup (1/2 stick) butter

1½ cups roasted garlic, divided

Juice of 1 orange

1 cup light corn syrup

2 tablespoons Grand Marnier

2 pounds baby spinach

2 tablespoons chopped garlic

Oil for sautéing

■ Combine 2 quarts of the orange juice, 1 quart of the soy sauce, the garlic cloves, and the ducks in a large container and refrigerate for 2 days.

■ When ready to serve, bring the chicken broth to a boil over medium heat in a large saucepan. Add the grits and bring to a simmer. Cook, stirring, for 2 to 5 minutes or until the desired consistency is reached. Stir in the butter and ½ cup of the roasted garlic. Spread the grits evenly in a baking pan and refrigerate.

■ Preheat the oven to 375 degrees. Remove the ducks from the marinade. Tie the legs together using string, then tuck the wings under the body to secure. Score each duck breast in a crosshatch pattern. Place the duck in a roasting pan. Squeeze the juice of ½ orange over each duck. Bake for 45 to 60 minutes, or until the duck legs are loose and the skin is golden brown. Cut the ducks in half and refrigerate. Maintain the oven temperature.

■ In a medium saucepan, bring the corn syrup to a simmer over medium heat. Add the Grand Marnier and ignite. When the flames have subsided add the remaining ½ cup orange juice and the remaining 2 tablespoons soy sauce. Cook the sauce until it is reduced by half. Remove from the heat and let cool. Add the remaining 1 cup roasted garlic. (This should make a paste.)

■ Once the garlic paste has cooled completely, remove the duck and the grits from the refrigerator. Cut the grits into 8 triangles and heat in a greased sauté pan over medium heat. Spread a thick layer of the garlic paste over each duck half and return to the oven. Cook until the garlic paste starts to crisp. In a large pan, sauté the spinach and chopped garlic in oil until the spinach is wilted.

■ To serve, place the hot grits on a plate. Top with the duck and the sautéed spinach.

**MAKES 4 SERVINGS**

## Applewood-Smoked Bacon and Garlic-Wrapped Jumbo Shrimp

*Shrimp:*

16    slices applewood-smoked bacon

6    elephant garlic bulbs

16    (U-10) shrimp, peeled and deveined

Extra-virgin olive oil

Salt and pepper to taste

*Smashed Potatoes:*

2    pounds red bliss potatoes

3    cups heavy cream

1/2    cup (1 stick) butter

4    ears sweet corn

2    bunches scallions, thinly sliced

Salt and pepper to taste

*Sauce:*

3    large ripe tomatoes

10    garlic cloves, peeled

2    cups white wine

2    cups heavy cream

1 1/2    cups (3 sticks) unsalted butter

Kosher salt and fresh cracked black pepper to taste

■ For the shrimp, preheat the oven to 400 degrees. Lay the bacon on a nonstick baking sheet, and cook until the slices just start to crisp. Remove from the pan and place on paper towels to drain and cool.

■ Preheat a grill to high heat. Slice the elephant garlic paper-thin using a chef's knife or a mandolin. Layer the garlic slices on top of each piece of bacon, leaving 1 inch uncovered at each end. Season the shrimp with salt and pepper to taste. Wrap each shrimp with a bacon slice, making sure to enclose all the garlic. Secure the bacon with a metal skewer. Repeat with all of the shrimp, dividing the shrimp evenly onto 4 skewers. Brush each skewer with olive oil and season with salt and pepper. Grill for 4 to 5 minutes on each side.

■ For the smashed potatoes, boil the potatoes until tender; drain. In a large bowl, mash the potatoes with the heavy cream and butter; set aside. Boil the corn for 1 1/2 minutes. Let cool and then remove the kernels from the cob. Set aside a small amount of scallions for garnish. Mix the remaining scallions and the corn into the smashed potatoes. Season with salt and pepper.

■ For the sauce, fold a 3-foot piece of aluminum foil in half twice. Place the foil directly on a grill heated to high. Place the tomatoes on the foil and close the lid of the grill. Grill for 10 minutes or until the skin starts to char. Once cool enough to handle, roughly chop the tomatoes and place in a heavy-bottom pot over high heat. Add the garlic and sauté for 1 minute. Pour in the white wine. Cook until the wine is reduced by half. Add the heavy cream and cook until reduced by half. Dice the butter into 1-inch cubes. Carefully pour the tomato mixture into a blender and blend on medium speed. Add the butter, one piece at a time, and season with salt and pepper. Blend until thoroughly mixed.

■ To serve, using a 2-ounce ladle, spoon the sauce onto 4 plates. Place a healthy scoop of the smashed potatoes in the center of the plate and top with one skewer of the wrapped shrimp. Sprinkle the plates with the reserved scallions.

**MAKES 4 SERVINGS**

## DID YOU KNOW?

Garlic is a member of the lily family, as is the onion.

# March

# Highland Maple Festival

**WHERE:** Monterey, McDowell, and Blue Grass, Virginia

**WHEN:** The second and third weekends in March (Saturday and Sunday)

These three towns in the Virginia Mountains are referred to as "Virginia's Switzerland," and they are the largest producers of maple syrup in the South. As many as 60,000 people have attended the festival in a good year (defined as good weather and no snow) to enjoy one of the region's largest arts and crafts fairs, dances, live entertainment, clogging, and tours to the sugar camps to view the process of maple syrup making. In case you were wondering, you will definitely find all the pancakes you could possibly eat.

For more information, please visit
*www.highlandcounty.org/maple.htm*.

**DID YOU KNOW?**

It takes 30 to 50 gallons of sap to make one gallon of maple syrup.

## Praline Cheesecake

*Crust:*

1/4 cup (1/2 stick) margarine

1 cup graham cracker crumbs

2 tablespoons brown sugar

*Filling:*

24 ounces cream cheese, softened

1 1/4 cups firmly packed brown sugar

2 tablespoons all-purpose flour

4 eggs

1 1/2 teaspoons vanilla extract

3/4 cup pecans, chopped

3 tablespoons maple syrup

◼ To make the crust, preheat the oven to 350 degrees. Melt the margarine in a saucepan. Stir in the graham cracker crumbs and brown sugar. Press into the bottom of an ungreased 9-inch springform pan. Bake for 10 minutes. Let the crust cool. Maintain the oven temperature.

◼ For the filling, in a large mixing bowl beat the cream cheese, brown sugar, and flour together at medium speed until blended. Add the eggs, one at a time, beating until blended after each addition. Mix in the vanilla and nuts. Pour the mixture over the crust. Bake for 50 to 60 minutes or until firm. Chill. Spread the maple syrup over the top of the cooled cheesecake. Chill until ready to serve.

**MAKES 12 SERVINGS**

## Johnny Cake Cornbread

3 eggs, beaten

1 cup milk

1/3 cup maple syrup

3/4 cup vegetable shortening, melted

2 cups all-purpose flour

4 1/2 teaspoons baking soda

3/4 teaspoon salt

1 cup cornmeal

◼ Preheat the oven to 400 degrees. Grease a 9 x 9-inch baking pan. In a large bowl combine the eggs, milk, maple syrup, and melted shortening. In a separate bowl combine the flour, baking soda, salt, and cornmeal. Stir the wet ingredients into the dry ingredients. Pour the batter into the prepared pan and bake for 30 minutes. Cut into 1 1/2-inch squares.

**MAKES 25 SQUARES**

## Maple Fudge

1  cup granulated sugar

1  cup firmly packed brown sugar

2  teaspoons vinegar

1/2  cup maple syrup

1/2  cup water

   Maple flavoring to taste (optional)

1/2  cup chopped walnuts

■ In a large saucepan combine the granulated sugar, brown sugar, vinegar, maple syrup, and water. Place over medium heat and cook uncovered, scraping down the sides of the pan often, until the mixture comes to a slow boil. Cover with a lid and cook for 1 minute. Uncover and continue cooking until the fudge reaches 228 degrees on a candy thermometer. Let cool in the pan. When the fudge is cool, beat until it loses its gloss and the consistency becomes fudge-like. Stir in maple flavoring to taste, if desired, and the nuts. Pour the fudge into a buttered 8 x 8-inch pan. Allow to cool until the fudge is set. Cut into 1-inch squares.

**MAKES 64 PIECES**

## Maple Carrots

10  carrots, sliced into rounds (do not use baby carrots)

1  garlic clove, crushed

1/4  teaspoon garlic salt

1/3  cup maple syrup

2  tablespoons butter

■ In a frying pan, combine the carrots, garlic, garlic salt, maple syrup, and butter and cook over medium-low heat. Stir occasionally until the carrots are cooked to the desired doneness, or approximately 5 to 7 minutes.

**MAKES 4 TO 6 SERVINGS**

**DID YOU KNOW?**
A gallon of maple syrup weighs 11 pounds.

# World Championship Étouffée Cook-Off

**WHERE:** Eunice, Louisiana

**WHEN:** Last Sunday in March (the festival moves to the third Sunday in March if the fourth Sunday happens to be Easter Sunday)

The good folks who participate in the World Championship Étouffée Cook-Off are serious about their Cajun food. More than 100 teams compete for bragging rights at the World Champion Crawfish Étouffée Cook-Off each and every year. Teams also compete for the best decorated booth. But the real winners at this festival are the thousands of people who come each year to taste all the entries. Festival attendees also enjoy dancing to the music of Cajun and Zydeco bands.

For more information, please visit *www.eunice-la.com*.

## DID YOU KNOW?

Étouffée is a Creole seafood dish typically served over rice. The primary difference between an étouffée and a gumbo is the roux. An étouffée is made with a blonde roux, which is about the color of a paper bag. A gumbo is made with a typical Creole roux, which is a darker brown.

## Crawfish Étouffée

1     cup (2 sticks) butter
1     cup finely chopped onion
1/3   cup chopped celery
1     cup chopped shallots
1     teaspoon minced garlic
2     tablespoons all-purpose flour
1     cup canned whole tomatoes
2     cups fish stock
1     teaspoon salt
1     teaspoon black pepper
      Dash cayenne pepper
1     teaspoon Worcestershire sauce
1 1/2 to 2 pounds crawfish meat

■ In a large saucepan over medium-high heat, melt the butter. Add the onion, celery, and shallots and sauté until transparent. Add the garlic and cook a few minutes more. Stir in the flour and continue stirring until the flour is a deep brown. Add the tomatoes. Add the fish stock. Reduce the heat to medium and simmer for 20 minutes. Add the salt, black pepper, cayenne pepper, and Worcestershire sauce and cook slowly for 20 minutes more. Stir in the crawfish and cook 10 minutes longer, stirring often.

**MAKES 6 TO 8 SERVINGS**

## Easy Shrimp Étouffée

1/2   cup (1 stick) butter
1     cup finely chopped onion
3     tablespoons all-purpose flour
1     teaspoon paprika
1     (14-ounce) can chicken broth
1     pound shrimp
      Salt and pepper to taste
      Finely chopped green onion tops
      Chopped fresh parsley
      Hot cooked rice`

■ Melt the butter in a heavy saucepan over medium heat. Add the onion and sauté until wilted and starting to disintegrate. Add the flour and stir constantly until well mixed. Add the paprika and broth and simmer for 20 minutes. Stir in the shrimp and salt and pepper and simmer for another 20 minutes. Just before serving, sprinkle with green onions and parsley. Serve over hot rice.

**MAKES 4 SERVINGS**

# April

# Big Squeeze Juice Festival

**WHERE:** Palm Bay, Florida

**WHEN:** First weekend in April (Thursday through Sunday)

"The Big Squeezer" is the coveted title that contestants in the juice-squeezing competition are after when they see how much juice they can squeeze—one handed—from oranges in 60 seconds. Other highlights of this festival include the Big Squeeze Bake-Off; live music; arts and crafts; carnival rides; helicopter and pony rides; a business fair; car, bike, and boat shows; and of course, free juice samples.

For more information, please visit *www.palmbaychamber.com*.

## DID YOU KNOW?

About 90 percent of the Florida orange crop is used to make orange juice.

# Claire's Orange Lime Cake

*Cake:*

| | |
|---|---|
| 2 | cups (4 sticks) margarine, softened |
| 2 | cups sugar |
| 6 | eggs |
| 2 | teaspoons grated orange zest |
| 2 | teaspoons grated lime zest |
| 3 | teaspoons vanilla extract |
| 4 | cups all-purpose flour, sifted |
| 2 | teaspoons baking powder |
| 3/4 | cup fresh squeezed orange juice |
| 1/4 | cup fresh lime juice |

*Frosting:*

| | |
|---|---|
| 4 | cups confectioners' sugar |
| 1/2 | cup (1 stick) margarine, softened |
| 5 | tablespoons lime juice |
| 2 | teaspoons anise extract |

■ For the cake, preheat the oven to 350 degrees. Grease and lightly flour two 9-inch round cake pans. In a mixing bowl beat the margarine on medium speed until smooth. Add the sugar, beating until fluffy. Beat in the eggs, one at a time. Add the orange zest, lime zest, and vanilla and mix well. In a separate bowl combine the flour with the baking powder. Gradually add the flour mixture, one cup at a time, to the batter, alternating with the orange juice and lime juice. Continue to mix until the batter falls slowly like a ribbon. Pour the batter into the prepared pans. Bake for 35 minutes or until a toothpick comes out clean when inserted in the middle of the cake. Let cool completely before frosting.

■ For the frosting, in a mixing bowl combine the confectioners' sugar, margarine, lime juice, and anise extract. Spread on the top and side of the cooled cake.

**MAKES 16 SERVINGS**

# Orange Squeeze Cake

*Cake:*

1   (18.25-ounce) package butter cake mix (such as Duncan Hines)

1/2   cup cooking oil

4   eggs

1/2   cup sugar

1   (11-ounce) can mandarin oranges, undrained

*Filling:*

1   (11-ounce) can mandarin oranges, drained

1   (3-ounce) box vanilla instant pudding mix

1   (12-ounce) container whipped topping

■ For the cake, preheat the oven to 325 degrees. Grease two 9–inch cake pans. In a large mixing bowl combine the cake mix, oil, eggs, sugar, and mandarin oranges and juice and beat until smooth. Pour the batter into the prepared pans. Bake for 30 minutes. Remove from the oven and let cool.

■ For the filling, reserve a few mandarin oranges for a garnish. Chop the remaining mandarin oranges. In a large bowl combine the chopped mandarin oranges, pudding mix, and whipped topping. Spread the filling between the layers and on the top and side of the cake. Decorate the top of the cake with the reserved mandarin oranges.

**MAKES 16 SERVINGS**

**DID YOU KNOW?**
The largest orange juice glass in the world stood over 8 feet tall and could hold more than 730 gallons of orange juice.

# Newport Pig Cooking Contest

**WHERE:** Newport, North Carolina

**WHEN:** First weekend in April (Friday and Saturday—unless that weekend happens to be Easter weekend—then the festival is the last weekend in March)

Since 1978, as many as 15,000 people have made their way in early April to Newport to view the largest whole hog cooking contest in the United States. And yes, that's just what it sounds like—a whole pig, split down the middle and placed on the cooker (but with no head or feet). The contestants start cooking the pigs late Friday night and the judging is early Saturday morning. In addition to the competition that draws entrants from many states, visitors can enjoy crafts, live music, carnival rides, bake sales, and the Pig Cooking King and Queen contest, which raises funds for local organizations.

For more information, please visit *www.newportpigcooking.com*.

## DID YOU KNOW?

Big Bill was the largest pig that ever lived. He was a Poland-China hog and weighed 2,552 pounds. His shoulders were 5 feet high and he was 9 feet long. He was so big he dragged his belly on the ground when he walked.

*There is a great debate among barbecue lovers as to which state produces the best sauce—Texas, Tennessee, or North Carolina. The North Carolina sauces are vinegar based. Here are three versions of North Carolina barbecue sauces.*

## North Carolina Hot Barbecue Sauce

2    quarts cider vinegar

1/4  cup crushed red pepper

     Salt and pepper to taste

■ In a large bowl combine the cider vinegar, red pepper, and salt and pepper and mix well. Use to baste pork. Pour any remaining sauce into small jars to serve or to use another time.

**MAKES 2 QUARTS**

## Carolina Pig Sauce

1    gallon cider vinegar

1/2  cup salt

2    tablespoons cayenne pepper

2    tablespoons red pepper flakes

1    cup firmly packed brown sugar

■ In a large bowl combine the vinegar, salt, cayenne pepper, red pepper flakes, and brown sugar and mix well. Let stand 3 to 4 hours before using.

**MAKES 1 GALLON**

## Eastern NC BBQ Sauce

1    cup white vinegar

1    cup cider vinegar

1    tablespoon brown sugar

3/4  tablespoon cayenne pepper

1    tablespoon hot pepper sauce

3/4  teaspoon salt

1    teaspoon ground black pepper

■ Combine the white vinegar, cider vinegar, brown sugar, cayenne pepper, hot pepper sauce, salt, and pepper in a jar or bottle with a tight-fitting lid. Refrigerate for at least 1 day before using. The sauce will keep up to 2 months in the refrigerator.

**MAKES 2 CUPS**

## Southern-Fried Pork Chops

4    medium bone-in pork chops

1/2   teaspoon salt

1/2   teaspoon pepper

1/2   teaspoon onion salt

1    cup all-purpose flour

1/2   cup (1 stick) butter

■ Rinse the pork chops well and drain on a plate. Combine the salt, pepper, onion salt, and flour together in plastic or paper bag. Put the pork chops in the bag and shake well to season and fully coat the pork chops.

■ Melt the butter in a large skillet over medium heat. Place the coated pork chops in the butter and fry for 20 minutes or until done, turning occasionally.

**MAKES 4 SERVINGS**

## Southern Baked Pork Chops

6    bone-in pork chops

     Salt and pepper to taste

1    tablespoon vegetable oil

3/4   cup water

1/4   cup chopped celery

2    tablespoons brown sugar

1    tablespoon dry mustard

1    (8-ounce) can tomato sauce

■ Preheat the oven to 350 degrees. Sprinkle the pork chops with salt and pepper. Heat the oil in a skillet over medium-high heat and brown the pork chops on both sides. Place the pork chops in a shallow baking dish. Combine the water, celery, brown sugar, dry mustard, and tomato sauce in a bowl. Pour over the chops. Cover and bake for 1 hour, or until the chops are tender, basting occasionally.

**MAKES 6 SERVINGS**

> ### DID YOU KNOW?
> The first book on raising pigs was written in 3468 BC by Emperor Fo Hi of China.

# World Catfish Festival

**WHERE:** Belzoni, Mississippi

**WHEN:** First Saturday in April (unless Easter falls that weekend—then the festival is the following weekend)

For more than 30 years, tens of thousands of people have made the pilgrimage to Belzoni to celebrate the catfish. Well, they do more eating than celebrating. In fact, the annual catfish-eating contest (where you try to eat a mere 3 pounds of fried catfish in 10 minutes) is one of the highlights of this festival, which includes the Miss Catfish Pageant, a children's play, and arts and crafts.

For more information, please visit *www.catfishcapitalonline.com*.

## DID YOU KNOW?

*Malapterurus electricus*, the electric catfish, can generate an electric charge of up to 350 volts, which is enough to stun a human being. It is native to Africa.

# Grilled Smoked Catfish with Horseradish Cream

*Horseradish Cream:*

1    cup crème fraîche

1/2  cup prepared horseradish, drained

1    teaspoon Dijon mustard

1    teaspoon chopped fresh dill

1    teaspoon lemon juice

1    teaspoon salt

1    teaspoon pepper

*Smoked Catfish:*

2    cups water

1    cup lemon juice

5    garlic cloves, sliced

4    shallots, sliced

2    tablespoons salt

2    tablespoons sugar

2    tablespoons chopped fresh dill

6    catfish fillets

■ For the horseradish cream, mix the crème fraîche, horseradish, mustard, dill, lemon juice, salt, and pepper in a small bowl. Cover and refrigerate overnight. Let come to room temperature before serving.

■ For the smoked catfish, mix the water, lemon juice, garlic, shallots, salt, sugar, and dill in a small bowl. Place the catfish fillets in a shallow dish and pour the marinade over them. Cover with plastic wrap and refrigerate for 4 to 5 hours to marinate.

■ Prepare a charcoal grill for grilling, letting the fire burn until the coals are medium to low heat (250 degrees to 300 degrees on a barbecue thermometer or you can hold your hand, palm down, about 5 inches above the coals for 5 seconds before removing it). Place the catfish on an oiled grill rack over the coals. Cover the grill and cook for 25 minutes or until the fish flakes easily when tested with a fork. Place the fillets on serving plates and spoon the horseradish cream over the top.

**MAKES 4 SERVINGS**

## DID YOU KNOW?
Catfish do not have true scales and are distinguished by their barbells, or "whiskers."

## Delta Bisque

1    tablespoon plus 1/3 cup butter, divided

3    green onions, chopped

2    celery ribs, finely chopped

2    catfish fillets, cut into 1-inch pieces

1/3    cup all-purpose flour

4    cups milk

1    cup heavy cream

1    teaspoon Tabasco sauce

1    tablespoon chopped fresh parsley

1    bay leaf

1    tablespoon chopped fresh chives

1    teaspoon salt

■  Melt 1 tablespoon of the butter in a Dutch oven or a large, heavy saucepan over medium-low heat. Add the green onions, celery, and catfish pieces and sauté for 3 to 4 minutes; do not brown. Remove the catfish and vegetables from the pan. Add the remaining 1/3 cup butter to the pan and cook over medium heat until melted. Add the flour and stir for 2 to 3 minutes. Gradually stir in the milk and cream, stirring well after each addition. Cook, stirring constantly until thickened. Return the catfish and vegetables to the pan. Stir in the Tabasco sauce, parsley, bay leaf, chives, and salt. Simmer for 15 minutes. Remove the bay leaf and serve. The bisque can be covered and refrigerated for up to 3 days.

**MAKES 6 SERVINGS**

## Beer Batter Fried Catfish

1/2    cup all-purpose flour

1/2    cup cornstarch

2    tablespoons Cajun seasoning

1    tablespoon garlic powder

1    teaspoon baking powder

1    teaspoon paprika

1/2    teaspoon salt

1/3    teaspoon ground white pepper

1/3    teaspoon ground red pepper

1/3    teaspoon dried oregano leaves, crushed

3/4    cup beer, at room temperature

1    large egg, slightly beaten
       Vegetable oil for deep-frying

1    pound catfish fillets, cut into 3- to 4-inch-thick strips

■  In a medium bowl combine the flour, cornstarch, Cajun seasoning, garlic powder, baking powder, paprika, salt, white pepper, red pepper, and oregano. In a separate bowl whisk the beer and egg together until smooth. Add to the dry ingredients. Cover and refrigerate for 1 to 2 hours.

■ In a deep skillet or large pan, pour vegetable oil to a depth of 3 inches; heat to 375 degrees. Stir the batter and fold in the catfish. When the oil is hot, lift the fish strips with tongs, draining any excess batter. Place the catfish in the oil, several pieces at a time (do not overcrowd). Fry until well browned on all sides, about 3 minutes. Remove to paper towels to drain. Keep warm and repeat with the remaining catfish.

**MAKES 4 SERVINGS**

# Fried Catfish Fingers with Spicy Dipping Sauce

*Fried Catfish Fingers:*

2    cups white cornmeal
     Salt and freshly ground black pepper to taste

2    pounds catfish fillets, cut into 1-inch-thick strips
     Peanut oil for deep frying

*Spicy Dipping Sauce:*

3/4   cup white wine vinegar

1/2   teaspoon salt

1/2   teaspoon coarsely ground black pepper

1    shallot, finely chopped

2    garlic cloves, finely chopped

2    green onions, thinly sliced

1    tablespoon finely chopped fresh parsley

■ For the catfish fingers, place the cornmeal in a shallow dish. Season with salt and pepper. Dredge the catfish strips in the cornmeal mixture, shaking off any excess. Set aside on a waxed paper-lined baking sheet.

■ Pour 2 inches of peanut oil into a deep fryer or large, heavy skillet and heat to 375 degrees on a deep-frying thermometer. Add the catfish strips to the hot oil, three at a time. Fry in a single layer for 5 minutes, turning to cook evenly, until golden brown and the fish flakes easily when tested with a fork. Drain on paper towels and sprinkle lightly with salt.

■ For the dipping sauce, 1 minute before serving the catfish fingers mix the vinegar, salt, pepper, shallot, garlic, green onions, and parsley in a small bowl. Taste and adjust seasonings if necessary. Serve with the catfish fingers.

**MAKES 8 SERVINGS**

## Catfish Fillet Sandwiches with Red "Firecracker" Sauce

*Red "Firecracker" Sauce:*

2    tablespoons lime or lemon juice

2    teaspoons Dijon mustard

1½   teaspoons chili powder

1    teaspoon ground cumin

¼    teaspoon cayenne pepper

⅛    teaspoon garlic powder

¼    cup olive oil
     Salt and freshly ground black pepper

*Catfish Sandwiches:*

4    (4- to 5-ounce) catfish fillets, frozen

1    teaspoon dried oregano
     Salt and freshly ground black pepper

4    teaspoons olive oil

4    soft sandwich rolls
     Lettuce leaves, alfalfa sprouts, or coleslaw

8    slices ripe avocado
     Salt and pepper to taste

4    thin slices red onion

4    teaspoons sour cream or plain yogurt

■ For the sauce, combine the lime juice and mustard in a medium glass bowl. Using a wire whisk, mix until smooth. Whisk in the chili powder, cumin, cayenne pepper, and garlic powder. Gradually whisk in the olive oil until a smooth, slightly thickened sauce forms. Season with salt and pepper to taste. Cover and set aside. The sauce can be prepared up to 3 days in advance and stored in the refrigerator. If the sauce separates, whisk until blended.

■ For the catfish, preheat the oven to 425 degrees. Place the frozen catfish fillets in a single layer in a baking pan. Sprinkle with the oregano and season with salt and pepper. Drizzle the fillets with the olive oil. Bake for about 12 minutes or until the fish flakes easily when tested with a fork. Set aside to cool. The catfish can be prepared up to 1 day in advance and kept in the refrigerator.

■ To serve, cut the cooled catfish fillets in half lengthwise and coat each piece with some of the sauce. Spread a small amount of the sauce on the bottom of each roll and top with lettuce, sprouts, or coleslaw. Place two pieces of the dressed fillets on top of the greens on each roll. Place 2 avocado slices on top of each sandwich. Season with salt and pepper. Place 1 red onion slice on top of the avocado and add 1 teaspoon of sour cream or yogurt. Top with the remaining half of the roll. Cut the sandwiches in half and serve. This sandwich can also be made with warm or hot catfish.

**MAKES 4 SERVINGS**

# National Grits Festival

**WHERE:** Warwick, Georgia
**WHEN:** Second Saturday in April

Grits, the official prepared food of the state of Georgia (it's in the law books), is celebrated each year in tiny Warwick (population 500), which is located between Cordele and Albany. Thousands converge on this spring day to enjoy a grits breakfast, an arts and crafts show, pony rides, and lots more. Unique to the festival is a grits cooking contest, antique tractor and car show, and the parade of the "Grits Queens." But the must-see event occurs in the afternoon with the Quaker Instant Grits contest; that's when contestants roll around in a cattle trough of cooked grits.

For more information, please visit *www.gritsfest.com.*

## DID YOU KNOW?

When most people talk about "grits," they are referring to hominy grits. But the word "grits" is actually the term for any coarsely ground grain, be it rice, oats, corn, or any other.

## Baked Bacon Eggs and Grits

1    cup white hominy grits or white hominy quick grits

4    tablespoons butter, divided

4    slices bacon, crisp-cooked and crumbled

6    eggs

     Black pepper to taste

■ Preheat the oven to 350 degrees. Prepare the grits according to the package directions. Stir in 2 tablespoons of the butter and the bacon. Pour the grits mixture into an ungreased 11 x 7-inch baking dish. Make 6 depressions with the back of a spoon, about 2 inches apart, in the grits. Carefully break 1 egg into each depression. Melt the remaining 2 tablespoons butter and pour over the eggs. Sprinkle with pepper. Bake uncovered for 15 minutes or until the eggs are done.

**MAKES 6 SERVINGS**

## Sausage and Cheese Grits Casserole

1    pound breakfast sausage

1    cup uncooked grits

1    cup grated Cheddar cheese

1/2  cup (1 stick) butter

2    large eggs, beaten

1/2  cup milk

1    garlic clove, minced

■ Form the sausage meat into 8 patties. Heat a skillet over medium heat and fry the patties until brown. Drain on paper towels. Crumble the sausage in a bowl.

■ Preheat the oven to 350 degrees. Prepare the grits according to the package directions. When the grits thicken, remove from the heat and stir in the cheese. Cover and let stand several minutes. Stir in the butter, eggs, milk, and garlic until well blended. Stir in the sausage meat. Pour into a buttered baking dish and bake until lightly brown, about 1 hour.

**MAKES 12 SERVINGS**

## Baked Grits with Green Onions

2    cups water

1/2    cup quick grits

1/4    teaspoon salt

1    cup shredded sharp Cheddar cheese

1/4    cup sliced green onions

1/4    cup (1/2 stick) butter

1    egg, beaten

1/4    teaspoon red pepper sauce

Green onion strips for garnish

■ Heat the oven to 350 degrees. Grease a 1-quart round casserole dish. In a large saucepan, bring the water to a boil. Stir in the grits and salt. Return to a boil, and then reduce the heat. Cook, uncovered for 2 1/2 to 5 minutes, stirring occasionally. Stir in the cheese, green onions, butter, egg, and red pepper sauce. Continue cooking over low heat until the cheese is melted. Pour into the prepared dish. Bake for about 30 minutes. Garnish with strips of green onions.

**MAKES 6 SERVINGS**

## Grits Biscuits

1/2    cup grits

1/2    cup sugar

2    teaspoons salt

1/2    cup vegetable shortening

2    cups milk

1    package yeast

1/4    cup warm water

2    eggs, beaten

4    cups all-purpose flour

■ Combine the grits, sugar, salt, shortening, and milk in a medium saucepan and cook until thick (like cooked cereal). Remove from the heat and cool to lukewarm. Dissolve the yeast in the warm water. Add the dissolved yeast and the eggs to the grits mixture. Beat thoroughly with a whisk. Add the flour and mix to form a soft dough. Knead well on a lightly floured board. Place in a bowl, cover, and let rise to double its bulk. Punch down the dough and roll out to 1-inch thickness. Cut with a biscuit cutter and place on a greased cookie sheet. Cover and let rise again.

■ Preheat the oven to 375 degrees. Bake for 15 minutes.

**MAKES 36 BISCUITS**

## Fried Grits

5      cups water

2      teaspoons salt

1      cup grits

5      tablespoons butter, divided

1      egg, lightly beaten

2      tablespoons cold water

1/2    cup all-purpose flour

■ Bring the water and salt to a boil in a heavy 2-quart saucepan over high heat. Stir in the grits slowly so that the water continues to boil. Reduce the heat and cover. Cook, stirring occasionally, for 30 minutes. Stir in 1 tablespoon of the butter and spoon into a greased 9 x 13-inch baking dish. Smooth the top with the back of a spoon and cool to room temperature. Cover with foil and refrigerate for at least 4 hours.

■ Cut the grits into 2-inch squares with a sharp knife. In a small bowl combine the egg and water. Dip the grits in the egg mixture, and then roll in the flour. Melt the remaining 4 tablespoons butter in a heavy 12-inch skillet over moderate heat. Add 7 or 8 of the grits squares and cook for about 3 minutes on each side or until brown, turning with a spatula. Remove from the skillet and keep warm.

Repeat with the remaining grits squares, adding butter to the skillet as needed. Place on a heated platter and serve.

**MAKES 24 2-INCH SERVINGS**

## Grits Pie

3      eggs

1      cup cooked grits

1/2    cup firmly packed light brown sugar

1/3    cup heavy cream

1      unbaked (8 to 9-inch) piecrust

1/2    cup sliced fresh strawberries

■ Preheat the oven to 400 degrees. Put the eggs in a mixing bowl and beat until blended and smooth. Stir in the grits, brown sugar, and cream and mix until blended. Pour the mixture into the piecrust. Gently stir in the strawberries and bake for about 40 minutes or until the center is slightly jiggly, but most of the filling is set. Cool for 5 minutes after removing from the oven. Serve warm or cold.

**MAKES 8 SERVINGS**

# Baked Triple Cheese Grits

| | |
|---|---|
| 1 | cup quick grits |
| 1/3 | cup butter |
| 3/4 | cup shredded mozzarella cheese, divided |
| 3/4 | cup shredded Cheddar cheese, divided |
| 1/2 | cup fresh shredded Parmesan cheese |

▪ Preheat the oven to 350 degrees. Prepare the grits according to the package directions. Remove from the heat. Stir in the butter. Spread half of the grits into a greased 2-quart baking dish. Top with 1/2 cup of the mozzarella cheese and 1/2 cup of the Cheddar cheese. Add the remaining half of the grits. Top with the remaining 1/4 cup mozzarella cheese and the remaining 1/4 cup Cheddar cheese. Sprinkle with the Parmesan cheese. Bake for 30 minutes.

**MAKES 12 SERVINGS**

# Grits Muffins

| | |
|---|---|
| 1 | cup cooked grits |
| 1 | cup all-purpose flour |
| 3 | teaspoons baking powder |
| 2 | tablespoons sugar |
| 1/4 | teaspoon salt |
| 3 | tablespoons vegetable shortening |
| 1 | cup milk |

▪ Preheat the oven to 350 degrees. Combine the grits, flour, baking powder, sugar, salt, shortening, and milk in a bowl and mix well. Pour into a well-greased muffin pan and bake for 20 minutes.

**MAKES 12 MUFFINS**

---

**DID YOU KNOW?**

The Waffle House restaurant chain serves more than 3.2 million pounds of grits each year.

# Chicken and Egg Festival

**WHERE:** Moulton, Alabama

**WHEN:** Second full weekend in April (Saturday and Sunday)

I checked. The chicken bowling at this festival has nothing to do with rolling a bowling ball into a group of live chickens. It's just that the bowling pins have pictures of chickens attached. More than 10,000 people visit this festival each year to watch or participate in activities like the hard-boiled-egg-eating contest, the chicken wing–eating contest, an exhibit (make that "eggshibit") of more than 100 live exotic bantam chickens, beauty pageants, agricultural photography contests, a motorcycle run, an egg drop for future engineers, live entertainment, and the chicken clucking contest.

For more information, please visit
*www.alabamachickenandeggfestival.com.*

## DID YOU KNOW?

You shouldn't feel cheated if you find an egg in your carton that looks smaller than the rest. Egg sizing is based on the weight of an egg, not its circumference.

# Country Fried Chicken with Gravy

*Chicken:*

| | |
|---|---|
| 3 | pounds chicken, cut up |
| 1 | cup buttermilk |
| 2 | cups all-purpose flour |
| 1 | teaspoon salt |
| 1 | teaspoon pepper |
| 1/2 | teaspoon garlic powder |
| 1 | teaspoon paprika |
| 1/4 | teaspoon ground sage |
| 1/4 | teaspoon ground thyme |
| 1/8 | teaspoon baking powder |
| | Vegetable oil for frying |

*Gravy:*

| | |
|---|---|
| 3 | tablespoons reserved pan drippings |
| 3 | tablespoons reserved seasoned flour |
| 2 | cups milk |

For the chicken, rinse the chicken and pat dry with paper towels. Place the chicken in a large shallow dish. Add the buttermilk, turning to coat all sides of the chicken. Cover and refrigerate for at least 1 hour. Drain the chicken, discarding the buttermilk.

Combine the flour, salt, pepper, garlic powder, paprika, sage, thyme, and baking powder in a double-strength paper bag. Set aside 3 tablespoons of the seasoned flour for the gravy. Add the chicken pieces to the seasoned flour, one at a time, and shake to coat well. Arrange the chicken on a baking sheet and allow the coating to dry.

Pour 1/2 inch of vegetable oil in a heavy skillet and heat over medium-high. Fry the chicken, several pieces at a time, for about 3 minutes on each side. Be careful not to overcrowd. Reduce the heat to medium and return all the chicken to the pan. Cook the chicken, turning occasionally, for 25 to 35 minutes or until the juices run clear and the chicken is tender. Remove to a paper towel-lined platter. Reserve 3 tablespoons of the drippings for the gravy.

For the gravy, heat the reserved drippings in a skillet over medium-high heat. Add the reserved seasoned flour, stirring constantly until brown, about 1 minute. Slowly stir in the milk and continue stirring for about 3 minutes or until the gravy is smooth and thickened. Serve the gravy with the chicken, over mashed potatoes or biscuits.

**MAKES 6 SERVINGS**

## Southern Chicken Casserole

1 (10½-ounce) can cream of mushroom soup
1 cup sour cream
3 cups chopped cooked chicken
½ cup (1 stick) butter, softened
1⅓ cups crushed Ritz crackers
1 tablespoon poppy seeds

■ Preheat the oven to 350 degrees. Combine the soup and sour cream in a bowl and mix well. Arrange the chicken in a 1½-quart baking dish. Pour the soup mixture over the chicken. In a separate bowl combine the butter with the cracker crumbs and poppy seeds. Sprinkle over the top of the chicken mixture. Bake for 30 to 40 minutes.

**MAKES 8 SERVINGS**

## Oven-Barbecued Chicken

Oil for frying
1 large (2 to 2½-pound) chicken, cut up
2 tablespoons sugar
¼ cup cider vinegar
⅓ cup Worcestershire sauce
1 garlic clove, minced
1 cup ketchup
1 teaspoon salt
½ cup water

■ Preheat the oven to 325 degrees. Heat oil in a skillet and brown the chicken on all sides. Place the chicken in a greased 9 x 13-inch baking dish. In the same skillet, add the sugar, vinegar, Worcestershire sauce, garlic, ketchup, salt, and water. Stir until thoroughly mixed and pour over the chicken. Bake for 1½ hours or until the chicken is done.

**MAKES 6 SERVINGS**

**DID YOU KNOW?**
The color of the eggshell and yolk vary depending on the diet of the hen.

# Alma Spinach Festival

**WHERE:** Alma, Arkansas

**WHEN:** Third Saturday in April

You know a town is serious about spinach when it has a statue of Popeye in its fountain. For more than 20 years people have been coming to Alma to honor the spinach farmers and to enjoy the annual Spinach Festival. Among the most popular events are carnival rides, arts and crafts, live entertainment, a car show, a spinach cook-off, and a spinach-eating contest.

For more information, please visit *www.almachamber.com*.

## DID YOU KNOW?

In the 1930s, Popeye was credited with increasing the consumption of spinach in the United States by 33 percent, thereby saving the spinach industry.

## Parmesan Spinach Dip

1  (10-ounce) package frozen chopped spinach, thawed

1  (8-ounce) can water chestnuts, drained

1  cup sour cream

1  cup mayonnaise

2  tablespoons grated Parmesan cheese

1  (1.4-ounce) package vegetable soup mix

1  tablespoon finely chopped onion

■  Drain the spinach, pressing to remove the excess liquid. Coarsely chop the water chestnuts. Combine the spinach, water chestnuts, sour cream, mayonnaise, Parmesan cheese, soup mix, and onion in a bowl. Cover and refrigerate overnight. Serve with assorted crackers, pita chips, or vegetables.

**MAKES 12 SERVINGS**

## Sausage Spinach Balls

2  (10-ounce) packages frozen chopped spinach, thawed

2  cups crushed herb stuffing mix (place the stuffing in a plastic bag and crush with a wooden spoon)

1  cup grated Parmesan cheese

4  eggs, beaten

4  green onions, chopped

1/2  pound hot Italian sausage, casings removed

■  Drain the spinach and squeeze dry. Combine the spinach, herb stuffing mix, Parmesan cheese, eggs, and green onions in a large bowl. Cook the sausage in a heavy skillet over high heat until no longer pink, crumbling with a fork, about 4 minutes. Add the sausage and drippings to the spinach mixture, mixing well. Form the mixture into 1-inch balls and place on a baking sheet. Cover and chill overnight.

■  Preheat the oven to 350 degrees. Bake for 15 minutes or until golden. Serve hot. The sausage spinach balls may be frozen after baking.

**MAKES 48 SAUSAGE BALLS**

# Red Potatoes with Wilted Spinach

2    pounds small red potatoes

2    tablespoons unsalted butter

1    tablespoon olive oil

2    garlic cloves, minced

12    ounces packed spinach leaves, stems removed

    Salt and pepper to taste

■ In a medium saucepan bring the potatoes with enough salted water to cover by 1/2 inch to a boil. Reduce the heat and simmer for 15 minutes or until tender; drain. When cool enough to handle, cut each potato in half.

■ In a heavy skillet, heat the butter and oil over moderate heat until the foam subsides. Cook the potatoes cut-sides down, for about 5 minutes or until golden. Loosen the potatoes from bottom of the skillet with a spatula. Add the garlic and cook until the garlic is pale gold. Add the spinach and cook, covered, for 3 minutes or until the spinach is wilted. Season with salt and pepper and stir well.

**MAKES 8 SERVINGS**

# Spinach and Bacon Chicken

7    slices bacon

4    boneless, skinless chicken breasts, cut into 2-inch strips

2    cups all-purpose flour

1    cup white wine

1    (8-ounce) bunch fresh spinach, stems removed

1    cup heavy whipping cream

■ In a large skillet, fry the bacon until the desired degree of doneness. Remove the bacon, reserving the drippings, and drain on paper towels. Dredge the chicken strips in flour, then brown in the reserved bacon drippings until crispy on each side. Remove the chicken and drain on paper towels. Pour out the remaining drippings. Add the wine and spinach to the skillet. Cover and simmer over medium-low heat until the spinach is wilted. Add the cream and chicken strips to the skillet. Crumble the bacon and add to the skillet. Cover and simmer for about 5 minutes longer.

**MAKES 6 SERVINGS**

# The Great American Pie Festival

**WHERE:** Celebration, Florida

**WHEN:** Third weekend in April (Saturday and Sunday)

If pie eating rates right up there in your list of favorite things to do, you'll want to make room on your calendar for Florida's Great American Pie Festival. If you have ever dreamed of a never-ending buffet of pies, toppings, ice cream, and beverages, your dream will come true at this event. Between bites of chocolate cream, lemon meringue, apple, and pecan pies, attendees can enjoy live music, cooking demonstrations for both adults and children, children's games, arts and crafts, and as you might expect, a pie-eating contest. All this leads up to the National Pie Championships where amateur and professional bakers and chefs compete for bragging rights and prize money.

For more information, please visit *www.piecouncil.org*.

## DID YOU KNOW?

A survey by the American Pie Council and Crisco found that apple pie is the favorite flavor among one out of four Americans, followed by pumpkin, chocolate, lemon meringue, and cherry.

# Strawberry Cream Delight

## Crust:

| | |
|---|---|
| 1 | cup all-purpose flour |
| 1/4 | cup crushed vanilla wafers |
| 1/2 | teaspoon salt |
| 1/3 | cup vegetable shortening |
| 3 | to 4 tablespoons cold water, divided |

## Strawberry Layer:

| | |
|---|---|
| 3/4 | cup sugar |
| 1/4 | cup cornstarch |
| 1/8 | teaspoon salt |
| 1 1/2 | cups water |
| 1 | (3-ounce) package strawberry Jell-O |
| 2 | cups frozen unsweetened strawberries |

## Cream Layer:

| | |
|---|---|
| 1 | (3-ounce) package cream cheese, softened |
| 1/3 | cup confectioners' sugar |
| 1 | teaspoon vanilla extract |
| 1/8 | teaspoon salt |
| 1 | cup whipping cream, whipped |
| | Whipped cream for garnish |
| | Fresh strawberries for garnish |

■ For the crust, preheat the oven to 350 degrees. In a mixing bowl, combine the flour, crushed wafers, and salt. Cut in the shortening until the pieces are the size of small peas. Sprinkle 1 tablespoon of the water over mixture. Gently toss with a fork. Repeat with the remaining 2 to 3 tablespoons water until the dough is moistened. Form the dough into a ball. On a lightly floured surface, flatten the dough and roll into a 12-inch circle. Transfer to a 9-inch pie plate. Trim the edge and flute. Prick the bottom and side with a fork. Bake for 10 to 12 minutes or until golden brown. Cool.

■ For the strawberry layer, combine the sugar, cornstarch, and salt in a medium saucepan over medium heat. Gradually stir in the water. Cook and stir until the mixture comes to a boil and is thick and clear. Add the Jell-O and stir until dissolved. Add the frozen strawberries and refrigerate until slightly thickened.

■ For the cream layer, combine the cream cheese, confectioners' sugar, vanilla, and salt in a medium bowl and beat until smooth. Fold in the whipped cream.

■ To serve, spoon half of the cream mixture into the prepared crust. Top with half of the strawberry mixture. Repeat the layers. Garnish with additional whipped cream and fresh strawberries.

**MAKES 8 SERVINGS**

# Appealing Apple Caramel Pie

*Crust:*

2    cups all-purpose flour

1/2  teaspoon salt

2/3  cup vegetable shortening

1    teaspoon vanilla extract

6    tablespoons cold water

*Filling:*

2    tablespoons all-purpose flour

1    cup sugar

1    teaspoon apple pie spice (a mixture of ground cinnamon, ginger, nutmeg, and allspice)

2    tablespoons butter, softened

8    apples, sliced

     Additional butter, cut into small pieces

     Milk for brushing

     Sugar for sprinkling

     Caramel for drizzling

■ For the crust, mix the flour and salt in large bowl. Cut in the shortening with a pastry blender or two knives until the mixture resembles coarse meal. Add the vanilla and cold water. Mix until the dough is moist. Form the dough into a ball and divide in half. Wrap each half in plastic wrap and refrigerate for 30 to 40 minutes.

■ Unwrap 1 portion of the dough and place on waxed paper, sprinkling the dough and waxed paper with flour. Roll the dough into an 11-inch circle. Lift the dough into 9-inch pie pan and gently press into the bottom of the pan.

■ For the filling, preheat the oven to 400 degrees. In a medium bowl combine the flour, sugar, apple pie spice, and butter. Add the apple slices and mix well. Spoon the filling into the prepared pie pan. Dot the apple filling with additional butter.

■ Unwrap the remaining dough portion and place on waxed paper, sprinkling the dough and waxed paper with flour. Roll out the dough and cut into 1/2-inch-thick strips. Lay 2 strips in an "X" shape in the center of the filling. Place the remaining strips in a lattice design over the filling. Seal the dough strips to the edge of the crust. Brush the lattice with milk and sprinkle with sugar.

■ Bake the pie for about 50 minutes or until the crust is golden. Just before serving, drizzle caramel on top of the pie.

MAKES 8 SERVINGS

## Classic Cherry Cherry Bang Bang Pie

*Piecrust:*

3    cups all-purpose flour

1    teaspoon salt

1    teaspoon sugar

1    cup plus 2 tablespoons butter-
     flavored Crisco shortening

1/3  cup plus 1 tablespoon apple juice

1    extra-large egg white, well beaten
     Sugar for sprinkling

*Filling:*

4      cups red tart cherries, pitted

1/2    teaspoon almond extract

1 1/4  cups sugar

3      tablespoons cornstarch

2      tablespoons unsalted butter, melted

2      tablespoons wild chokecherry jelly
       Dash of salt

■ For the crust, sift the flour, salt, and sugar into a large mixing bowl. Cut in the shortening with a pastry blender until the mixture resembles cornmeal. Combine the apple juice and egg white in a small bowl. Sprinkle the mixture, one tablespoon at a time, over the flour mixture, tossing with a fork to form a soft dough. Divide the dough into thirds and shape into 3 disks. Wrap in plastic wrap and chill for 3 to 24 hours. Extra pastry may be frozen for a later use.

■ For the filling, preheat the oven to 425 degrees. In a large bowl combine the cherries, almond extract, sugar, cornstarch, butter, jelly, and salt together; set aside.

■ Roll out 1 pastry disk into a circle and fit into a 9-inch pie plate. Pour the filling into the pie plate. Roll out a second disk and place over the filling. Pressing the edges of the dough together, flute. Cut several slits in the top to vent. You may also cut the crust into strips and arrange in a lattice design. Brush with the beaten egg white and sprinkle with sugar. Bake for 10 minutes. Reduce the oven temperature to 350 degrees and bake an additional 30 to 35 minutes. Remove from the oven. Cool on a wire rack.

MAKES 8 SERVINGS

## Jammin' Banana Cream Pie

*Piecrust:*

1 1/3  cups all-purpose flour

1/2  teaspoon salt

1/2  cup vegetable shortening

3  tablespoons cold water

*Filling:*

2/3  cup Splenda

3  tablespoons cornstarch

1  tablespoon all-purpose flour

1/2  teaspoon salt

3  cups 2% milk

3  egg yolks, lightly beaten

1  tablespoon butter

1 1/2  teaspoons vanilla extract

3/4  cup sugar-free blackberry jam

3  bananas, sliced

Whipped topping for garnish

Blackberries (optional)

■  For the crust, preheat the oven to 425 degrees. Mix the flour and salt in a large bowl. Cut in the shortening with a pastry blender until the mixture resembles peas. Add the water, 1 tablespoon at a time, until the dough forms a ball. Roll the dough onto a floured surface into a 10-inch circle. Place into a 9-inch pie plate and flute the edges. Prick the bottom and side of the piecrust. Bake for 12 to 15 minutes. Remove from the oven and cool on a wire rack.

■  For the filling, combine the Splenda, cornstarch, flour, and salt in a saucepan. Gradually add the milk and stir until smooth. Bring to a boil. Cook and stir for 2 minutes or until thickened. Remove from the heat. Gradually add 1 cup of the hot filling to the egg yolks, stirring constantly. Return the mixture to the pan, stirring constantly. Bring to a gentle boil. Cook and stir for 2 minutes. Remove from the heat. Stir in the butter and vanilla. Set aside to cool, stirring often. When cooled, spoon the jam into the prepared piecrust. Layer the bananas over the jam. Add the cooled filling. Chill for at least 3 hours. Garnish with whipped topping and blackberries, if desired.

**MAKES 8 SERVINGS**

# The Ramp Festival

**WHERE:** Elkins, West Virginia

**WHEN:** The fourth weekend in April (Friday and Saturday)

Much like the plant this festival is named after, the Ramp Festival is small but packs quite a punch. Now in its second decade, the Ramp Festival draws thousands to Elkins each year for such kids' activities as a climbing wall, as well as arts and crafts, live music, and of course, the ever-popular ramp cook-off.

For more information, please visit www.randolphcountywv.com/festivalsandevents/rampfestival.htm.

## DID YOU KNOW?

The flavor and odor of ramps is usually compared to a combination of garlic and onions.

## Ramp Casserole

3   tablespoons butter

8   medium bunches ramps, diced into 1-inch pieces

2   garlic cloves, minced

1/4   cup heavy cream

1/2   cup freshly grated Parmesan cheese, divided

1   tablespoon oil

2   cups fresh bread crumbs

■ Preheat the oven to 350 degrees. In a skillet melt the butter over medium heat. Add the ramps and garlic and cook for about 5 minutes or until tender. Stir in the cream and 1/4 cup of the Parmesan cheese. Pour the mixture into a 1-quart baking dish. In the same skillet, heat the oil over medium heat until hot, but not yet smoking. Sauté the bread crumbs, stirring constantly, for about 3 minutes or until golden brown. Top the casserole with the bread crumbs and the remaining 1/4 cup Parmesan cheese. Bake for 20 minutes.

**MAKES 6 TO 8 SERVINGS**

## Ramp Sausage Hash

1   pound pork sausage (hot or mild is fine)

1/2   cup chopped ramps

2   medium carrots, grated

1   medium green bell pepper, chopped

3   cups diced cooked potatoes

1/2   teaspoon salt

1/4   teaspoon pepper

1   cup shredded Cheddar cheese

■ Brown the sausage in a skillet over medium heat. Add the ramps, carrots, and green pepper and cook until tender. Stir in the potatoes, salt, and pepper. Reduce the heat. Cook, stirring frequently, for 20 minutes or until lightly browned and heated through. Top with the Cheddar cheese.

**MAKES 8 SERVINGS**

# Ramp Dip

· · · · · · · · · · · · · · · · · · · · · · · · · · · · ·

| 1 | pound sour cream |
| 1/2 | pound bacon, cooked crisp and finely diced |
| 1 | green bell pepper, finely chopped |
| 4 | ramps, smashed and chopped |
| | Tabasco sauce to taste |

■ In a large bowl combine the sour cream, bacon, green pepper, ramps, and Tabasco sauce. Cover and refrigerate overnight for best results. Serve with crackers or vegetables.

**MAKES 10 SERVINGS**

---

**DID YOU KNOW?**

Native Americans used ramps in medicines that treated coughs and colds. They also used the juice of a ramp to make a poultice to lessen the pain and itching of bee stings.

# North Carolina Pickle Festival

**WHERE:** Mount Olive, North Carolina

**WHEN:** Last full weekend in April (Friday and Saturday)

"Eat some pickles. Have some fun." Those are the words used to welcome everybody to the North Carolina Pickle Fest in Mount Olive. That slogan must be working since more than 20,000 people show up each and every year. Of course, there's plenty of pickle eating at this fest, but attendees also enjoy pig and duck races, carnival rides, a mechanical bull, a Harley motorcycle show, pony rides, the Pickle Derby, live music, live animals (a petting zoo), and a pickle treasure hunt. And you get to meet the pickle princesses.

For more information, please visit *www.ncpicklefest.org*.

## DID YOU KNOW?

Around the time of Columbus's discovery of America, many crews on transoceanic voyages suffered from scurvy. Amerigo Vespucci, the man who stocked the *Niña*, *Pinta*, and *Santa Maria*, stored ample quantities of vitamin C–rich pickles on board, helping to prevent scurvy. America's name derives from this man who stocked the pickles and later became an explorer himself.

## Pick-a-Pepper Corn Cheese Muffins

1   (8-ounce) box corn muffin mix
    (such as Jiffy)

1   cup sweet 'n hot salad peppers,
    drained and chopped

1   egg

1   cup shredded sharp Cheddar cheese

1/4   cup milk

1/2   cup sour cream

■ Preheat the oven to 375 degrees. Spray a muffin tin with cooking spray. In a large bowl combine the corn muffin mix, salad peppers, egg, cheese, milk, and sour cream and mix until smooth. Pour the batter into the prepared pan, filling the muffin cups 2/3 full. Bake for 15 minutes.

**MAKES 1 DOZEN**

## Deviled Eggs

12   eggs

1/3   cup ranch-style salad dressing

4   ounces cream cheese, softened

1/2   cup chopped onion

1   dill pickle, finely chopped

■ Place the eggs in a large saucepan and cover with cold water. Bring the water to a boil and immediately remove from the heat. Cover and let the eggs stand in hot water for 10 to 12 minutes. Remove the eggs from the hot water. When cool enough to handle, peel the eggs. Slice the eggs in half lengthwise and remove the yolks. Place the yolks in a medium bowl. Mash together with the dressing. Mix in the cream cheese, onion, and dill pickle. Spoon the yolk mixture evenly into the egg whites.

**MAKES 24 DEVILED EGGS**

## Unusual Apple Salad

1/2   cup sugar

1/2   cup distilled white vinegar

3   tart apples, peeled, cored, and
    julienned

2/3   cup chopped onion

1/2   cup chopped dill pickles

■ In a small bowl combine the sugar and vinegar. In a medium bowl mix together the apples, onion, and pickles. Add the vinegar mixture and toss to coat. Refrigerate until thoroughly chilled.

**MAKES 8 SERVINGS**

## Southwest Banana Pepper Dip

2/3  cup mild banana pepper rings, coarsely chopped

16   ounces sour cream

1/4  cup Southwest seasoning

1    (10-ounce) can diced tomatoes with onion, drained

1    cup shredded Cheddar cheese

■ In a large bowl combine the banana peppers, sour cream, Southwest seasoning, diced tomatoes, and cheese until well blended. Store in the refrigerator in an airtight container until ready to serve. Serve with tortilla chips.

**MAKES 10 SERVINGS**

## Festival Vegetable Dip

1    (12-ounce) jar sweet 'n hot salad peppers

2    (15-ounce) cans black beans, rinsed and drained

1    (15-ounce) can whole kernel corn, rinsed and drained

2    (10-ounce) cans diced tomatoes and green chiles, drained

1    chopped green onions

1    cup zesty Italian dressing

1    teaspoon lime juice

Salt and pepper to taste

■ Drain off most of the liquid of the salad peppers. Chop the peppers to the size of the other ingredients. In a large bowl lightly mix the peppers with the remaining liquid, the beans, corn, tomatoes, green onions, salad dressing, and lime juice. Season with salt and pepper. Chill before serving. Serve with tortilla chips.

**MAKES 16 SERVINGS**

---

### DID YOU KNOW?

The phrase "in a pickle" was first introduced by Shakespeare in his play *The Tempest:* "How cam'st thou in this pickle?" and "I have been in such a pickle."

# Mountain Mushroom Festival

**WHERE:** Irvine, Kentucky

**WHEN:** Last full weekend in April (Saturday and Sunday)

Mountain mushrooms—specifically, the morel mushroom—are why more than 20,000 people come to Irvine every year on the last weekend in April. What do they do when they get there? Why, the 5K Fungus marathon race, of course, along with a variety of activities like the Miss Mushroom Festival pageant, a parade, an engine and tractor show, live musical entertainment, arts and crafts, a gem and mineral show, and the mushroom cook-off.

For more information, please visit
*www.estillonline.com/mountain_mushroom_festival.htm.*

## DID YOU KNOW?

It is probably wisest to buy mushrooms from a reputable farm or market and not hunt for them yourself, unless you are an expert in all types of mushrooms, especially poisonous ones.

# Fried Morel Mushrooms

1    pound fresh morel mushrooms

1    teaspoon salt

1    cup all-purpose flour

2    tablespoons milk

1    egg, beaten

1/2    cup finely crushed cracker crumbs

1    cup vegetable oil

■ Wash the mushrooms and slice lengthwise. Soak the mushrooms in salted water; drain and rinse again. Drain the mushrooms on paper towels. Combine the salt with the flour in a shallow dish. In a small bowl combine the milk and egg. Roll the mushrooms in the seasoned flour, then dip the mushrooms in the liquid. Roll in the cracker crumbs.

■ Heat the oil in a skillet over medium-high heat. Add the mushrooms and fry in the hot oil until golden.

**MAKES 4 SERVINGS**

# Morel Mushroom Soup

4    cups sliced fresh morel mushrooms, washed well and patted dry

1    small onion, chopped

2    celery ribs, chopped

4    tablespoons whole wheat flour

4    cups milk

Salt and pepper to taste

■ In a saucepan over medium heat sauté the morels, onion, and celery in a small amount of oil until barely tender. Stir in the flour. Gradually add the milk and salt and pepper. Simmer until slightly thickened.

**MAKES 4 SERVINGS**

**DID YOU KNOW?**
The best mushroom harvesting is done while it is raining.

# Mushroom and Bacon Pasta

4   ounces fresh morel mushrooms (or 1 ounce dried morels)

3/4   cup hot chicken broth, divided

6   slices bacon

1   small red bell pepper, diced

2   garlic cloves

1/4   cup brandy

1/3   teaspoon dried thyme

1/2   cup whipping cream

8   ounces pasta (any shape), cooked

■   If using dried morels, soak them in 1/4 cup of the chicken broth until soft; drain. Cut the mushrooms into bite-size pieces; set aside.

■   Cook the bacon in a skillet until crisp. Drain, reserving all but 1 tablespoon of the drippings. Crumble the bacon and set aside. Using the same skillet, sauté the bell pepper, garlic, and mushrooms in the reserved bacon drippings over medium heat for 5 minutes. Remove from the pan. Add the brandy and scrape the pan, reducing to a glaze. Return the bell pepper mixture to the pan. Add the remaining 1/2 cup chicken broth and thyme. Simmer for 10 minutes or until reduced by half. Reduce the heat to low and add the cream. Simmer until warm. Toss with the cooked pasta and the crumbled bacon.

**MAKES 2 SERVINGS**

## DID YOU KNOW?

There are over 38,000 known varieties of mushrooms around the world. North America is home to more than 3,000 of them, with diverse colors, textures, and flavors. Some rare species grow for only one week each year.

# National Cornbread Festival

**WHERE:** South Pittsburgh, Tennessee
**WHEN:** The last weekend in April (Saturday and Sunday)

Every year, during the last full weekend in April, the smells of cornbread fill the air in South Pittsburgh where cast-iron skillets are made. This festival even has its own Cornbread Festival theme song. Each year, tens of thousands of cornbread lovers come to enjoy great food, arts and crafts, a Cornbread 5K race, and even a Cornbread Kids' corner. People with a competitive streak can enter the cornbread-eating contest and buttermilk chug or the ice cream–eating contest. Adjacent to the festival grounds is a full-size carnival midway.

For more information, please visit *www.nationalcornbread.com.*

## DID YOU KNOW?

Cornbread became very popular during the Civil War because it was inexpensive to make and could be prepared in many different forms.

# Caribbean Cornbread Crab Cakes

1     (6-ounce) package country or buttermilk cornbread mix (such as Martha White)

*Salsa:*

3     tablespoons fresh lime juice

1     tablespoon honey

1     teaspoon freshly grated ginger

1/8   teaspoon salt

2     tablespoons chopped fresh cilantro

1/2   cup chopped red bell pepper

2     mangos, peeled and cubed

1     cup chopped fresh pineapple

*Crab Cakes:*

2     eggs

1     cup mayonnaise

1     tablespoon fresh lemon juice

1     teaspoon seafood seasoning

1/2   teaspoon dry mustard

1/4   cup sliced green onions

2     (6-ounce) packages lump crabmeat, lightly drained
      Black pepper to taste

1/2   cup oil

■ In an 8-inch cast-iron skillet bake the cornbread according to the package directions. Cool and crumble.

■ For the salsa, in a medium bowl, whisk together the lime juice, honey, ginger, and salt. Add the cilantro, bell pepper, mangos, and pineapple; stir. Refrigerate.

■ For the crab cakes, in a large bowl combine the eggs, mayonnaise, lemon juice, seafood seasoning, and dry mustard; mix well. Stir in the crumbled cornbread. Fold in the green onions and crabmeat. Season with pepper. Heat the oil in a cast-iron skillet over medium heat. Form the crab mixture into 12 cakes. Cook in the hot oil for 3 to 4 minutes on each side or until lightly browned. Drain on paper towels. Serve topped with the salsa.

**MAKES 6 SERVINGS**

## Chicken Taco Cornbread Wedges with Ranchero Cilantro Drizzle

*Dressing:*

1/2    cup ranch dressing

1/2    cup salsa verde

1    cup tightly packed cilantro leaves

*Filling:*

2    tablespoons extra-virgin olive oil

1/2    cup finely chopped onion

1/4    cup finely chopped red bell pepper

1    tablespoon finely chopped jalapeño chile

2    cups shredded rotisserie chicken

3    tablespoons finely chopped fresh cilantro leaves

1/2    teaspoon salt

1/2    teaspoon cumin

1/4    teaspoon black pepper

1    (14 1/2-ounce) can diced tomatoes with green chiles, undrained

*Crust:*

1    egg

1    (7-ounce) package sweet yellow cornbread mix (such as Martha White)

1/2    cup milk

3/4    cup crushed corn tortilla chips

1/2    cup shredded mozzarella cheese

1/2    cup shredded Cheddar cheese

3    cups shredded romaine

1    cup chopped tomatoes

■    For the dressing, combine the ranch dressing, salsa verde, and cilantro leaves in a small food processor or blender. Process until well blended. Pour into a bowl. Cover and refrigerate.

■    For the filling, in a 10-inch cast-iron skillet heat the olive oil over medium heat. Add the onion, bell pepper, and jalapeño and cook for 3 to 5 minutes or until tender, stirring frequently. Stir in the chicken, cilantro, salt, cumin, pepper, and tomatoes with juice; cook for 5 minutes. Remove from the skillet and let cool. Wipe out the skillet with a paper towel; grease generously.

■    For the crust, preheat the oven to 400 degrees. In a large bowl, beat the egg. Add the cornbread mix and milk; mix well. Place the tortilla chips into the greased skillet. Pour the cornbread mixture over the chips. Spoon the filling over the cornbread mixture; sprinkle with the mozzarella and Cheddar cheeses. Bake for 16 to 20 minutes or until golden brown.

■    To serve, cut into wedges. Top with the romaine and tomatoes; drizzle with the dressing.

**MAKES 6 SERVINGS**

## Monte Cristo Cornbread Skillet Supper

1   (6-ounce) package country cornbread mix (such as Martha White)

1½  cups chopped cooked turkey

½   cup chopped cooked ham

1½  cups shredded Swiss cheese

4   eggs

1   cup milk

2   tablespoons mayonnaise

2   tablespoons honey mustard, divided

1½  teaspoons salt

½   teaspoon pepper

½   cup currant jelly

    Confectioners' sugar for dusting

■ Prepare the cornbread according to the package directions, baking it in a 10½-inch cast-iron skillet. (The cornbread will be thin.) Remove the cornbread from the skillet and cut into cubes. Wipe out the skillet with paper towels; grease generously.

■ Preheat the oven to 350 degrees. Place the cornbread cubes in the skillet. Top with the turkey, ham, and cheese. In a medium bowl whisk together the eggs, milk, mayonnaise, 1 tablespoon of the honey mustard, the salt, and pepper until well blended. Pour evenly into the skillet. Bake for 30 to 35 minutes or until set and lightly browned.

■ Warm the currant jelly slightly to melt. Add the remaining 1 tablespoon honey mustard; whisk to blend. Set aside.

■ Remove the skillet from the oven. Cut the cornbread into wedges and sprinkle with confectioners' sugar. Serve with the currant jelly and mustard sauce.

**MAKES 4 SERVINGS**

### DID YOU KNOW?

"Cornbread" is a generic name for any number of quick breads containing cornmeal. (A quick bread is leavened chemically, rather than by yeast.)

## Alabama Country Supper

*Filling:*

1½   pounds pork sausage patties

6     cups sliced, peeled Golden Delicious
      or Granny Smith apples

½     cup dried cherries

1     cup sugar

¼     cup (½ stick) butter or margarine

*Topping:*

½     cup milk

1     (6-ounce) package buttermilk or
      country cornbread mix (such as
      Martha White)

2     tablespoons butter or margarine,
      melted

1     egg, beaten

■ For the filling, preheat the oven to 425
degrees. In a 10-inch cast-iron or ovenproof
skillet, cook the sausage patties over medium
heat until thoroughly cooked, turning once.
Remove from the skillet and drain on paper
towels. Discard the drippings. In the same
skillet, combine the apples, cherries, sugar,
and butter. Cook over medium heat until the
apples are tender, stirring occasionally. Add the
cooked sausage to the skillet, tucking the patties under the apples and continue cooking.

■ For the topping, in a medium bowl, combine the milk, cornbread mix, melted butter,
and egg; stir until smooth. Pour evenly over
the sausage mixture. Bake for 15 to 20 minutes
or until golden brown.

**MAKES 8 SERVINGS**

## Festive Good Luck Cornbread Skillet

*Filling:*

1     pound smoked sausage

½     cup chopped onion

1     to 2 garlic cloves, minced

2     cans (15-ounce) black-eyed peas,
      rinsed and drained

1     can (14.5-ounce) fat-free, less-
      sodium chicken broth

10    ounces frozen chopped collard
      greens, thawed

½     teaspoon hot pepper sauce

*Topping:*

2     cups self-rising cornmeal mix

2     teaspoons sugar

1½   cups buttermilk

¼     cup vegetable oil

1   egg, beaten

2   ounces shredded Cheddar cheese

1/4   cup finely chopped fresh parsley or cilantro

Sour cream for garnish (optional)

Pickled jalapeño chile slices for garnish (optional)

■ For the filling, preheat the oven to 400 degrees. Cut the sausage in half lengthwise; cut crosswise into 1/4-inch slices. In a 12-inch cast-iron or ovenproof skillet, combine the sausage, onion, and garlic. Cook over medium heat until the sausage is browned and the onion is tender, stirring occasionally. Add the black-eyed peas, chicken broth, collard greens, and hot pepper sauce and mix well. Bring to a boil. Reduce the heat to low and simmer for 10 minutes.

■ For the topping, in a large bowl combine the cornmeal mix, sugar, buttermilk, oil, egg, cheese, and parsley; stir until smooth. Spoon the batter evenly over the filling in the skillet. Bake for 30 to 40 minutes or until golden brown. If desired, garnish with sour cream and pickled jalapeño chile slices.

**MAKES 8 SERVINGS**

## Sausage Gravy Breakfast Skillet

1   pound hot pork sausage

1   (2.64-ounce) package country gravy mix

3 1/3   cups milk, divided

4   hard-boiled eggs, peeled and diced

2   (6-ounce) packages Martha White Cornbread Creations Extra Rich Buttermilk Cornbread Mix

2   tablespoons sugar

■ Heat a 10-inch cast-iron skillet over medium heat. Add the sausage and cook until browned. Meanwhile, in a medium bowl combine the gravy mix and 2 cups of the milk; whisk until smooth. Pour over the sausage in the skillet. Cook and stir over medium heat until thick and bubbly. Stir in the eggs. Remove from the heat. In a medium bowl combine the cornbread mix and sugar with the remaining 1 1/3 cups milk. Stir until smooth. Pour evenly over the sausage mixture. Bake for 22 to 28 minutes or until the cornbread is golden brown.

**MAKES 8 SERVINGS**

## Cornbread Supreme

3    thick slices bacon

4    eggs

1/4    cup milk

1/2    cup (1 stick) butter, melted and cooled

1    (6-ounce) package buttermilk or country cornbread mix (such as Martha White)

6    dashes hot pepper sauce

1    medium onion, chopped

10    ounces frozen chopped broccoli or frozen spinach, thawed and well drained

1    pound peeled and deveined shrimp, cooked and coarsely chopped

2    cups (8 ounces) finely shredded Cheddar cheese, divided

     Chopped fresh parsley

■ Preheat the oven to 375 degrees. Cook the bacon in a 10 1/2-inch cast-iron skillet until crisp. Drain on paper towels, reserving 1 table-spoon of the drippings. When cool, crumble the bacon and set aside. Place the skillet with the reserved bacon drippings in the oven.

■ Beat the eggs in a large bowl. Add the milk, butter, cornbread mix, and hot pepper sauce; stir until well blended. Stir in the onion, broccoli, shrimp, and 1 1/2 cups of the cheese. Pour the batter into the hot skillet. Sprinkle the remaining 1/2 cup cheese evenly over the top. Bake for 30 to 35 minutes or until set and golden brown. Sprinkle with the bacon and parsley.

**MAKES 8 SERVINGS**

## Pesto Cornbread with Chicken and Sun-Dried Tomato Streusel

1    (6-ounce) package yellow cornbread mix

1    egg, beaten

1/2    cup milk

1/2    cup pesto sauce

1 1/2    cups chopped grilled chicken

1    cup marinated sun-dried tomatoes, finely chopped

1/2    cup grated Parmesan cheese

2    tablespoons olive oil

1    cup mozzarella cheese

2    tablespoons chopped fresh basil

■ Preheat the oven to 425 degrees. In a large bowl combine the cornbread mix, egg, milk, and pesto sauce. In a separate large bowl combine the chicken, sun-dried tomatoes, and Parmesan cheese. Heat the oil in a 10-inch cast-iron skillet in the oven for 8 to 10 minutes. Pour the cornbread batter into the hot skillet. Immediately spoon the chicken mixture evenly on top of the cornbread batter. Bake for 15 to 20 minutes or until golden brown. Sprinkle with the mozzarella cheese and basil and return to oven for 2 to 3 minutes longer or until the cheese is melted.

**MAKES 6 SERVINGS**

# White Chicken Chili with Cheddar Hushpuppy Crust

*Filling:*

1    tablespoon olive oil

1    cup finely chopped onion

2    garlic cloves, minced

1    medium green bell pepper, chopped

1/2  teaspoon cumin

1    tablespoon chili powder

2    tablespoons lime juice

1    (19-ounce) can cannellini beans, rinsed and drained

2    cups chopped cooked chicken

1    (14-ounce) can chicken broth

1    (4.5-ounce) can mild green chiles, drained

*Crust:*

1    egg

1/2  cup milk

3    tablespoons butter or margarine, melted

1    (6-ounce) package country cornbread mix (such as Martha White)

1/4  cup finely chopped onion

1    cup shredded Cheddar cheese

     Sour cream (optional)

     Salsa (optional)

     Chopped fresh cilantro (optional)

For the filling, preheat the oven to 400 degrees. In a 10 1/2-inch cast-iron skillet, heat the olive oil over medium heat. Add the onion, garlic, bell pepper, cumin, and chili powder and cook for about 3 to 5 minutes or until the vegetables are tender. Add the lime juice, beans, chicken, chicken broth, and chiles and simmer for about 10 minutes.

For the crust, in a medium bowl beat the egg. Add the milk, butter, and cornbread mix; mix well. Stir in the onion and cheese. Pour over the filling in the skillet. Bake for 25 to 30 minutes or until the cornbread is golden brown. Serve with small bowls of sour cream, salsa, and cilantro, if desired.

**MAKES 6 SERVINGS**

## Coastal Carolina Skillet Supper

*Filling:*

16  ounces hot and spicy-flavored sausage links

1  cup chopped onion

14  ounces raw large shrimp, peeled and deveined

2  cups frozen corn, thawed

*Cornbread:*

2  cups buttermilk self-rising cornmeal mix (such as Martha White)

1 1/3  cups milk

1/3  cup vegetable oil

1  tablespoon seafood seasoning

2  eggs, beaten

*Pimiento-Mayonnaise Sauce:*

2  cups mayonnaise

2  ounces chopped pimientos, undrained

3  tablespoons chopped fresh chives

2  tablespoons fresh lemon juice

1/8  teaspoon cracked black pepper

■  For the filling, cook the sausage links in a 10 1/2-inch cast-iron or ovenproof skillet over medium heat until thoroughly cooked, turning frequently. Remove from the skillet; drain on paper towels. Cut the sausage links into 1-inch pieces and place in a large bowl; set aside. Cook the onion in the same skillet over medium-low heat until tender, stirring occasionally. Add the cooked onion to the large bowl. Heat the same skillet over medium-high heat until hot. Add the shrimp and cook for about 2 minutes or just until the shrimp turn pink, stirring constantly. Add the cooked shrimp to the large bowl; mix well. Stir in the corn.

■  For the cornbread, preheat the oven to 425 degrees. In a medium bowl, combine the corn meal mix, milk, vegetable oil, seafood seasoning, and eggs; stir until smooth. Spoon half of the cornbread batter into the skillet; spread evenly over the bottom. Spoon the shrimp mixture over the batter to within 1 inch of the side of the skillet. Spoon the remaining batter evenly over the shrimp mixture, spreading the batter to the edge of the skillet. Bake for 30 to 35 minutes or until golden brown. Let stand 15 minutes before serving.

■  For the sauce, in a small bowl combine the mayonnaise, pimientos and liquid, chives, lemon juice, and black pepper; blend well.

■  To serve, cut the cornbread into 6 wedges. Top with the pimiento-mayonnaise sauce.

**MAKES 6 SERVINGS**

# Vidalia® Onion Festival

**WHERE:** Vidalia, Georgia

**WHEN:** The last weekend in April (Friday through Sunday)

The springtime Vidalia Onion Festival celebrates the annual harvest of Georgia's official state vegetable, the sweet Vidalia onion. First organized in 1978 by local civic groups to promote the Vidalia onion and raise funds for the community, this festival now attracts as many as 75,000 visitors. Onion lovers are able to enjoy freshly cooked Vidalia onion rings, an onion-eating contest, and onion cooking demonstrations. Other festival activities include a street dance, a rodeo, a children's parade, an air show, fireworks, carnival rides, train rides, and the Vidalia Onion Arts and Crafts Festival.

For more information, please visit *www.vidaliaonionfestival.com*.

## DID YOU KNOW?

Onions must be harvested by hand due to their delicate nature.

## Vidalia and Sausage Casserole

4    cups thinly sliced green onion tops

2    cups sliced Vidalia onions

1/2    teaspoon salt

1/2    teaspoon black pepper

1    tablespoon hot sauce

1/4    teaspoon ground red pepper

1/2    teaspoon garlic powder

2    tablespoons Worcestershire sauce

1/2    teaspoon Louisiana Cajun seasoning

1    tablespoon lemon juice

1    tablespoon teriyaki sauce

3    or 4 medium baking potatoes, peeled and sliced

Salt and pepper to taste

2    pounds sausage meat, browned and drained

2    (10 1/2-ounce) cans Cheddar cheese soup

2    cups shredded Cheddar cheese

■ Preheat the oven to 400 degrees. Layer the green onions and Vidalia onions in a deep 9 x 13-inch baking pan. Sprinkle the Vidalia onions with the salt, black pepper, hot sauce, red pepper, garlic powder, Worcestershire sauce, Louisiana Cajun seasoning, lemon juice, and teriyaki sauce. Arrange the potatoes over the onion layer. Season with salt and pepper. Layer the sausage on top of the potatoes. Pour the Cheddar cheese soup on top of the sausage meat. Cover and bake for 35 minutes. Uncover and continue to bake for an additional 35 minutes. Remove the casserole from the oven and sprinkle with the shredded cheese on top. Bake for 10 more minutes or until the cheese is completely melted.

**MAKES 12 SERVINGS**

## Vidalia Casserole in a Jiffy

1    (8 1/2-ounce) box Jiffy corn muffin mix

2    (15-ounce) cans cream-style corn

1/4    cup (1/2 stick) butter, softened

1    large Vidalia onion, chopped

1    (4-ounce) jar chopped pimientos, drained

1/2    green bell pepper, chopped

Salt and pepper to taste

1    Vidalia onion, sliced

■ Preheat the oven to 350 degrees. Grease a 9 x 13-inch pan. Prepare the muffins according to the package directions. Add the corn, butter, chopped onion, pimientos, green pepper, and salt and pepper to taste. Mix well. Pour into the prepared pan. Top with the sliced onion. Bake for 35 to 40 minutes or until golden brown.

**MAKES 12 SERVINGS**

## Vidalia Brie Surprise

1 sheet frozen puff pastry, thawed
1 (8-ounce) round Brie cheese
1/4 cup raspberry preserves
1/2 cup chopped Vidalia onion
1/4 cup sliced almonds, toasted
2 egg whites, lightly beaten

■ Preheat the oven to 350 degrees. Place the puff pastry on a lightly greased baking sheet. Place the cheese in the center of the pastry. Spread the raspberry preserves over the cheese. Top with the onion and almonds. Wrap the puff pastry around the cheese, trimming the excess. Seal the seams by moistening the edges with water and pressing together with your fingers. Baste lightly with the egg whites. Bake for 30 to 40 minutes or until the pastry is golden brown. Serve with crackers.

**MAKES 8 SERVINGS**

## Vidalia Onion Shrimp Pasta

1 pound rotini pasta
1 pound shrimp, peeled and deveined
  Olive oil for sautéing
1 cup mayonnaise
1 cup coleslaw dressing (such as Marzetti's)
1 cup golden raisins
1 cup dried cranberries
1 (20-ounce) can pineapple tidbits, drained
1 cup grapes, sliced
1 large Vidalia onion, chopped

■ Cook the pasta according to the package directions; drain. Sauté the shrimp in olive oil. Set aside to cool. Combine the mayonnaise, dressing, raisins, cranberries, pineapple, grapes, onion, pasta, and shrimp together in a large bowl. Cover and chill overnight.

**MAKES 8 SERVINGS**

## Cream of Vidalia Onion Soup

3/4 cup (1 1/2 sticks) butter, divided

3 cups chopped Vidalia onions

1/4 cup all-purpose flour

1/4 teaspoon salt

1/2 teaspoon pepper

2 1/2 cups milk

1 1/2 cups half-and-half

Shredded cheese to taste (your choice)

Vidalia onion tops or parsley for garnish

■ Melt 1/2 cup of the butter in a skillet over medium heat. Add the onions and sauté until tender. Set aside. Melt the remaining 1/4 cup butter in a Dutch oven. Add the flour, salt, and pepper and stir until smooth. Cook for 1 minute stirring constantly. Gradually add the milk and half-and-half. Cook over medium heat, stirring constantly until thickened. Stir in the sautéed Vidalia onions. Reduce the heat and simmer. Sprinkle with cheese to taste and garnish with Vidalia onion tops or parsley.

**MAKES 6 SERVINGS**

## Savory Stuffed Vidalia Onions and Shrimp

4 large Vidalia onions, peeled

1 to 3 ounces cream cheese, softened

3 slices bacon, cooked and crumbled

1/4 cup chives

1/4 cup sliced fresh mushrooms

1/2 teaspoon salt

1/4 teaspoon pepper

1/2 teaspoon garlic salt

2 drops red pepper sauce

1/4 cup heavy whipping cream

1/4 cup shredded Cheddar cheese

20 boiled shrimp for garnish

Parsley for garnish

■ Wrap each onion in a damp paper towel. Microwave on high for 10 minutes or until tender. Scoop out the inside, leaving 3 outer layers of onion. You should have a circular opening. Place the onions in a microwave-safe dish. Set aside.

■ Combine the cream cheese, bacon, chives, mushrooms, salt, pepper, garlic salt, red pepper sauce, cream, and cheese in a large bowl; mix well. Spoon the mixture evenly into each onion. Microwave on high for 2 to 3 minutes until well heated.

■ Garnish each onion with 5 boiled shrimp around the top edge of the onion. Sprinkle the center with parsley.

**MAKES 4 SERVINGS**

## Sweet Vidalia Pie

| | |
|---|---|
| 1 | cup shredded mozzarella cheese |
| 1 | cup shredded Cheddar cheese |
| 1 | cup mayonnaise |
| 3 | large tomatoes, thinly sliced and drained |
| 1 | cup thinly sliced Vidalia onions |
| 1 | (9-inch) deep-dish piecrust, baked |
| 1 | pound bacon, fried and crumbled |

■ Preheat the oven to 350 degrees. In a large bowl combine the mozzarella cheese, Cheddar cheese, and mayonnaise. Place the tomatoes and onions in the baked piecrust. Spread the mayonnaise mixture over the top. Sprinkle with the bacon. Bake for 30 to 40 minutes.

**MAKES 8 SERVINGS**

## DID YOU KNOW?

When farmer Mose Coleman discovered in 1931 that the onions he had planted were sweet instead of hot, that was the beginning of the Vidalia onion. Although marketing a sweet onion wasn't easy, Coleman persevered and sold his first crop of Vidalia onions for $3.50 per 50-pound bag, a very good price for onions at that time.

# West Tennessee Strawberry Festival

**WHERE:** Humboldt, Tennessee

**WHEN:** Starts the first Sunday in May and runs through the following Sunday (an 8-day festival)

One of Tennessee's oldest festivals, the West Tennessee Strawberry Festival has been around since 1934. More than 100,000 visitors come every year to Humboldt to participate in arts and crafts shows, a walking horse show, an antique tractor show, a classic car show, a barbecue cook-off contest, a checker tournament, parades, beauty pageants, a carnival, a recipe contest, and much, much more!

For more information, please visit *www.wtsf.org*.

## DID YOU KNOW?

Strawberries are a member of the rose family.

# Strawberry Crunch

*Crust:*

2    cups self-rising flour

1    cup chopped pecans

1    cup (2 sticks) margarine, softened

*Strawberry Filling:*

3    (8-ounce) containers frozen whipped topping, thawed and divided

1    (8-ounce) package cream cheese, softened

3    cups confectioners' sugar

1    quart strawberries, puréed

2    (8-ounce) containers strawberry glaze

     Sliced strawberries for garnish

     Finely chopped pecans for garnish

▮   For the crust, preheat the oven to 350 degrees. Combine the flour and pecans together in a large bowl. Cut in the margarine using a pastry blender or two knives until the mixture resembles coarse meal. Press into a 9 x 13-inch baking dish. Bake for 25 minutes. Cool completely.

▮   For the filling, in a mixing bowl beat 1 container of the whipped topping with the cream cheese and confectioners' sugar. Spread the mixture over the cooled crust. Pour the puréed strawberries on top of the cream cheese mixture. Spread the glaze over the strawberries. Spread the remaining 2 containers whipped topping over the strawberries and glaze. Garnish with sliced strawberries and finely chopped pecans.

**MAKES 8 SERVINGS**

# Sassy Berry Salsa

2    quarts strawberries, chopped

1/2  cup minced garlic

4    teaspoons kosher salt

2    teaspoons cumin

1/4  cup lime juice

1    large white onion, chopped

5    jalapeño chiles, minced

5    bunches minced fresh cilantro

▮   In a large bowl combine the strawberries, garlic, salt, cumin, lime juice, onion, jalapeños, and cilantro and mix well. Let marinate 1 to 2 hours before serving. Serve with chips.

**MAKES 12 SERVINGS**

## Strawberry Paradise Surprise

1    angel food cake

1    (8-ounce) container frozen whipped topping, thawed

1    (3-ounce) package vanilla instant pudding mix

1    quart strawberries, sliced

1½   teaspoons almond extract

Whole strawberries for garnish

■ Slice the cake horizontally into 3 layers. In a bowl combine the whipped topping, pudding mix, sliced strawberries, and almond extract. Spread the mixture between the layers and on top of the cake. Garnish with whole strawberries.

**MAKES 12 SERVINGS**

## Strawberry Cookies

1    (18.25-ounce) package strawberry cake mix

1    egg

1    egg white

½    cup oil

■ Preheat the oven to 350 degrees. Combine the cake mix, egg, egg white, and oil together in a bowl. Shape the batter into small balls. Place the balls on a cookie sheet and bake for 15 minutes.

**MAKES 36 COOKIES**

## Springtime Strawberry Spinach Salad

1    tablespoon olive oil

1    (10-ounce) package fresh spinach, torn

2    cups fresh strawberries, sliced

½    cup chopped walnuts

⅓    cup vegetable oil

3    tablespoons raspberry vinegar

1    teaspoon sugar

⅓    teaspoon salt

■ In a large bowl combine the olive oil, spinach, strawberries, and walnuts. In a jar with a lid combine the vegetable oil, vinegar, sugar, and salt. Shake well. Drizzle the dressing over the salad and toss to coat.

**MAKES 8 SERVINGS**

## Strawberry Cheese Ball

12  ounces cream cheese, softened

1  (8-ounce) can crushed pineapple, drained

1  cup chopped fresh strawberries

■ In a large bowl combine the cream cheese, pineapple, and strawberries; mix well. Shape into a ball and refrigerate overnight. Serve with crackers.

**MAKES 10 SERVINGS**

## Strawberry Bread

*Bread:*

3  cups self-rising flour

2  teaspoons ground cinnamon

3  eggs, beaten

1/2  teaspoon salt

2 1/4  cups sugar

1 1/3  cups oil

2 1/2  cups fresh strawberries, chopped and juice reserved for glaze

1  cup chopped pecans

*Topping:*

1/2  cup sugar

1/3  cup all-purpose flour

1/4  cup (1/2 stick) butter

1 1/2  teaspoons ground cinnamon

*Glaze:*

1  cup confectioners' sugar

Reserved juice from strawberries

■ For the bread, preheat the oven to 350 degrees. Grease and flour 2 loaf pans. Combine the flour, cinnamon, eggs, salt, sugar, and oil in a large bowl. Fold in the strawberries and pecans. Pour the batter into the prepared loaf pans and bake for 1 hour. Maintain the oven temperature.

■ For the topping, combine the sugar, flour, butter, and cinnamon in a bowl and mix together with a fork. Sprinkle the topping over the bread. Bake for an additional 20 minutes.

■ For the glaze, combine the confectioners' sugar and the reserved strawberry juice in a small bowl. Drizzle the glaze over the warm bread.

**MAKES 16 SERVINGS**

## Strawberry Gooey Butter Cookies

1    (8-ounce) package cream cheese, at room temperature

1/2  cup (1 stick) butter, at room temperature

1    egg

1    teaspoon vanilla extract

1    (18.25-ounce) package moist strawberry cake mix
     Confectioners' sugar

▩ In a mixing bowl cream together the cream cheese and butter until smooth. Beat in the egg and vanilla. Beat in the cake mix. Cover and refrigerate for 2 hours or until firm.

▩ Preheat the oven to 350 degrees. Roll the chilled batter into small balls and then roll them in confectioners' sugar. Place on an ungreased cookie sheet, 2 inches apart. Bake for 12 minutes.

**MAKES 36 COOKIES**

## Strawberry Jam-N-Cheese Cake

*Cake:*

2    (18.25-ounce) packages strawberry cake mix

1 1/4 cups water

2/3  cup buttermilk

1    cup (2 sticks) butter, softened

1/4  cup rum

1    (21-ounce) can strawberry pie filling

1    cup chopped walnuts

*Icing:*

2    pounds confectioners' sugar

1/2  cup crushed strawberries

1    cup (2 sticks) butter, softened

4    ounces cream cheese, softened

1/4  teaspoon vanilla extract

1/2  cup chopped walnuts (optional)

*Topping:*

2    tablespoons cornstarch

1½   cups water

½    cup sugar

1    (3-ounce) package strawberry Jell-O

1½   cups chopped strawberries, juice
     reserved

1    (7-ounce) package ladyfingers

     Whipped topping for garnish
     (optional)

     Whole strawberries for garnish
     (optional)

■ For the cake, preheat the oven to 350 degrees. Grease and flour three 9-inch round cake pans. In a mixing bowl beat the cake mix, water, buttermilk, butter, and rum together until smooth. Fold in the pie filling and walnuts. Pour the batter into the prepared pans and bake for 30 minutes or until the cake springs back. Let cool completely.

■ For the icing, in a mixing bowl combine the confectioners' sugar, strawberries, butter, cream cheese, and vanilla. Spread the icing in between each layer and on the side of the cooled cake. Sprinkle with the chopped walnuts, if desired.

■ For the topping, combine the cornstarch, water, and sugar in a saucepan. Mix well. Cook over medium heat until clear. Add the Jell-O, stirring until dissolved. Stir in the chopped strawberries. Spread on the top of the cake. Place the ladyfingers vertically on the side of the cake. Brush them with the reserved strawberry juice. If desired, decorate the top of the cake with whipped topping and whole strawberries.

**MAKES 16 SERVINGS**

**DID YOU KNOW?**
Strawberries were grown in ancient Rome, and in the 13th century they were used as a medicinal herb.

# May

# Poke Salat Festival

**WHERE:** Arab, Alabama

**WHEN:** First weekend of May (Friday and Saturday)

Any food festival originated by a group calling themselves the Liars Club just has to be fun. Such is the case with the Poke Salat Festival in Arab, where more than 5,000 folks gather to enjoy an art show, a womanless beauty pageant (the festival says a beauty pageant with real women is in the planning stages), a best-dressed pet contest, a stroller strut, street dances, a quilt display, a classic car show, a parade, a wackiest hat contest, and a motorcycle rally. They used to have a poke salat cooking contest, but a woman named Granny Nell won it every year for more than 20 years, so they called off the contest and just let Granny Nell give cooking demonstrations.

For more information, please visit *www.pokesalatfestival.com*.

## DID YOU KNOW?

Some supporters of James K. Polk, the 11th president of the United States, wore poke leaves during his campaign. (Poke is sometimes spelled "polk.")

**NOTE:** *Poke can be poisonous and have possible ill effects if not picked at the right stage and prepared properly. Anyone who prepares poke salat should take great care to ensure it is prepared correctly and is safe to eat. Your local agricultural department is a good source of information on methods of preparing this Southern delicacy.*

## Poke Salat and Eggs

1 1/2  pounds poke salat

3  slices bacon

6  tablespoons oil

1  cup chopped green onions

4  eggs

■ Wash the poke salat well. In a large saucepan combine the poke salat and water and bring to a rapid boil for 20 minutes. Drain and rinse with cold water. Bring the poke salat to a rapid boil again, starting with cold water, for 20 minutes. Drain and rinse with cold water. For the third time, bring the poke salat to a rapid boil using cold water and boil for 20 minutes longer. Drain and rinse with cold water. Let drain completely.

■ In a skillet fry the bacon until crisp. Crumble and set aside. Heat the oil in the same skillet and fry the poke salat. Add the onions and bacon and fry for 10 minutes. Add the eggs and cook until scrambled. Serve hot.

**MAKES 4 SERVINGS**

## Poke and Ham Hot Pocket

1  frozen biscuit, thawed

1  cup packed poke salat

2  tablespoons chopped ham

2  tablespoons grated Cheddar cheese

2  tablespoons chopped onion

■ Wash the poke salat well. In a large saucepan combine the poke salat and water and bring to a rapid boil for 20 minutes. Drain and rinse with cold water. Bring the poke salat to a rapid boil again, starting with cold water, for 20 minutes. Drain and rinse with cold water. For the third time, bring the poke salat to a rapid boil using cold water and boil for 20 minutes longer. Drain and rinse with cold water. Let drain completely.

■ Preheat the oven to 375 degrees. Roll the biscuit until it is about 1/4 inch thick (it should be about the size of a saucer). Pat the boiled poke salat dry with a paper towel and place it in the center of the biscuit. Spoon the ham, cheese, and onion over the poke salat. Fold the crust together, pressing the edges with a fork to form a pastry that resembles a semicircular fried pie. Place on a greased baking pan and bake for 15 minutes or until golden brown.

**MAKES 1 SERVING**

## Poke Salat

. . . . . . . . . . . . . . . . . . . . . . . . . . . . .

| | |
|---|---|
| 1 | to 2 pounds poke salat |
| 6 | to 8 slices bacon |
| 1 | large onion, quartered |
| 1/4 | cup water |
| | Salt to taste |
| 2 | sliced hard-cooked eggs |

■ Wash the poke salat well. In a large saucepan combine the poke salat and water and bring to a rapid boil for 20 minutes. Drain and rinse with cold water. Bring the poke salat to a rapid boil again, starting with cold water, for 20 minutes. Drain and rinse with cold water. For the third time, bring the poke salat to a rapid boil using cold water and boil for 20 minutes longer. Drain and rinse with cold water. Let drain completely.

■ In a skillet fry the bacon until crisp. Remove from the skillet and drain on paper towels, reserving the drippings. Heat the reserved drippings in the skillet and add the poke salat to the skillet. Add the onion, water, and salt. Sauté until the onion is tender, about 15 to 20 minutes.

■ To serve, crumble the bacon. Top the poke salat with the hard-cooked eggs and crumbled bacon.

**MAKES 4 SERVINGS**

### DID YOU KNOW?

Poke was a favorite of early settlers in North America. After a long winter without fresh fruit and vegetables, the vitamin-rich greens were considered a good spring tonic.

# Florida Citrus Festival

## Winter Haven, Florida

*Ron Manville*

Orange Pecan Pound Cake (recipe on page 4).

# Chocolate Lovers Festival

**Fairfax, Virginia**

*Left page:* Entries in the Chocolate Challenge art contest.

*Right page:* The Taste of Chocolate, where visitors sample the wares of chocolate vendors.

*Photos by Chris Fow, City of Fairfax Community Relations Office. Photo copyright owned by the City of Fairfax.*

# Highland Maple Festival

## Monterey, McDowell, and Blue Grass, Virginia

*Ellen Phillips*

*J. Jacenich*

*Top:* Making maple syrup the old-fashioned way.

*Bottom:* Cooking pancakes for the festival.

# Vidalia® Onion Festival

## Vidalia, Georgia

*Courtesy of Vidalia® Onion Committee, VidaliaOnion.org*

Sweet Vidalia Pie (recipe on page 75).

# Chicken and Egg Festival

## Moulton, Alabama

*Roland Langley*

*Roland Langley*

*Left page, top*: Poultry display.

*Left page, bottom:* Enjoying exotic drinks at the food booths.

*Right page, top:* Barbecue contest.

*Right page, bottom:* Chicken wing–eating contest.

*Roland Langley*

*Roland Langley*

# National Cornbread Festival

## South Pittsburgh, Tennessee

*Left page, top:* Jenny Flake, winner of the 2007 National Cornbread Cook-Off.

*Left page, bottom:* Caribbean Cornbread Crab Cakes (recipe on page 63).

*Right page:* Chicken Taco Cornbread Wedges with Ranchero Cilantro Drizzle (recipe on page 64).

*Courtesy of National Cornbread Festival*

*Courtesy of National Cornbread Festival*

# Shenandoah Apple Blossom Festival

**Winchester, Virginia**

*Ron Manville*

# Poke Salat Festival

## Arab, Alabama

*Top:* Contestant in the best-dressed pet contest.

*Bottom:* King and queen of the festival.

*Donna Gentry*

*Donna Gentry*

# Sand Mountain Potato Festival

**Henagar, Alabama**

Ron Manville

Green Beans and New Potatoes (recipe on page 135).

# Ham and Yam Festival

**WHERE:** Smithfield, North Carolina

**WHEN:** First weekend in May (Saturday and Sunday)

Teeming with fresh ham and biscuits, barbecued pork, and of course, yams, the Smithfield Ham and Yam Festival draws more than 20,000 people each year to downtown Smithfield to hear nationally known musical acts, as well as contestants in the Ham and Yam Idol competition. Visitors can also enjoy antique truck, car, and tractor shows; a Harley ride-in; a petting zoo; and a barbecue cooking contest.

For more information, please visit *www.downtownsmithfield.com*.

## DID YOU KNOW?

Yams and sweet potatoes are often mistaken for each other. The truth is that the two are different vegetables. The vegetables found in U.S. markets are usually sweet potatoes, although they may be labeled "yams." True yams are grown in the tropics and are not related to the sweet potato.

## Yam Hushpuppies

1    (16-ounce) can yams, drained and mashed (see note)

2    tablespoons self-rising cornmeal

4    tablespoons all-purpose flour

2    tablespoons honey
     Milk

2    tablespoons vegetable oil

■ Combine the yams, cornmeal, flour, and honey in a large bowl. Add enough milk to the mixture to moisten to the consistency of cookie dough. Heat the oil in a skillet over medium-high heat. Drop the dough by spoonfuls into the hot oil. Fry until crispy and brown. Serve immediately. (The hushpuppies can be fried in a deep fryer.)

**MAKES 6 SERVINGS**

Note: *Canned sweet potatoes can be substituted for canned yams.*

## Double Praline Raisin and Coconut Yam Casserole

*Filling:*

3    cups cooked mashed yams

1/2  teaspoon salt

2    tablespoons margarine, melted

2    tablespoons brown sugar

2    teaspoons ground cinnamon

1    egg, beaten

2    tablespoons caramel sauce

*Topping:*

1/4  cup (1/2 stick) margarine, melted

6    tablespoons brown sugar

2/3  cup chopped pecans

1/2  teaspoon ground cinnamon

1/2  cup shredded coconut

1/4  cup raisins

■ For the filling, preheat the oven to 350 degrees. In a large bowl combine the yams, salt, margarine, brown sugar, cinnamon, egg, and caramel sauce and mix well. Pour the filling into a 9 x 9-inch baking dish.

■ For the topping, in a bowl combine the margarine, brown sugar, pecans, cinnamon, coconut, and raisins. Spread the topping over the yam filling. Bake for 35 minutes.

**MAKES 10 SERVINGS**

# Ham and Swiss Pie

1 tablespoon margarine

1/2 cup chopped onion

1/2 pound fresh mushrooms, sliced

2 tablespoons all-purpose flour

1/2 cup heavy cream

2½ cups chopped cooked ham

1 cup diced Swiss cheese

1 (9-inch) uncooked piecrust

■ Preheat the oven to 350 degrees. In a large skillet, melt the margarine over medium heat. Add the onion and mushrooms and cook for 3 to 4 minutes or until tender. Sprinkle the flour over the vegetables and cook for 1 minute. Stir in the cream and continue stirring until thickened. Remove from the heat and let cool. Stir in the ham and cheese. Spoon the filling into the piecrust and bake for 30 minutes.

**MAKES 8 SERVINGS**

# Yam Blueberry Cream Cheese Pudding Bread

1 (18-ounce) box blueberry muffin mix

3/4 cup water

1/3 cup oil

2 eggs

1/2 cup blueberries

8 ounces cream cheese, softened

1/4 cup sugar

3/4 cup grated yams

Confectioners' sugar for dusting

■ Preheat the oven to 350 degrees. In a large bowl combine the muffin mix, water, oil, and eggs. Fold in the blueberries. Pour half of the batter into a bread loaf pan. In a separate mixing bowl beat together the cream cheese, sugar, and yams until combined. Pour over the batter. Top with the remaining half of the batter. Bake for 1 hour and 20 minutes. Dust with confectioners' sugar.

**MAKES 10 SERVINGS**

**DID YOU KNOW?**
Yams are generally sweeter than the sweet potato and can grow over 7 feet long.

# Shenandoah Apple Blossom Festival

**WHERE:** Winchester, Virginia

**WHEN:** First week in May (Tuesday through Sunday. This festival is always the week prior to Mother's Day)

Started in 1927, the Shenandoah Apple Blossom Festival is one of the oldest and largest festivals in the South, drawing more than a quarter of a million people each year to Winchester to celebrate the blooming of the state's apple trees. In addition to nationally known entertainers and parades with celebrity grand marshals, festival-goers can enjoy beauty pageants, carnival rides, a pro-am golf tournament, tours of historic churches and Civil War sites, an apple pie baking contest, live music, band and drill team competitions, a fire truck rodeo, dances of all kinds from square dancing to disco, a 10K run, a circus, and fireworks.

For more information, please visit *www.thebloom.com*.

## DID YOU KNOW?

2,500 varieties of apples are grown in the United States. 7,500 varieties of apples are grown throughout the world.

## Apple Pecan Crumb Pie

*Filling:*

| | |
|---|---|
| 1/4 | cup chopped pecans |
| 1 | (9-inch) deep-dish piecrust, unbaked |
| 1 | cup sugar |
| 2 | teaspoons all-purpose flour |
| 1/3 | teaspoon nutmeg |
| 1/2 | teaspoon ground cinnamon |
| 6 | cups York or Golden Delicious apples, peeled and sliced |
| 2 | tablespoons margarine |

*Crumb Topping:*

| | |
|---|---|
| 1/2 | cup firmly packed brown sugar |
| 1/4 | cup (1/2 stick) margarine, softened |
| 1/3 | cup all-purpose flour |
| 1/4 | teaspoon ground cinnamon |
| 1/4 | cup chopped pecans |

■  For the filling, preheat the oven to 425 degrees. Sprinkle the pecans in the piecrust. In a large bowl combine the sugar, flour, nutmeg and cinnamon. Toss with the apples. Spoon the apple mixture into the piecrust. Dot with the margarine.

■  For the topping, blend the brown sugar, margarine, flour, cinnamon, and pecans together with a fork until the size of peas. Sprinkle over the pie. Bake for 40 to 45 minutes.

**MAKES 8 SERVINGS**

## Apple Cobbler

| | |
|---|---|
| 4 | cups thinly sliced, peeled apples |
| 1/2 | cup sugar |
| 1/2 | teaspoon ground cinnamon |
| 1 | cup sifted all-purpose flour |
| 1 | teaspoon baking powder |
| 1/4 | teaspoon salt |
| 1 | egg, well beaten |
| 1/2 | cup evaporated milk |
| 1/4 | cup melted butter |

■  Preheat the oven to 325 degrees. Place the apples in the bottom of a greased 81/4 x 13/4-inch round baking dish. Sprinkle with a mixture of the sugar and cinnamon. In a bowl combine the flour, baking powder, and salt. In a separate bowl combine the egg, evaporated milk, and butter. Add the dry ingredients to the wet ingredients and mix until smooth. Pour over the apples. Bake for 1 hour or until a toothpick inserted in the middle comes out clean. Serve warm.

**MAKES 8 SERVINGS**

# Turkey Waldorf Salad

*Yogurt Dressing:*

| | |
|---|---|
| 1/2 | cup plain nonfat yogurt |
| 3 | tablespoons reduced-calorie mayonnaise |
| 3 | tablespoons cider vinegar |
| 1 | tablespoon sugar |
| 1/4 | teaspoon ground black pepper |

*Salad:*

| | |
|---|---|
| 2 | cups sliced celery |
| 2 | cups cooked small shell pasta |
| 2 | cups (12 ounces) diced cooked turkey breast |
| 2 | cups diced unpeeled Fuji apples |
| 1/4 | cup sliced green onions |
| 1/3 | cup chopped walnuts |

■ For the dressing, in a bowl combine the yogurt, mayonnaise, vinegar, sugar, and pepper and mix well.

■ For the salad, in a large bowl combine the celery, pasta, turkey, apples, green onions, and walnuts. Add the yogurt dressing and toss to coat thoroughly.

**MAKES 4 SERVINGS**

# Fried Apples

| | |
|---|---|
| 2 | tablespoons bacon drippings |
| 2 | teaspoons butter |
| 6 | large tart apples, cut into thick slices |
| 1/4 | cup water |
| 1/2 | cup sugar |
| 1/4 | teaspoon salt |
| | Juice of 1/2 lemon (optional) |
| | Butter |

■ Heat the bacon drippings and butter in a heavy iron skillet. Add the apples, water, sugar, and salt. Cover and steam the apples over high heat for about 6 minutes. Remove the lid. Reduce the heat to medium and continue frying until the apples are tender and transparent. The syrup should be thick enough to gel when the apples are done. Add the lemon juice if needed to thicken the syrup. Pour the apples and syrup into a serving dish. Dot with additional butter on top. The apple skins add to the flavor and color of this dish.

**MAKES 4 TO 6 SERVINGS**

# Fried Apple Pies

3 medium Golden Delicious apples

1/3 cup sugar

2 teaspoons cornstarch

1 teaspoon lemon juice

1/2 teaspoon ground cinnamon

1/4 teaspoon nutmeg

1 1/2 cups all-purpose flour

1 teaspoon baking powder

1/2 teaspoon salt

1/3 cup vegetable shortening

1/3 to 1/2 cup milk

Vegetable oil for frying

■ Peel, core, and cut each apple into 1/2-inch cubes. In a 2-quart saucepan combine the sugar, cornstarch, lemon juice, cinnamon, and nutmeg. Stir in the apples until moistened. Cover and cook the apples over low heat until tender and bubbly, about 20 minutes, stirring continuously to keep the apples from sticking to the pan. Remove from the heat and cool at room temperature for 1 hour. Refrigerate.

■ In a medium bowl combine the flour, baking powder, and salt. Cut in the shortening with a pastry blender until the mixture resembles coarse crumbs. Gradually stir in enough milk while mixing with a fork until the dough forms a ball. Shape the dough into a ball. Flatten and wrap in plastic. Chill for 30 minutes.

■ Cut the dough into 16 equal portions. Shape each portion into a ball. Using a floured rolling pin, roll each portion into a 4 1/2-inch circle on a floured surface. Spoon about 1 tablespoon filling in the center of each circle. Moisten the edge of the dough with milk. Fold the dough over the filling to form a semicircle. Press the edges together with a floured fork to seal.

■ Heat the vegetable oil to 375 degrees in a deep fryer. Fry 2 or 3 pies at a time for about 1 minute. Drain on paper towels.

**MAKES 16 PIES**

**DID YOU KNOW?**
The largest apple ever picked weighed three pounds.

# West Virginia Strawberry Festival

**WHERE:** Buckhannon, West Virginia

**WHEN:** Third weekend in May (Wednesday through Sunday)

If you like strawberries, you will love the West Virginia Strawberry Festival. If you like strawberries and parades, you will think you have died and gone to heaven at the West Virginia Strawberry Festival (like the song says, "Almost heaven, West Virginia"). As you might imagine, there are plenty of strawberry and strawberry-flavored dishes to be had here. But this festival is also the host to three parades during its five-day run. And if that's not enough, there are carnival rides, a golf tournament, an art show, a strawberry basket auction, live music, fireworks, a gospel singing, a horse pull, a canoe race, a pistol shooting competition, as well as the "Strawberry Party Gras" and pageants galore, including the strawberry blonde competition.

For more information, please visit *www.wvstrawberryfestival.com*.

## DID YOU KNOW?
Strawberries are the only fruit with seeds on the outside.

# Strawberry Pretzel Salad

2    cups crushed salted pretzels

3/4  cup (1 1/2 sticks) butter, melted

3    tablespoons plus 1 cup sugar, divided

8    ounces cream cheese, softened

1    (8-ounce) container frozen whipped topping, thawed

1    (6-ounce) package strawberry Jell-O

2    cups boiling water

2    (10-ounce) packages halved or whole frozen strawberries, thawed

■ Preheat the oven to 400 degrees. In a bowl combine the pretzels, butter, and 3 tablespoons of the sugar. Press into a 9 x 13-inch pan and bake for 8 minutes; cool. In a mixing bowl beat the cream cheese and the remaining 1 cup sugar together. Fold in the whipped topping. Spread over the cooled pretzel crust. In a bowl mix together the Jell-O and boiling water. When blended, stir in the strawberries. Pour the mixture over the cream cheese filling. Refrigerate until firm. Cut into squares and serve on lettuce-lined plates for a salad or serve as a dessert.

**MAKES 12 SERVINGS**

# Strawberry Pancakes with Strawberry Topping

3/4  cup low-fat cottage cheese

1/4  cup all-purpose flour

1/3  cup nonfat dry powdered milk

1/4  cup low-fat milk

1/3  teaspoon ground cinnamon or nutmeg

3    eggs, separated

1    cup strawberries, thinly sliced

1    cup strawberries, puréed

1/2  cup plain low-fat yogurt

■ Combine the cottage cheese, flour, milks, and cinnamon in a large mixing bowl. Add the egg yolks and beat until smooth. In a separate bowl beat the egg whites until stiff peaks form. Gently fold the egg whites into the cottage cheese mixture. Drop by spoonfuls into a hot lightly greased nonstick skillet. Cook slowly over medium-low so the pancakes can cook through. Turn once. Top the pancakes with the sliced strawberries.

■ Make the strawberry sauce by combining the pureed strawberries and yogurt. Serve the pancakes immediately with the sauce.

**MAKES 8 SERVINGS**

## Southern Strawberry Shortcake

*Strawberries:*

1    quart fresh strawberries, stemmed, or 1 quart frozen strawberries, thawed

1/2    cup sugar

*Shortcake:*

2    cups all-purpose flour

1/2    cup vegetable shortening

1/4    cup sugar

1/3    teaspoon salt

1/2    cup warm water

    Whipped topping

For the strawberries, combine the strawberries and sugar in a bowl. Set aside.

For the shortcake, preheat the oven to 350 degrees. Combine the flour, shortening, sugar, and salt in a large bowl. Mix together until the dough is of the consistency of cornmeal. Stir in the water. Roll out the dough into a rectangle and cut it into bite-size squares. Arrange the squares on a cookie sheet. Bake for 12 to 15 minutes or until golden brown. Allow the shortcakes to cool before removing from the cookie sheet. Break into bite-size pieces into 4 individual dessert bowls. Spoon the strawberries over the shortcake and then top with a dollop of whipped topping.

**MAKES 4 SERVINGS**

## Strawberry Pie

3/4    cup sugar

2    tablespoons cornstarch

1    tablespoon light corn syrup

1    cup water

3    tablespoons strawberry gelatin

1    quart whole strawberries, stemmed

1    (9-inch) piecrust, baked

    Whipped topping

Combine the sugar, cornstarch, corn syrup, and water in a saucepan. Bring to a boil over medium-high heat. Cook until clear and thickened, stirring constantly. Remove from the heat and stir in the gelatin until dissolved. Set aside to cool. Arrange the strawberries in the piecrust. Pour the gelatin mixture over the strawberries. Chill until firm. Top with whipped topping.

**MAKES 6 SERVINGS**

## Deep-Fried Strawberries

1     cup pancake mix

1/2    cup plus 2 tablespoons milk

24    large strawberries, stemmed

       Vegetable oil

■ Combine the pancake mix and milk in a large bowl, stirring well. Dip the strawberries into the pancake mixture. Heat the oil in a deep skillet until it registers 375 degrees on a thermometer. Fry the strawberries until golden brown. Drain on paper towels.

**MAKES 8 SERVINGS**

### DID YOU KNOW?
The average strawberry has 200 seeds.

# Blue Crab Festival

**WHERE:** Little River, South Carolina

**WHEN:** The third weekend in May (Saturday and Sunday)

For more than 25 years, festivalgoers have come to the Blue Crab Festival to have a good time, enjoy delicious food, and support the town of Little River. It seems to be working; the festival started out as a small event with a few vendors set up under a live oak tree but now draws more than 50,000 people every year. In addition to the delicious crabs, attendees also enjoy the Little River Blue Crab Pageant, live music, a 5K run along the historic Little River waterfront, arts and crafts, a kids' zone, and the World Series of Gospel Music.

For more information, please visit *www.bluecrabfestival.org*.

## DID YOU KNOW?

The blue crab has 10 legs and is related to the shrimp, lobster, and crayfish.

## Steamed Blue Crabs

1   cup white vinegar

1   cup beer

3   tablespoons kosher salt

1   garlic clove, minced

1   bay leaf

3/4   tablespoon Old Bay seasoning or crab boil

1   dozen live blue crabs, well rinsed

In a large bowl combine the vinegar, beer, salt, garlic, bay leaf, and Old Bay. Carefully place half of the crabs on the bottom of a large stockpot with a lid. Pour half of the vinegar mixture into the pot. Add the remaining crabs and the remaining liquid. Cover and steam until the crabs become bright red, about 20 to 25 minutes. Discard the bay leaf before serving.

**MAKES 4 SERVINGS**

## Blue Crab Cakes

3   cups blue crab meat

1   medium potato, boiled and mashed

1/2   cup cooked onion

1   cup unseasoned bread crumbs, divided

3   eggs, divided

1   tablespoon garlic powder

1/2   cup (1 stick) butter

1/2   cup sweet vermouth

Place the crabmeat, mashed potato, onion, and 1/2 cup of the bread crumbs in a bowl. Add 2 of the eggs to the mixture and mix well. Form the crab mixture into 8 patties. Sprinkle the patties with the garlic powder. Beat the remaining 1 egg in a bowl. Pour the remaining 1/2 cup bread crumbs into another bowl. Dip the crab cakes in the egg. Press both sides into the bread crumbs. Melt the butter in a frying pan over medium-high heat. Add the crab cakes and cook for 3 minutes on each side or until brown. Remove the crab cakes from the pan. Add the vermouth to the pan and deglaze. Return the crab cakes to the pan and cook for 2 additional minutes. Serve hot.

**MAKES 8 SERVINGS**

## Low Country Crab Boil

6    large potatoes, halved

4    large sweet onions, halved

1    tablespoon salt

1    dozen live blue crabs, well rinsed

1    (3-ounce) package crab boil

3    whole garlic cloves

4    lemons, halved

1    cup vinegar

1    dozen ears of corn

5    pounds unpeeled shrimp

    Melted butter for serving

■ Fill a 5- to 6-gallon pot with water and bring to a boil until the water level is two-thirds full. Add the potatoes, onions, and salt. Cover and cook over high heat for 20 minutes. Stir in the crabs, crab boil, garlic, lemons, and vinegar. Cook an additional 10 minutes. Reduce the heat. Add the corn and cook 5 minutes longer. Remove from the heat and add the shrimp. Let stand in the water for 5 minutes; drain. Serve with melted butter.

**MAKES 12 SERVINGS**

## Cream of Blue Crab Soup

1    pound blue crab meat

1/4    cup chopped onion

1/4    cup melted fat or oil

2    tablespoons all-purpose flour

1    teaspoon salt

1/4    teaspoon celery salt

    Dash of pepper

4    drops hot pepper sauce

1    quart milk

1    cup chicken broth

    Chopped parsley

■ Pick through the crabmeat and remove any shells or cartilage; set aside.

■ In a stockpot cook the onion in the melted fat until tender. Blend in the flour, salt, celery salt, pepper, and hot pepper sauce. Add the milk and broth gradually and cook until thickened, stirring constantly. Add the crabmeat and cook until heated through. Garnish with parsley.

**MAKES 6 SERVINGS**

# Blue Crab Stuffing

| | |
|---|---|
| 1 | pound blue crab claw meat |
| 1/4 | cup finely chopped onion |
| 1/4 | cup finely chopped celery |
| 1/4 | cup finely chopped green bell pepper |
| 1 | garlic clove, minced |
| 2 | cups crushed cracker crumbs |
| 2 | tablespoons chopped fresh parsley |
| 1 | teaspoon dry mustard |
| 1/4 | teaspoon salt |
| | Dash of cayenne pepper |
| 1 | egg, beaten |
| 1/4 | cup milk |
| 1/2 | cup melted butter |
| 1 | teaspoon Worcestershire sauce |

■ Preheat the oven to 350 degrees. Place the crabmeat in a large mixing bowl. Remove any remaining shells and cartilage. Stir in the onion, celery, bell pepper, garlic, cracker crumbs, parsley, dry mustard, salt, and cayenne pepper. Add the egg, milk, melted butter, and Worcestershire sauce and mix thoroughly. Place the mixture into a casserole dish and bake for 20 minutes or until golden brown on top and heated through.

**MAKES 10 SERVINGS**

---

**DID YOU KNOW?**

The blue crab uses its three middle pairs of legs to walk sideways and its sharp front pincer claws to grasp prey and defend itself.

# June

# Virginia Pork Festival

Calling itself the world's largest outdoor barbecue, the Virginia Pork Festival is unique in many ways. First of all, it's on a Wednesday. In 1974 the tradition in South Virginia was to "roll up the sidewalks" and enjoy an afternoon off from work. Thus Wednesday was chosen as the most appropriate day for the event. Lasting for only about four hours, the Virginia Pork Festival limits the number of tickets to 15,000—and it does sell out. People come from all across the United States to enjoy the ribs, sausage, country ham, chitterlings, chops, and everything in between, including pork skins. But Emporia packs a lot into those few hours, including cooking up 43,000 pounds of pork—nearly 3 pounds of pork per person. All food and drink is included with the price of your ticket, as well as music from five different stages.

For more information, please visit *www.vaporkfestival.com*.

## DID YOU KNOW?
The pig is rated the fourth most intelligent animal.

## Cinnamon Apple Pork Tenderloin

1   to 1 1/2 pounds pork tenderloin

2   tablespoons cornstarch

1   teaspoon ground cinnamon

2   tablespoons brown sugar

2   cooking apples, peeled, cored, and sliced

2   tablespoons dried cranberries

■ Preheat the oven to 400 degrees. Place the pork tenderloin in a roasting pan or casserole dish. Combine the cornstarch, cinnamon, brown sugar, apples, and cranberries in a bowl and mix well. Spoon the apple mixture around the pork tenderloin. Cover and bake for 30 minutes. Uncover and spoon the apple mixture over the tenderloin. Return to the oven and bake for 15 to 20 minutes longer, or until the pork tenderloin is browned and cooked through. A meat thermometer inserted in the center should register at least 150 to 160 degrees. Slice the tenderloin and spoon the cooked apple and cranberry mixture over the meat.

**MAKES 6 SERVINGS**

## Bacon-Wrapped Pork Tenderloin

1   tablespoon garlic powder

1   teaspoon Lawry's seasoned salt

1   teaspoon dried crumbled leaf basil

1/3  teaspoon dried crumbled leaf oregano

1   teaspoon black pepper

1   pork tenderloin, cleaned and trimmed

4   slices bacon

1/4  cup olive oil

■ Preheat the oven to 375 degrees. Combine the garlic powder, seasoned salt, basil, oregano, and black pepper in a bowl. Rub the seasoning over the pork tenderloin. Wrap the bacon slices around the tenderloin and secure with toothpicks. Coat with the olive oil. Place the tenderloin in a 9 x 13-inch pan and bake, uncovered, for 45 to 60 minutes, or until a thermometer inserted into the tenderloin registers about 155 degrees. Remove the bacon and let the pork stand for 10 minutes before slicing.

**MAKES 2 TO 4 SERVINGS**

## Smothered Pork Chops

4     pork loin chops

1     teaspoon plus 1 tablespoon salt, divided

1     teaspoon plus 1 tablespoon ground black pepper, divided

2     cups plus 2 tablespoons all-purpose flour, divided

1/2   cup vegetable oil

1     large onion, coarsely chopped

1     green bell pepper, coarsely chopped

1     celery rib, coarsely chopped

2     cups water

■  Trim the excess fat from the edges of the pork chops. Sprinkle 1 teaspoon of the salt and 1 teaspoon of the pepper evenly over each pork chop. Combine 2 cups of the flour with the remaining 1 tablespoon salt and the remaining 1 tablespoon pepper. Dredge the chops in the flour until coated on all sides, shaking off the excess. Heat the vegetable oil in a deep, heavy cast-iron skillet over medium-high heat. Add the pork chops and fry for about 5 minutes on both sides or until well-browned, turning once. Remove the pork chops to a plate.

■  Pour off all but 1/4 cup of the drippings from the skillet. Reduce the heat to medium and add the onion, green pepper, and celery. Cook for about 10 minutes or until brown and soft. Sprinkle the remaining 2 tablespoons flour over the vegetables and in the bottom of the skillet. Cook, stirring, until the flour is golden brown. Slowly pour in the water. Stir, cooking until thickened. Place the pork chops in the skillet on top of the gravy and vegetables. Cover tightly and cook over low heat until the pork chops are cooked through, about 15 minutes.

**MAKES 4 SERVINGS**

### DID YOU KNOW?
Pork is the world's most widely eaten meat.

## Barbecued Country-Style Ribs

| | |
|---|---|
| 3 | to 4 pounds country-style pork ribs with bones |
| 1 | (8-ounce) can tomato sauce |
| 1 | large onion, chopped |
| 1/2 | cup dark corn syrup |
| 2 | tablespoons Worcestershire sauce |
| 1/3 | cup cider vinegar |
| 1 | teaspoon salt |
| 1 | teaspoon dry mustard |
| 1/2 | teaspoon chili powder |

■ Place the ribs in a large Dutch oven or stockpot. Add water to the depth of about 1 inch. Cover and bring to a boil. Reduce the heat and simmer for 1 hour.

■ In a 1-quart saucepan, mix together the tomato sauce, onion, corn syrup, Worcestershire sauce, vinegar, salt, dry mustard, and chili powder. Simmer for 10 minutes. Drain the ribs and brush with the sauce. Grill the ribs for about 20 minutes or until browned, basting with the sauce and turning frequently.

**MAKES 8 SERVINGS**

### DID YOU KNOW?

In ancient times, sea captains kept pigs aboard their ships. They believed that pigs always swam toward the nearest shore and that in the event of a shipwreck, the crew could follow the pigs to dry land.

# Bradley County Pink Tomato Festival

**WHERE:** Warren, Arkansas

**WHEN:** Second full weekend in June (Friday and Saturday)

The oldest continuously running festival in Arkansas, the Bradley County Pink Tomato Festival started more than 50 years ago and has evolved into one of the most anticipated events in the state. Attendees, who can number more than 30,000, enjoy a beauty pageant, arts and crafts shows, a Civil War reenactment, a quilt show, a parade, dunking booths, lawn mower races, car shows, concerts, a fish fry, a pancake breakfast, and of course, plenty of food featuring the pride of Bradley County, the Bradley County Pink Tomato—which is both the official fruit and the official vegetable of the State of Arkansas.

For more information, please visit *www.bradleypinktomato.com*.

## DID YOU KNOW?

The tomato is the world's most popular fruit—even more popular than apples, bananas, and oranges.

## Marinated Carrots

2    pounds peeled carrots, thinly sliced

1    medium green bell pepper, sliced

1    medium onion, sliced into rings

1/2   cup salad oil

3/4   cup sugar

3/4   cup vinegar

1    teaspoon Worcestershire sauce

1    (10³/4-ounce) can tomato soup

1    teaspoon prepared mustard

■ Cook the carrots in boiling, salted water until barely tender. Drain and let cool.

■ Layer the carrots, green pepper, and onion in a shallow bowl. Combine the oil, sugar, vinegar, Worcestershire sauce, tomato soup, and mustard in a saucepan and bring to a boil. Pour over the vegetables. Refrigerate, covered, overnight. Drain most of the marinade before serving.

**MAKES 12 SERVINGS**

## Cornbread Salad

1    (7-ounce) package Mexican cornbread mix (such as Martha White)

     Bacon slices to taste

1    medium onion, chopped

1    (15-ounce) can whole kernel corn, drained

1    medium green bell pepper, chopped

1    medium tomato, chopped

1    cup Miracle Whip salad dressing

■ Prepare the cornbread according to the package directions. Set aside to cool.

■ Cook the bacon and crumble. Crumble the cooled cornbread in a large bowl. Add the crumbled bacon, onion, corn, bell pepper, tomato, and Miracle Whip and stir together. Chill. Serve with white or pinto beans.

**MAKES 12 SERVINGS**

---

**DID YOU KNOW?**
Tomatoes were first cultivated in AD 700 by Aztecs and Incas.

## Heavenly Tomato Cake

*Cake:*

1/2   cup (1 stick) butter, softened

1/2   cup oil or vegetable shortening

2     cups sugar

2     eggs

1/4   cup cocoa

2     cups all-purpose flour

1     teaspoon baking soda

1/2   cup tomato juice

1     cup hot water

1 1/2 cups miniature marshmallows

1     teaspoon vanilla extract

*Tomato Icing:*

1/2   cup (1 stick) butter

1/4   cup tomato juice

2     tablespoons water

1/4   cup cocoa

1/4   teaspoon salt

1     (1-pound) box confectioners' sugar

1     cup chopped toasted pecans

■  For the cake, preheat the oven to 350 degrees. Grease and flour a 15 1/2 x 10 1/2 x 1-inch pan. Cream together the butter, oil, and sugar in a large mixing bowl. Add the eggs, one at a time, beating well after each addition. Sift together the cocoa, flour, and baking soda. Add to the creamed mixture, mixing thoroughly. In a bowl combine the tomato juice, hot water, and marshmallows. Fold into the batter. Mix in the vanilla. The batter will be thin and the marshmallows will rise to the top. Pour into the prepared pan. Bake for 35 minutes.

■  For the icing, combine the butter, tomato juice, water, cocoa, and salt in a saucepan. Bring to a boil. Pour over the confectioners' sugar in a large mixing bowl and beat well. Fold in the pecans. Spread on the hot cake.

**MAKES 16 SERVINGS**

## Green Tomato Pie

3     cups sliced green tomatoes

1/4   cup lemon juice

4     teaspoons grated lemon peel

1 1/3 cups sugar

3     tablespoons all-purpose flour

3/4   teaspoon ground cinnamon

1/4   teaspoon salt

3     tablespoons butter, melted

2     (9-inch) piecrusts, uncooked

Preheat the oven to 450 degrees. Combine the tomatoes, lemon juice, and lemon peel together in a bowl. In a separate bowl mix the sugar, flour, cinnamon, salt, and butter together. Add to the tomato mixture and pour into 1 of the piecrusts. Roll out the remaining piecrust and place over the filling, pressing the edges of the dough together. Pierce the crust to allow steam to escape. You may also cut the crust into strips and arrange in a lattice design. Bake for 10 minutes. Reduce the heat to 350 degrees and bake for another 30 minutes.

**MAKES 16 SERVINGS**

## Open-Faced Tomato Sandwiches

| | |
|---|---|
| 1/2 | cup sour cream |
| 1/2 | cup mayonnaise |
| 1 | teaspoon dried dill weed |
| 1 | loaf sandwich bread (white or wheat) |
| 2 | pounds Roma tomatoes, sliced thin |
| | Fresh basil leaves for garnish |

Combine the sour cream, mayonnaise, and dill weed in a small bowl. Trim the crusts from the bread and cut into circles just large enough to hold 1 tomato slice. Spread the bread with the sour cream-mayonnaise mixture and top with a tomato slice. Garnish with fresh basil.

**MAKES 40 SANDWICHES**

## Bradley County Caviar

| | |
|---|---|
| 1 | (15-ounce) can black-eyed peas, rinsed and drained |
| 1 | (11-ounce) can Mexican corn, drained |
| 3 | Bradley County tomatoes, chopped |
| 1 | cup salsa |
| 2 | garlic cloves, minced |
| 2 | tablespoons fresh lime juice |
| 1 | small sweet onion, chopped |
| 1/4 | cup chopped fresh cilantro for garnish |
| | Tortilla chips for serving |

Combine the peas, corn, tomatoes, salsa, garlic, lime juice, and onion in a serving bowl. Cover and chill for at least 2 hours. Garnish with the cilantro. Serve with tortilla chips.

**MAKES 12 SERVINGS**

# Louisiana Corn Festival

**WHERE:** Bunkie, Louisiana

**WHEN:** Second full weekend in June (Friday through Sunday)

While Bunkie's Louisiana Corn Festival gives the 15,000 or so people who attend each year the opportunity to pay tribute to the area's corn farmers, it also offers almost all attendees a chance to be a winner through such marvelous competitions as corn eating, corn shucking, corn cooking, corn creatures, and lizard races. There is also softball, a wonderful talent contest called Corn Idol, live music, street dances, carnival rides, arts and crafts, a parade, and pirogue races on the Bayou.

For more information, please visit *www.bunkie.com*.

**DID YOU KNOW?**
An ear of corn averages 800 kernels in 16 rows.

# Corn and Pasta Salad

1½   cups bow tie pasta

2    cups fresh corn

1    cup chopped cooked chicken

1    large tomato, seeded and chopped

½    cup olive oil

3    tablespoons cider vinegar

2    tablespoons pesto

1    tablespoon chicken broth

¼    teaspoon salt

⅛    teaspoon pepper

2    tablespoons Parmesan cheese
     Chopped fresh basil for garnish

■ Cook the pasta according to the package directions. Drain and rinse with cold water. Cook the corn in boiling water for 10 minutes or until tender; drain. In a large bowl combine the pasta, chicken, tomato, and corn. In a jar with a tight-fitting lid combine the olive oil, vinegar, pesto, chicken broth, salt, and pepper. Cover and shake well. Pour over the pasta mixture. Toss gently to coat. Cover and chill for at least 2 hours. Arrange the salad on a serving plate. Sprinkle with the Parmesan cheese and garnish with basil.

**MAKES 8 SERVINGS**

# Southern-Fried Corn

6    ears of corn

¼    cup bacon drippings or vegetable oil

2    tablespoons all-purpose flour

1    tablespoon sugar

1    cup water

¼    cup milk
     Salt and pepper to taste

■ Cut the kernels off of the cobs, scraping the juice out of the corncobs into the corn. Heat the bacon drippings in a large heavy skillet over medium-high heat. Add the corn and juice, the flour, sugar, water, milk, and salt and pepper to taste. Bring the mixture to a boil, stirring constantly. Reduce the heat and simmer, covered, until the corn is tender, about 20 to 25 minutes. Add a little hot water if necessary to thin.

**MAKES 6 SERVINGS**

**DID YOU KNOW?**
A pound of corn consists of approximately 1,300 kernels.

## Pan-Fried Catfish with Crab and Corn Topping

*Crab and Corn Topping:*

| | |
|---|---|
| 1 | (4-ounce) sleeve saltine crackers, finely crumbled and divided |
| 1 | (5-ounce) can evaporated milk |
| 1½ | cups fresh corn |
| 2 | tablespoons butter |
| | Salt to taste |
| | Red pepper to taste |
| 2 | cans lump crabmeat |
| ¼ | cup chopped onion |

*Catfish:*

| | |
|---|---|
| 2 | eggs, beaten |
| ½ | cup milk |
| | Salt to taste |
| | Red pepper to taste |
| 2 | to 4 catfish fillets |
| 1 | cup all-purpose flour |
| | Reserved cracker crumbs |
| ½ | cup corn oil |

■ For the topping, measure ¼ cup of the cracker crumbs for use in the topping. Set aside the remaining crumbs for the catfish. Pour the evaporated milk into a heavy saucepan and heat over medium-low. Add the corn, butter, salt, and red pepper. Cook over medium-low heat for 20 minutes, stirring often. Add the crabmeat and onion and cook for 10 to 15 minutes longer. Add the cracker crumbs as needed if the topping needs thickening.

■ For the catfish, in a bowl combine the eggs, milk, salt, and red pepper. Coat the catfish fillets in the flour, then dip in the egg mixture. Next, dredge the fillets in the reserved cracker crumbs, coating both sides well. Heat the oil in a skillet and cook the catfish for 3 to 4 minutes on each side. Drain on paper towels. Serve hot with the Crab and Corn Topping.

**MAKES 4 SERVINGS**

## Fresh Corn Pudding

| | |
|---|---|
| 2½ | cups fresh corn |
| 2 | tablespoons all-purpose flour |
| 1 | teaspoon salt |
| | Dash of cayenne pepper |
| ¼ | teaspoon nutmeg |
| 1½ | tablespoons sugar |
| 2 | eggs, slightly beaten |
| 1¼ | cups milk |
| ¼ | cup (½ stick) butter, softened |

■ Preheat the oven to 350 degrees. In a large bowl combine the corn, flour, salt, cayenne pepper, nutmeg, and sugar. Mix in the eggs, milk, and butter. Pour into a buttered casserole dish and bake for 30 to 40 minutes or until firm.

**MAKES 8 SERVINGS**

## Corn Fritters

1    cup fresh corn or 1 cup frozen or canned corn kernels

1    egg

1/3    teaspoon salt

1/2    teaspoon baking powder

1/4    cup milk

1/4    cup all-purpose flour
      Vegetable oil for frying

■ Combine the corn, egg, salt, baking powder, milk, and flour together, forming a batter. Heat 1/2-inch of oil in a deep skillet over medium-high heat. Drop the batter by spoonfuls into the hot oil. Fry until golden brown on both sides.

**MAKES 12 FRITTERS**

### DID YOU KNOW?
The Indians showed the early settlers in North America how to grow corn. They dug a small hole and dropped in a few kernels along with a small fish, which acted as fertilizer.

# RC and Moon Pie Festival

**WHERE:** Bell Buckle, Tennessee

**WHEN:** Third Saturday in June

You can't get much more Southern than an RC Cola and a Moon Pie. Writers and musicians have rhapsodized about this combination for decades, and now tiny Bell Buckle dedicates the third Saturday in June to paying homage to this Southern tradition. In addition to cutting and serving the world's largest Moon Pie, the more than 15,000 people who visit this festival each year also enjoy arts and crafts, a 10K run, clogging, the RC Moon Pie Parade, the coronation of the RC King and Queen, the watermelon seed–spitting contest, the hog-calling contest, live music, and what has probably become the signature event of this festival, synchronized wading. And that doesn't even include such RC Cola–Moon Pie games as the Moon Pie toss, the RC Dash, and Moon Pie Hoops.

For more information, please visit
*www.bellbucklechamber.com/events.html.*

## DID YOU KNOW?

Moon Pies are a unique creation of the South, where they have been a favorite since they came on the market. It is rare to find these chocolate-covered graham cracker and marshmallow pies sold anywhere other than the South, but thanks to the Internet, people from all over can now purchase them online.

## Deep-Fried Moon Pies

Oil for deep-frying

1 1/4 cups baking or pancake mix (such as Bisquick)

3/4 cup milk

1 large egg

1 tablespoon oil

1 (12-ounce) box 3-inch Moon Pies (8 in a box; frozen works best)

Flour for dusting

Confectioners' sugar for dusting

Heat the oil in a deep fryer to 375 degrees. Combine the baking mix, milk, egg, and oil in a large bowl. Mix until there are no lumps. Roll the Moon Pies in flour then dip in the batter. Drop the Moon Pies in the hot oil. Fry until golden brown on both sides. Remove to a wire rack or paper towels to drain. Dust with confectioners' sugar.

**MAKES 8 PIES**

## Deep-Fried RC Cola

2 cups all-purpose flour

1 teaspoon baking powder

2 eggs, lightly beaten

1 1/2 cups RC Cola or any cola

Oil for deep-frying

In a medium bowl mix together the flour and baking powder. Mix in the eggs and cola and stir until a smooth batter forms. Heat the oil in a skillet or deep fryer. Pour 1/3 cup of the batter into a funnel or turkey baster. In a circular motion, pour the batter into the hot oil. Fry for about 1 minute on each side and drain on paper towels. Repeat with the remaining batter.

**MAKES 10 SERVINGS**

## Southern Summertime Lemonade

Juice of 2 lemons (about 1/3 cup juice)

3/4 cup sugar

1 quart water

Sprigs of mint

Ice cubes

In a 2-quart pitcher combine the lemon juice, sugar, water, and mint. Stir until the sugar dissolves. Refrigerate for 30 minutes to 6 hours for the flavors to mellow. Pour over ice and serve.

**MAKES 4 SERVINGS**

## Moon Pie Bread Pudding

*Bread Pudding:*

7    eggs

2    cups whole milk

1/4  cup sugar

1/4  teaspoon ground cloves

1/4  teaspoon ground cinnamon

1/4  teaspoon vanilla extract

1/4  teaspoon baking powder

4    cups cubed French bread

7    regular (3-inch) Moon Pies (any flavor), diced

2    tablespoons butter

*Vanilla Cream Sauce:*

2    cups half-and-half

1    egg, beaten

1/2  cup sugar

3    tablespoons all-purpose flour

1    tablespoon vanilla extract
     Cinnamon-sugar mixture for
     sprinkling

■ For the bread pudding, in a large bowl combine the eggs, milk, sugar, cloves, cinnamon, vanilla, and baking powder and mix well. In a separate bowl combine the French bread and Moon Pies. Pour the liquid over the bread and Moon Pie mixture. Pour into a buttered 9 x 13-inch baking dish. Refrigerate for 1 1/2 hours.

■ Preheat the oven to 350 degrees. Cube the butter and distribute evenly over the top of the bread pudding. Bake in a water bath, uncovered, for 45 minutes or until a toothpick inserted in the center comes out clean.

■ For the sauce, combine the half-and-half, egg, sugar, and flour in a saucepan and bring to a boil. Add the vanilla.

■ To serve, pour the sauce over the bread pudding. Sprinkle cinnamon-sugar over the top.

**MAKES 12 SERVINGS**

# RC Cola Cake

*Cake:*

2   cups unsifted all-purpose flour

2   cups sugar

1   cup (2 sticks) butter

2   tablespoons cocoa

1   cup RC Cola or other cola (do not use diet colas)

1/2   cup buttermilk

2   eggs

1   teaspoon baking soda

1/4   teaspoon salt

1   teaspoon vanilla extract

1 1/4   cups miniature marshmallows

*Icing:*

1/2   cup (1 stick) butter

2   tablespoons cocoa

6   tablespoons RC Cola or other cola

1   (1-pound) box confectioners' sugar

1   cup chopped nuts

1   teaspoon vanilla extract

■   For the cake, preheat the oven to 350 degrees. Grease and flour a 9-inch cake pan. Sift the flour and sugar into a bowl. In a saucepan bring the butter, cocoa, and RC Cola to a boil. Pour over the sugar mixture. Add the buttermilk, eggs, baking soda, salt, and vanilla. Fold in the marshmallows. The batter will be thin and the marshmallows will float on top. Pour into the prepared pan and bake for 30 to 35 minutes.

■   For the icing, once the cake has finished baking, in a saucepan bring the butter, cocoa, and RC Cola to a boil. Combine the confectioners' sugar, nuts, and vanilla in a large bowl. Pour the hot liquid over the confectioners' sugar mixture and mix together. Spread over the warm cake.

**MAKES 12 SERVINGS**

**DID YOU KNOW?**

Legend has it that RC Cola became the drink of choice to accompany a Moon Pie because the bottles were typically larger than those of other colas.

# Alabama Blueberry Festival

**WHERE:** Brewton, Alabama

**WHEN:** Third Saturday in June

Whether you love blueberries because of their delicious taste or because of their health value, or both, you are welcome to visit Brewton and celebrate this fruit at the Alabama Blueberry Festival. More than 15,000 people come from all over to buy blueberries and to enjoy blueberry food items, as well as a motorcycle rally, an antique car show, a kids' zone, strolling magicians, arts and crafts, and live musical entertainment.

For more information, please visit *www.brewtonchamber.com*.

## DID YOU KNOW?

The blueberry is one of the few fruits native to North America (the others are cranberries and Concord grapes).

# Blueberry Cobbler

2 cups vanilla wafers, crushed

1/2 cup confectioners' sugar

1/2 cup (1 stick) butter, melted

8 ounces cream cheese, softened

3 eggs, beaten

1 cup granulated sugar

1 (21-ounce) can blueberry pie filling
Whipped cream

▪ Preheat the oven to 325 degrees. Mix the vanilla wafers, confectioners' sugar, and butter together in a bowl and spread into a 9 x 13-inch baking pan. In a mixing bowl beat the cream cheese, eggs, and granulated sugar together. Pour over the vanilla wafer mixture. Bake for 20 minutes. Set aside to cool. When cooled, spread the blueberry pie filling over the top. Top with whipped cream.

**MAKES 12 SERVINGS**

# Blueberry Yum Yum

2 cups fresh blueberries

2 cups sugar, divided

1/4 cup plus 3 tablespoons water, divided

1/4 cup cornstarch

1 cup all-purpose flour

1/2 cup (1 stick) butter, softened

3/4 cup chopped pecans

1 (8-ounce) package cream cheese, softened

1 (9-ounce) container frozen whipped topping, thawed

▪ Preheat the oven to 350 degrees. Combine the blueberries, 1 cup of the sugar, and 1/4 cup of the water in a medium saucepan. Cook over low heat for 15 minutes or until the blueberries are soft. Combine the cornstarch and the remaining 3 tablespoons water in a small bowl; stir well. Add the cornstarch mixture to the blueberry mixture. Cook, stirring constantly, until thickened. Remove from the heat to cool.

▪ Combine the flour, butter, and pecans in a separate bowl and mix well. Press into a 9 x 13-inch baking dish. Bake for 20 minutes. Let cool.

▪ In a mixing bowl combine the cream cheese and the remaining 1 cup sugar and beat until smooth. Fold in the whipped topping. Spread the topping evenly over the cooled crust. Pour the blueberry mixture evenly over the topping. Refrigerate. When chilled, cut and serve.

**MAKES 12 SERVINGS**

## Orange Blueberry Muffins

*Muffins:*

1  cup quick-cooking oats

1  cup orange juice

3  cups all-purpose flour

1  teaspoon baking powder

1  teaspoon salt

1/2  teaspoon baking soda

1  cup sugar

1  cup vegetable oil

3  eggs, beaten

11/3  cups fresh blueberries

1  tablespoon grated orange peel

*Topping:*

1/2  cup finely chopped pecans

1/3  cup sugar

1  teaspoon ground cinnamon

■ For the muffins, preheat the oven to 400 degrees. In a bowl combine the oats and orange juice; set aside. In a large mixing bowl combine the flour, baking powder, salt, baking soda, and sugar. Make a well in the center of the dry ingredients and add the oatmeal mixture, the oil, and eggs. Stir only until the ingredients are moistened. Carefully fold in the blueberries and orange peel. Spoon the batter into greased muffin tins, filling about 3/4 full.

■ For the topping, combine the pecans, sugar, and cinnamon. Sprinkle over the muffins and bake for 15 minutes or until the muffins test done. Remove from the tins and serve warm, if desired.

**MAKES 24 MUFFINS**

## Blueberry Pie

1/4  cup (1/2 stick) butter, softened

1  cup sugar

3/4  cup all-purpose flour

1  egg, beaten

1  teaspoon vanilla extract

1  pint blueberries

1  (9-inch) deep-dish piecrust, unbaked

■ Preheat the oven to 350 degrees. In a mixing bowl cream the butter and sugar together. Add the flour, egg, and vanilla and mix well. Fold in the blueberries. Pour into the piecrust. Bake for 50 minutes.

**MAKES 8 SERVINGS**

# Purple Hull Pea Festival

**WHERE:** Emerson, Arkansas

**WHEN:** Fourth weekend in June (Friday and Saturday)

If peas aren't reason enough to go to tiny Emerson to attend the Purple Hull Pea Festival, go for the World Championship Rotary Tiller Race. Now that's a festival. Join the thousands who also enjoy a cake auction, gospel singing, live entertainment, a fireworks show, a parade, a senior walk for "world peas," a cornbread cook-off, a pea-shelling competition, and a street dance.

For more information, please visit *www.purplehull.com*.

## DID YOU KNOW?

Purple hull peas, black-eyed peas, and crowder peas are all members of the cowpea or southern pea family.

# Purple Hull Pea Fritters

1     cup fresh shelled purple hull peas

1     egg, beaten

1/2   cup finely chopped onion

1     teaspoon salt

1/4   teaspoon ground red pepper
      Vegetable oil

■ If the peas are not very tender and young, simmer them in boiling water for 10 to 15 minutes. Process the peas in a blender or food processor. Combine the puréed peas with the egg, onion, salt, and ground red pepper in a large bowl and mix well. In a heavy frying pan, heat oil to 375 degrees, or until a smoky haze appears. Drop the mixture by teaspoonfuls into the hot oil and fry until golden brown on both sides. Drain on paper towels.

**MAKES 4 TO 6 SERVINGS**

# Purple Hull Pea Jelly

4     cups purple hull pea juice (see below)

1     envelope SureJell

1/2   teaspoon butter

5     cups sugar

■ This jelly is made from the hulls of the peas rather than the peas themselves. To make the juice, wash about a pound of empty hulls (or enough to fill a large stockpot) three or four times. Boil the hulls until tender. Strain the juice.

■ Return the juice to a stockpot and bring to a boil. Add the SureJell and butter. Bring to a rolling boil. Add the sugar. Return to a rolling boil. Let boil for 15 minutes. Remove from the heat and set aside for 5 minutes. Skim the top. Pour into jars and seal.

**MAKES 3 PINTS**

# Purple Hull Pea Dip

4     cups purple hull peas, cooked and drained

5     jalapeño chiles

1     tablespoon jalapeño juice

1/2   medium onion, chopped

1     (4-ounce) can green chiles

1     garlic clove

1/2   pound Old English sharp cheese

1/2   cup (1 stick) butter

■ Mix the peas, jalapeño chiles, jalapeño juice, onion, chiles, and garlic in a blender. Work with one-fourth to one-half of the mixture at a time if the amount is too large for the blender. Heat the cheese and butter in a double boiler until melted. Stir in the pea mixture. Serve in a chafing dish with chips.

**MAKES 12 SERVINGS**

## Purple Hull Pea Thermidor

2   cups fresh purple hull peas

3   cups chicken stock

1   whole clove

1   medium bay leaf

1   medium yellow onion, peeled

2   tablespoons dry English mustard powder

1   teaspoon or more water

1   cup freshly grated Parmesan cheese, divided

1   cup cooked and drained spinach leaves or collard greens

1/2   cup heavy cream
    Salt and freshly ground pepper to taste

■ Combine the peas and chicken stock in small stockpot or Dutch oven. Using the clove as a pin, attach the bay leaf to the onion. Add the studded onion to the pot and bring to a boil. Reduce the heat and cook, uncovered, until the peas are tender, 30 to 40 minutes. Drain the peas, reserving the stock in a bowl. Discard the studded onion. Return the peas to the pot and cover.

■ Preheat the oven to 400 degrees. Place the mustard powder in a small bowl and gradually mix in the water to make a loose paste, adding more water if needed. Fold the mustard paste, 1/2 cup of the Parmesan cheese, and the spinach into the reserved chicken stock. Mix the stock mixture back into the peas, then fold in the cream. Mix well. Season with salt and pepper. Pour the peas into a casserole dish. Sprinkle the top of the peas with the remaining 1/2 cup Parmesan cheese and bake for 30 minutes or until the cheese browns. Remove from the oven and serve immediately.

**MAKES 4 SERVINGS**

## Purple Hull Peas Creole

2   slices bacon

1   cup chopped onion

1   cup chopped green bell pepper

1   cup chopped celery

1   (20-ounce) can diced tomatoes

1   tablespoon sugar

1   large bay leaf

1/2   teaspoon dried sweet basil

Salt and freshly ground pepper to taste

2   (16-ounce) packages frozen purple hull peas

In a large saucepan fry the bacon until crisp. Remove from the pan, reserving the drippings. Drain on paper towels. Crumble the bacon. Brown the onion, bell pepper, and celery over medium heat in the reserved drippings. Add the crumbled bacon, tomatoes, sugar, bay leaf, sweet basil, salt, and pepper. Simmer for 5 minutes. Add the frozen purple hull peas. Cook slowly for 1 1/2 to 2 hours, adding water when necessary.

**MAKES 12 SERVINGS**

## DID YOU KNOW?

In the 4th century, Apicius authored Rome's first cookbook, which included nine recipes for peas. Some of the dishes paired peas with other vegetables and herbs, while others combined peas with meat or poultry.

# Georgia Peach Festival

**WHERE:** Byron and Fort Valley, Georgia

**WHEN:** The fourth weekend in June (Friday through Sunday)

The world's largest peach cobbler is just one reason to check out this festival, which began in 1986. Other events include a beauty pageant, a town parade, a 5K race, music, fireworks, arts and crafts, a best beard contest, square dancing, clogging, and an interdenominational choir program. The Georgia Peach Festival honors the role peach growers play in the economy of the Peach State—Georgia farmers harvest more than 1.7 million bushels of peaches annually.

For more information, visit *www.gapeachfestival.com.*

### DID YOU KNOW?

Peaches originated in China, where the fruit is traditionally believed to have mystical powers. Peaches are symbols of affection and fertility, and are thought to bring luck, wealth, and protection.

## Fresh Peach Pie

2     cups sugar

2     cups cold water

6     tablespoons cornstarch

1     (3-ounce) package peach Jell-O

2     pints fresh peaches, sliced

2     (9-inch) piecrusts, baked

1     (12-ounce) container frozen whipped topping, thawed

▇ Combine the sugar, water, cornstarch, and Jell-O in a saucepan. Bring to a boil and cook until thick and clear. Cool. Spoon the peaches into the piecrusts. Pour the Jell-O mixture over the peaches. Refrigerate until set. Spread the whipped topping evenly over each pie.

**MAKES 2 PIES**

## Homemade Peach Ice Cream

6     eggs

1     (14-ounce) can sweetened condensed milk

1½     cups sugar

2     to 3 cups sliced fresh or frozen peaches

2     quarts milk (or enough to reach the fill line in your ice cream freezer)

▇ In a blender, combine the eggs, condensed milk, sugar, and peaches. Pulse until smooth. Pour into the container of an ice cream freezer. Add enough milk to reach the fill line on the freezer. Freeze according to the manufacturer's directions.

**MAKES 16 SERVINGS**

---

**DID YOU KNOW?**
Fresh Georgia peaches are available only 16 weeks each year, from mid-May to August.

## Peach Bread Pudding

2  cups stale Italian bread

4  cups milk, heated

4  eggs, beaten

3  peaches, sliced

1  cup sugar

1/4  cup butter, melted

■ Preheat the oven to 400 degrees. Combine the bread, milk, eggs, peaches, sugar, and butter in a large bowl and mix well. Pour into a 9 x 13-inch baking dish and bake for 30 minutes or until firm.

**MAKES 12 SERVINGS**

## Peach Cobbler

1/2  cup (1 stick) butter

1  cup all-purpose flour

2  cups sugar, divided

3  teaspoons baking powder

1/2  teaspoon salt

1  cup milk

3  generous cups peeled, sliced peaches

1  teaspoon ground cinnamon

■ Preheat the oven to 350 degrees. Melt the butter in a 9 x 13-inch baking dish. Sift together the flour, 1 cup of the sugar, the baking powder, and salt. Blend with the milk. Pour the batter over the melted butter. Spread the peaches over the batter. Combine the remaining 1 cup sugar and cinnamon. Sprinkle over the peaches. Bake for 50 to 60 minutes or until a crust appears on top.

**MAKES 12 SERVINGS**

**DID YOU KNOW?**
The fragrant peach is a member of the rose family.

# July

# Sand Mountain Potato Festival

**WHERE:** Henagar, Alabama
**WHEN:** July 4

Thousands converge up on Sand Mountain every Fourth of July to celebrate the nation's independence and to honor the area's potato farmers. As you might expect, folks come for the big fireworks show, but there's also gospel singing, a car and tractor show, horseshoes, games for the kids, and, of course, a big parade.

For more information, please visit *www.800Alabama.com*.

### DID YOU KNOW?
Marie Antoinette popularized potatoes when she paraded in France wearing a crown of potato blossoms.

# Potato Pancakes

5    to 6 medium potatoes

2    tablespoons white vinegar

1    medium onion

1    large egg, beaten

1    tablespoon cream

2    tablespoons all-purpose flour

1    teaspoon baking soda

1    teaspoon salt

1/2  teaspoon ground black pepper

1/4  teaspoon paprika

4    teaspoons butter

▪ Peel the potatoes and grate using a food processor or by hand. Pour the potatoes into a large pot. Add the vinegar and mix. Add enough ice cold water to cover. Allow the potatoes to soak until the water reaches room temperature. Drain the potatoes. Using paper towels or a kitchen towel remove as much moisture from the potatoes as possible.

▪ Grate the onion using a food processor or by hand. In a medium bowl combine the grated potatoes, grated onion, egg, cream, flour, baking soda, salt, pepper, and paprika and mix well. Heat the butter in a large heavy bottom saucepan or a cast-iron skillet over medium heat. Drop 2 tablespoons of the mixture at a time into the hot butter in the skillet and then flatten with a pancake spatula. Cook the potato cakes as you would a pancake by cooking for about 3 to 5 minutes on each side or until brown.

**MAKES 18 PANCAKES**

# Hash Brown Potato Salad

1    (32-ounce) package frozen Southern-style hash browns

1    quart boiling water

3/4  cup Miracle Whip salad dressing

1/3  cup sliced celery

1/3  cup chopped green bell pepper

1/3  cup chopped onion

1/4  cup chopped pimientos

2    hard-cooked eggs, chopped
     Salt and pepper to taste

▪ Add the hash browns to the boiling water; return to a boil. Cover and cook for 2 minutes or until tender. Drain well. Combine the potatoes, Miracle Whip, celery, green pepper, onion, pimientos, and eggs; mix lightly. Season with salt and pepper to taste; chill.

**MAKES 8 TO 10 SERVINGS**

## Southern Potato Salad

1  pound red potatoes

1  large celery rib, finely chopped

1  hard-boiled egg, finely chopped

1/2  small onion, finely chopped

1/2  cup mayonnaise or Miracle Whip salad dressing

1  teaspoon yellow mustard

▪ Rinse the potatoes thoroughly under running water. While rinsing, gently scrub the potatoes to remove any dirt. Place the potatoes into a large pot and cover with at least 2 inches of cold water. Bring the water to a boil and cook the potatoes until tender. Drain the potatoes and set aside to cool before peeling.

▪ Once the potatoes have cooled, peel and mash them one at a time into the large pot. Add the celery, egg, onion, mayonnaise, and mustard and mix together thoroughly. Spoon the mixture into a suitable-size bowl with a lid. Cover and refrigerate.

**MAKES 4 SERVINGS**

## Hash Brown Casserole

1  (32-ounce) package frozen Southern-style hash browns, thawed

2  cups sour cream

2  cups shredded Cheddar cheese

1/2  cup chopped onion

1  (10.7-ounce) can cream of mushroom soup

1/4  cup bread crumbs

1/2  cup melted butter

Salt and pepper to taste

▪ Preheat the oven to 350 degrees. Mix the hash browns, sour cream, cheese, onion, and soup in a large bowl. Spread the mixture into a 9 x 13-inch baking dish. Top with the bread crumbs and melted butter. Season with salt and pepper. Bake for 1 hour.

**MAKES 12 SERVINGS**

---

**DID YOU KNOW?**
A potato is about 80 percent water and 20 percent solid.

# Green Beans and New Potatoes

2   pounds fresh green beans, trimmed

1/2   pound salt pork

1   teaspoon salt

6   or 7 medium new potatoes (red skin potatoes)

■ In a heavy Dutch oven, combine the beans, salt pork, and salt with enough water to cover. Over medium-high heat bring the beans to a boil and cover. Reduce the heat to low and cook for 1 hour. Add the potatoes. Cover and cook for an additional 45 minutes. Remove the lid and cook over low heat until the liquid is substantially reduced and the beans are very tender.

**MAKES 6 SERVINGS**

## DID YOU KNOW?

According to the *Guinness Book of World Records*, the largest potato ever was grown in England in 1795. It weighed 18 pounds, 4 ounces.

# Slugburger Festival

**WHERE:** Corinth, Mississippi

**WHEN:** Second weekend in July (Wednesday through Saturday)

What is a slugburger, and why would you want to eat one? The story goes that during the Depression when food budgets were tight, housewives made their beef stretch farther by adding pork and potato flour to the ground beef. The mixture took, and slugburgers have been a favorite to many ever since. Why do they call them slugburgers? Restaurants serving them charged a slug—a slang for a nickel. Now every year in Corinth people gather to celebrate the slugburger and to ride carnival rides, drink beer, and enjoy some wonderful live music.

For more information, please visit *www.corinth.net*.

### DID YOU KNOW?

If you placed all the hamburgers Americans eat each year (about 13 billion) end to end, they would circle the earth more than 32 times.

# Slugburgers

* * * * * * * * * * * * * * * * * * * * * * * *

*Slugburgers are served every day at Borroum's Drug Store in Corinth, Mississippi. The store purchases its meat in 100-pound increments from Rickman's Meat Company, which is also located in Corinth. Borroum's was nice enough to share its recipe for 100 pounds of Slugburger mix.*

| | |
|---|---|
| 50 | pounds ground pork |
| 10 | pounds soy meal |
| 15 | pounds all-purpose flour |
| 2 | pounds salt |
| 23 | pounds water |

*Here is a more manageable amount of Slugburger mix:*

| | |
|---|---|
| 1 1/2 | pounds ground pork |
| 1 1/4 | cups soy meal |
| 1 2/3 | cups all-purpose flour |
| 1 1/4 | tablespoons salt |
| 1 1/3 | cups water |

*To serve the burgers:*

**Buns**

**Mustard**

**Chopped onions**

**Pickles**

■ Combine the pork, soy meal, flour, salt, and water with your hands until the consistency of a meatball. Pat out into 1/4-inch-thick patties. Deep-fry or fry on a griddle or skillet (not a grill) for 3 to 5 minutes or until golden brown. Serve on a bun and MOP it (Mustard, Onion, and Pickles).

**100 POUNDS OF MIX MAKES 400 (4-OUNCE) BURGERS**

**"MANAGEABLE" MIX MAKES 12 (4-OUNCE) BURGERS**

---

### DID YOU KNOW?

The practice of putting cheese on a hamburger originated with chef Lionel Sternberger of Pasadena, California. He began serving "cheese hamburgers" in 1924.

# South Carolina Peach Festival

**WHERE:** Gaffney, South Carolina

**WHEN:** Second weekend in July through the following Saturday (starts on Friday and runs for 9 days)

Peaches are a real big deal in South Carolina, and they do things up big every year at the South Carolina Peach Festival. Events at past festivals have included the world's largest peach pie and a world record for having the most guitarists playing and vocalists singing "Louie, Louie." If you are one of the thousands who visit Gaffney each year to celebrate the peach, you can expect a great downtown festival with a car show, antique tractors, arts and crafts, rides for the children, and live music. Other highlights of this weeklong festival include the peach parade, talent shows, the mud bog, and Peach Beach—featuring beach music and shagging.

For more information, please visit *www.scpeachfestival.org*.

## DID YOU KNOW?

Peaches were introduced to the New World during the 1500s, when they were brought to Latin America by early Spanish colonists.

## Peach Dumplings

1  cup sugar

1  tablespoon butter

2  cups hot water

2  to 3 cups fresh sliced peaches, or frozen peaches, thawed

1  cup all-purpose flour

2  teaspoons baking powder

1/2  teaspoon salt

1  tablespoon sugar (optional)

1/2  cup milk or cream, more or less if needed

Cinnamon-sugar (optional)

■ In a medium saucepan over medium heat combine 1 cup sugar, butter, and hot water. Add the peaches and bring to a boil. In a medium bowl combine the flour, baking powder, salt, and 1 tablespoon sugar, if desired. Stir in enough milk to form a stiff batter. Drop the batter by large spoonfuls onto the boiling fruit. Cover and cook for about 20 minutes. Spoon out the dumplings and fruit into a bowl. If desired, sprinkle with cinnamon-sugar.

**MAKES 4 TO 6 SERVINGS**

## Baked Stuffed Peaches

6  large firm peaches, or 12 canned peach halves

2  tablespoons butter

1 1/2  tablespoons sugar

1  cup macaroon cookie crumbs

1  egg yolk, beaten

1  tablespoon cognac or apple juice

12  teaspoons sweet sherry or apple juice

1/4  cup water

■ Preheat the oven to 350 degrees. Peel the peaches, cut in half, and remove the pits. Scoop out some of the pulp to enlarge the hollow. Mash the pulp. In a mixing bowl cream the butter and sugar together. Add the cookie crumbs, peach pulp, egg yolk, and cognac and beat until smooth. Stuff the hollowed-out peaches with the mixture. Arrange the stuffed peaches in a buttered baking dish and sprinkle 1 teaspoon of sherry on each. Pour the water into the baking dish. Bake for 20 to 25 minutes if using fresh peaches, or until the peaches are tender but still firm. If using canned peaches, bake for 15 minutes.

**MAKES 12 SERVINGS**

## Peach Bread

1½   cups sugar

½    cup vegetable shortening

2    eggs

2    cups puréed peaches

2    cups all-purpose flour

1⅓   teaspoons ground cinnamon

1    teaspoon baking soda

1    teaspoon baking powder

¼    teaspoon salt

1½   teaspoons vanilla extract

1    cup chopped pecans or walnuts

■ Preheat the oven to 325 degrees. Grease and flour two 5 x 9-inch loaf pans.

■ In a large mixing bowl cream the sugar and shortening until light. Add the eggs and beat well. Add the peach purée, flour, cinnamon, baking soda, baking powder, and salt. Blend well. Stir in the vanilla and chopped pecans and mix until blended. Pour into the prepared pans. Bake for 55 to 60 minutes or until a wooden pick or cake tester inserted in the center comes out clean. Let the bread cool for 5 minutes before removing from the pans. Cool completely on wire racks.

**MAKES 2 LOAVES**

## Grilled Peaches

1    peach

     Juice of 1 lemon

½    cup sherry vinegar or balsamic vinegar

¼    cup firmly packed brown sugar

¼    teaspoon freshly ground black pepper

■ Halve the peach and remove the pit. Drizzle each peach half with about 2 teaspoons of the lemon juice. Cover with plastic wrap and set aside.

■ In a small saucepan, combine the vinegar, brown sugar, the remaining lemon juice, and the black pepper and boil until reduced by about half. Place the peaches cut-side down on a hot, lightly oiled grill. Cover and cook for about 2 minutes, or until there are grill marks. Turn over and baste the cut sides with the vinegar mixture. Cover the grill and cook for about 3 more minutes, or until peach halves are softened.

**MAKES 1 SERVING**

# Peach Pecan Muffins

*Muffins:*

1½  cups all-purpose flour

½  cup sugar

2  teaspoons baking powder

1  teaspoon ground cinnamon

¼  teaspoon salt

½  cup (1 stick) butter, melted

¼  cup milk

1  egg

2  medium peaches, peeled and diced
    (about 1 cup; can use fresh, frozen,
    or canned)

*Topping:*

½  cup chopped pecans

⅓  cup firmly packed brown sugar

¼  cup all-purpose flour

1  teaspoon ground cinnamon

2  tablespoons melted butter

■ For the muffins, preheat the oven to 400 degrees. Grease and flour 12 muffin cups or line with paper liners. Combine the flour, sugar, baking powder, cinnamon, and salt in a large bowl. In a separate bowl whisk together the butter, milk, and egg. Stir the liquid mixture into the dry mixture and blend just until moistened. Fold in the diced peaches.

■ For the topping, combine the pecans, brown sugar, flour, cinnamon, and butter in a bowl and mix until crumbly. Spoon the muffin batter into the muffin cups. Sprinkle evenly with the topping. Bake for 20 to 25 minutes, or until a wooden pick inserted in the center comes out clean. Remove from the pan.

**MAKES 12 MUFFINS**

**DID YOU KNOW?**

In ancient China, the peach was revered as a symbol of immortality. Archaeologists have found bowls of peaches entombed with Chinese dignitaries who died several centuries before Christ.

# Virginia Cantaloupe Festival

**WHERE:** South Boston, Virginia
**WHEN:** Fourth Friday in July

For more than a quarter of a century, Virginians have set aside the fourth Friday in July to show their appreciation to local cantaloupe growers for all their hard work. Besides all the good food, the thousands of attendees at this festival get to enjoy live music and dancing.

For more information, please visit *www.valopefest.com*.

## DID YOU KNOW?

Cantaloupes are named for the papal gardens of Cantaloupe, Italy, where some historians say this species of melon was first grown.

## Melon Meringue Pie

*Filling:*

1    cantaloupe, peeled, seeded, and cut into small chunks

1    cup sugar

3    tablespoons cornstarch

3    egg yolks

1/4    cup (1/2 stick) butter or margarine, melted

1    teaspoon vanilla extract

1/8    teaspoon salt

1    (10-inch) graham cracker piecrust

*Meringue:*

3    egg whites

1/4    cup sugar

1/2    teaspoon vanilla extract

■ For the filling, preheat the oven to 350 degrees. In a blender or food processor, process the cantaloupe until puréed. Pour the cantaloupe purée into a mixing bowl. Add the sugar, cornstarch, egg yolks, melted butter, vanilla, and salt. Mix with an electric mixer until well blended. Pour into the piecrust and place on a baking sheet. Bake for about 45 minutes or until a knife inserted in the center comes out clean.

■ For the meringue, beat the egg whites until soft peaks begin to form. Gradually add the sugar and then the vanilla. Spread the meringue over the filling and bake for another 15 minutes.

**MAKES 10 SERVINGS**

## Cantaloupe Bread

13/4    cups all-purpose flour

2    teaspoons baking powder

1/4    teaspoon salt

1/4    teaspoon baking soda

1/3    cup vegetable shortening

2/3    cup sugar

1    large egg

1    cup puréed cantaloupe

■ Preheat the oven to 350 degrees. Sift the flour, baking powder, salt, and baking soda together 3 times. In a separate bowl cream the shortening and sugar until light and fluffy. Add the egg and beat well. Add the puréed cantaloupe and mix. Add the flour mixture, 1/2 cup at a time, beating until smooth. Pour the batter into a well-greased loaf pan. Bake for 50 minutes.

**MAKES 8 SERVINGS**

## Cantaloupe Blueberry Salad

1    (8-ounce) carton vanilla low-fat yogurt

1    tablespoon lemon juice

1    teaspoon poppy seeds

1    teaspoon grated orange rind

1    medium cantaloupe, peeled and seeded

24   Boston lettuce leaves

2    cups fresh blueberries

■ Combine the yogurt, lemon juice, poppy seeds, and orange rind in a bowl and stir well. Cover and chill thoroughly. Cut the cantaloupe lengthwise into 20 to 25 slices. Arrange 3 to 4 slices on a lettuce-lined plate. Top each serving evenly with the blueberries and spoon the yogurt mixture on top.

**MAKES 8 SERVINGS**

## Cantaloupe Ice Cream

1    ripe cantaloupe

3    eggs

1/2  cup sugar

11/2 cups scalded milk

■ Peel, seed, and cut the cantaloupe into small chunks. Process in a food processor until smooth; set aside.

■ In a mixing bowl beat the eggs and sugar together. Whisk in the milk. Cook in a double boiler, stirring until thick. Cool and add to the processed cantaloupe in the food processor. Process until smooth. Pour the mixture into the container of an ice cream freezer and freeze according to the manufacturer's instructions.

**MAKES 1 QUART**

**DID YOU KNOW?**
What we call "cantaloupe" in the U.S. is actually a muskmelon.

# August

# West Virginia Blackberry Festival

**WHERE:** Nutter Fort, West Virginia

**WHEN:** First weekend in August (Thursday through Saturday)

Anyone who has ever picked wild blackberries knows that it's a lot of work, but that the rewards are awful sweet. Every year, more than 10,000 people, many of whom have never picked wild blackberries, come to Nutter Fort to enjoy the labors of those who are willing to put up with chiggers, snakes, briars, and other hazards that blackberry pickers know all too well. In addition to the delicious food, they enjoy midway rides, a car parade, musical entertainment, a pet parade, a 5K run, 4-H club exhibitions, pro wrestling, fireworks, and a talent contest.

For more information, please visit *www.wvblackberry.com*.

## DID YOU KNOW?
Blackberries belong to the rose family.

# Blackberry Jam Cake

*Cake:*

1¹/₂  cups (3 sticks) butter, softened

3    cups sugar

5    eggs

4¹/₂  cups all-purpose flour

1¹/₂  teaspoons baking soda

1    cup sour cream

1¹/₂  cups blackberry jam

1¹/₄  cups chopped pecans

1¹/₂  cups shredded coconut

1    cup raisins

*Filling:*

1    cup softened cream cheese

¹/₂   cup blackberry preserves

2    cups fresh blackberries

*Topping:*

1    (16-ounce) can butter cream frosting
     Additional blackberries for garnish

■ For the cake, preheat the oven to 350 degrees. Lightly grease two 10-inch round cake pans and set aside.

■ Cream together the butter and sugar. Add the eggs, one at a time, beating well after each addition. Sift together the flour and baking soda. Add the flour mixture to the creamed mixture alternately with the sour cream. Mix well. Fold in the jam, pecans, coconut, and raisins. Pour into the prepared pans. Bake for 35 minutes or until a toothpick inserted in the center comes out clean. Remove the cakes from the pans and allow to cool completely on wire racks.

■ For the filling, in a small bowl combine the cream cheese and preserves. Spread the filling on top of one of the cooled cake layers. Arrange the fresh blackberries on top. Place the remaining cake layer on top of the berries and press down lightly, making sure the cakes are "stuck" together.

■ For the topping, frost the cake with the butter cream frosting and top with additional blackberries.

**MAKES 20 SERVINGS**

## DID YOU KNOW?
Blackberry bushes are called "brambles."

# Blackberry Buckle

*Filling:*

1/4   cup (1/2 stick) butter

1/2   cup sugar

1   egg

1   cup all-purpose flour

1 1/2   teaspoons baking powder

1/8   teaspoon salt

1/3   cup milk

1   teaspoon vanilla extract

2   cups fresh blackberries

*Crumb Topping:*

1/2   cup sugar

1/4   cup (1/2 stick) butter, softened

1/3   cup all-purpose flour

1/2   teaspoon ground cinnamon

■ For the filling, preheat the oven to 375 degrees. Grease and flour a 7 x 7-inch pan. Cream the butter and sugar together. Add the egg; beat well. Sift the flour, baking powder, and salt together. Add the flour mixture to the creamed mixture alternately with the milk and vanilla. Pour the batter into the prepared pan; cover with the blackberries.

■ For the topping, combine the sugar, butter, flour, and cinnamon together in a bowl and mix until crumbly. Spread the topping over the blackberries and bake for 45 minutes or until done.

**MAKES 6 SERVINGS**

# Sour Cream and Blackberry Pie

4   cups fresh blackberries

1   (9-inch) piecrust, unbaked

1 1/3   cups sugar, divided

1   cup sifted all-purpose flour

1/4   teaspoon salt

1   cup sour cream

■ Preheat the oven to 450 degrees. Wash the blackberries and place in the piecrust. Reserve 2 tablespoons of the sugar. Sift the remaining sugar, the flour, and salt into a bowl. Add the sour cream and mix well. Pour over the blackberries. Sprinkle the reserved sugar over the top. Bake for 10 minutes. Reduce the oven temperature to 350 degrees. Bake for 30 minutes longer. Cool on a wire rack.

**MAKES 8 SERVINGS**

# Southern Blackberry Cobbler

| | |
|---|---|
| 1 | pint blackberries |
| 1 | cup all-purpose flour |
| 2 | teaspoons baking powder |
| 1 | cup sugar |
| 2 | eggs |
| 3/4 | cup milk |
| 1 | teaspoon vanilla extract |
| 1 | teaspoon grated lemon rind |
| 1 1/2 | cups heavy cream, chilled |
| 2 | tablespoon confectioners' sugar |

■ Preheat the oven to 350 degrees. Rinse and drain the fresh blackberries. Place in a 2-quart dish and set aside.

■ Sift the flour and baking powder into a large mixing bowl. Add the sugar, eggs, milk, vanilla, and lemon rind. Beat briskly until thoroughly combined. Pour the batter over the berries and bake in the center of the oven for 1 hour or until the top is crusty brown.

**MAKES 4 TO 6 SERVINGS**

# Natchez Food and Wine Festival and the Martha White Biscuit Cook-Off

**WHERE:** Natchez, Mississippi

**WHEN:** First weekend in August (Friday through Sunday)

You'll find no better place to enjoy the best biscuits in the world than among the antebellum mansions in Natchez. The biscuit cook-off is just one of the activities foodies can enjoy the first weekend in August. While the schedule differs a bit each year, previous visitors have had great fun with a food film festival, a British high tea (Natchez style), a beer and bocce ball competition, Southern cocktails, and tours of historic homes.

For more information, please visit *www.natchezfoodfest.com*.

## DID YOU KNOW?

Because of their size and rough surface, drop biscuits are sometimes referred to as "cat head biscuits."

## Southern Biscuits

2      cups all-purpose flour

1      tablespoon sugar

4      teaspoons baking powder

1/3    teaspoon salt

1/2    cup vegetable shortening

1      egg, beaten

2/3    cup milk

■ Preheat the oven to 450 degrees. In a bowl combine the flour, sugar, baking powder, and salt. Cut in the shortening until the mixture resembles coarse crumbs. In a separate bowl combine the egg and milk. Add to the flour mixture and mix until the dry ingredients are moistened. Turn the dough out onto a lightly floured surface. Knead and roll the dough a few times. Roll the dough to 3/4-inch thickness. Press a round cutter straight down, being careful not to twist. Place the biscuits on an ungreased baking sheet. Bake for 10 to 14 minutes or until golden brown.

**MAKES 16 BISCUITS**

## Southern Pecan Sweet Potato Biscuits

3/4    cup cold, mashed, cooked sweet potatoes

1/2    cup (1 stick) butter, melted and cooled

2      tablespoons brown sugar

1/2    cup milk

2      cups self-rising flour

1/2    cup chopped pecans

1      tablespoon all-purpose flour

■ Preheat the oven to 400 degrees. Combine the sweet potatoes, butter, and brown sugar in a large bowl. Stir in the milk until smooth. Add the self-rising flour and stir until moistened. Dust the pecans with the flour and add to the dough. Turn the dough out onto a lightly floured surface; knead a few times. Roll the dough to 1/2-inch thickness. Cut with a floured 2-inch round biscuit cutter. Bake on a lightly greased baking sheet for 15 to 18 minutes.

**MAKES 20 BISCUITS**

## Southern Raised Biscuits

2      (1/4-ounce) packages dry yeast
1/4    cup warm water (105 to 110 degrees)
2      cups buttermilk
5      cups all-purpose flour
1/3    cup sugar
1      tablespoon baking powder
11/4   teaspoons salt
1      teaspoon baking soda
1      cup vegetable shortening or unsalted
       butter

■ Dissolve the yeast in the warm water in a small bowl; let stand 5 minutes or until bubbly. Add the buttermilk and set aside.

■ Combine the flour, sugar, baking powder, baking soda, and salt in a large bowl. Cut in the shortening until the mixture resembles coarse meal. Add the yeast mixture gradually, gently combining with a fork. Turn the dough out onto a floured surface and knead lightly 4 or 5 times. Roll the dough to 1/2-inch thickness. Cut with a round biscuit cutter and place on a greased baking sheet. Cover and let rise for 1 hour.

■ Preheat the oven to 450 degrees. Bake for 10 to 12 minutes or until the biscuits are lightly browned.

**MAKES 40 BISCUITS**

## Buttermilk Biscuits

13/4   cups all-purpose flour
2      teaspoons baking powder
1      teaspoon salt
1/4    teaspoon baking soda
1/3    cup vegetable shortening
3/4    cup buttermilk

■ Preheat the oven to 400 degrees. In a large bowl combine the flour, baking powder, salt, and baking soda. Cut the shortening into the dry ingredients with a pastry blender until the mixture resembles crumbs. Stir in just enough buttermilk so the dough leaves the side of the bowl. Turn the dough out onto a floured surface. Knead 10 times. Roll to 1/2-inch thickness. Cut with 2-inch round biscuit cutter. Place on an ungreased cookie sheet and bake for 10 to 12 minutes.

**MAKES 16 BISCUITS**

## Beaten Biscuits

3 1/2 cups all-purpose flour

1/2 teaspoon baking powder

1/2 teaspoon salt

2 tablespoons sugar

1/2 cup vegetable shortening

3/4 cup very cold half-and-half

■ Preheat the oven to 325 degrees. Sift together the flour, baking powder, salt, and sugar in a large bowl. With a pastry blender cut in the shortening until the mixture resembles coarse meal. Add the half-and-half and stir until the dough is moistened. Knead the dough into a cohesive ball. Roll the dough out and fold 25 to 30 times. When the dough seems quite smooth, roll out to 1/2-inch thickness. Cut the dough with a round cutter and place on a baking sheet. Pierce each biscuit with a fork 2 or 3 times to allow air to escape from the layers during baking. Bake on the bottom rack for about 5 minutes. Move the pan to the top rack and bake 25 minutes.

**MAKES 36 BISCUITS**

## Garlic Cheddar Biscuits

2 cups baking mix (such as Bisquick)

2/3 cup milk

1/2 cup shredded Cheddar cheese

1/4 cup (1/2 stick) butter, melted

1/4 teaspoon garlic powder

■ Preheat the oven to 450 degrees. Mix the baking mix, milk, and cheese together in a large mixing bowl until a soft dough forms; beat vigorously for 30 seconds. Drop the dough by spoonfuls onto an ungreased baking sheet. Bake for 8 to 10 minutes or until golden brown.

■ Mix the melted butter and garlic powder in a small bowl. Brush the garlic mixture over the warm biscuits before removing from the baking sheet. Serve warm.

**MAKES 12 BISCUITS**

## Beer Biscuits

. . . . . . . . . . . . . . . . . . . . . . . . . . .

4      cups biscuit mix

1/3    cup sugar

1      cup beer, at room temperature

■ Preheat the oven to 375 degrees. Grease a baking sheet. Combine the biscuit mix, sugar, and beer in a mixing bowl. Stir until blended. Turn the dough out onto a floured surface. Roll to 1/2-inch thickness and cut with a round cutter. Place the biscuits on the prepared baking sheet and bake for 12 to 15 minutes.

**MAKES 12 BISCUITS**

### DID YOU KNOW?

Beaten biscuits differ from regular biscuits in that they are usually smaller and their texture is more like hardtack than soft bread. The dough is beaten against a hard surface or with a hard object for at least 30 minutes, and they are pricked with a fork before baking.

# Miss Martha's Ice Cream Crankin' Festival

**WHERE:** Nashville, Tennessee
**WHEN:** First Sunday in August

For more than 20 years, Miss Martha's Ice Cream Crankin' contest has brought people together from all over the South to crank homemade ice cream and serve it up to the masses for a good cause—the Martha O'Bryan Center, which supports families living in poverty. Visitors to this old-fashioned ice cream social also get to enjoy live music and a children's art show—as if homemade ice cream weren't reason enough to come together on a hot August afternoon.

For more information, please visit *www.marthaobryan.org*.

### DID YOU KNOW?

Nero is believed to have created the first frozen dessert, which was a mixture of snow (retrieved from the mountains by his slaves), nectar, fruit pulp, and honey.

## Banana Ice Cream

1   (14-ounce) can sweetened
    condensed milk

1   cup sugar

1   teaspoon vanilla extract

3   medium bananas, chopped
    Milk

■   Combine the sweetened condensed milk, sugar, vanilla, and bananas in a large bowl until well mixed. Pour into the container of a 1-gallon ice cream freezer. Add enough milk to almost fill the ice cream freezer. Freeze according to the manufacturer's instructions.

**MAKES 16 SERVINGS**

## Pineapple Ice Cream

1   (20-ounce) can crushed pineapple in
    heavy syrup

1   (3-ounce) package instant vanilla
    pudding mix

4   eggs

2   cups sugar

1   teaspoon vanilla extract

2   (14-ounce) cans sweetened
    condensed milk
    Milk

■   Combine the pineapple with syrup, pudding mix, eggs, sugar, vanilla, and sweetened condensed milk in a large bowl and mix well. Pour into the container of a 1-gallon ice cream freezer. Add enough milk to almost fill the ice cream freezer. Freeze according to the manufacturer's instructions.

**MAKES 16 SERVINGS**

## Coconut Ice Cream

2   (14-ounce) cans chilled unsweetened
    coconut milk

1   cup plus 3 tablespoons sugar

1   cup chilled half-and-half

■   Whisk the coconut milk, sugar, and half-and-half in a medium bowl until the sugar dissolves. Transfer the mixture to an ice cream freezer and freeze according to the manufacturer's instructions.

**MAKES 4 SERVINGS**

# White Chocolate Ice Cream

2    cups light cream

12    ounces white chocolate, coarsely chopped

4    eggs

1 1/3   cups sugar

2    cups heavy cream

■ Heat the light cream in the top of a double boiler set over simmering water. Add the white chocolate. Reduce the heat to a slow simmer and cook until the chocolate is melted, stirring occasionally. Remove from the heat.

■ Using an electric mixer, beat the eggs in a medium bowl. Add the sugar and continue beating until the sugar is dissolved. Slowly mix in the chocolate mixture. Beat in the heavy cream. Refrigerate until well chilled.

■ Pour the mixture into an ice cream freezer and freeze according to the manufacturer's instructions.

**MAKES 16 SERVINGS**

# Chocolate Ice Cream

2    cups whole milk

5    large egg yolks

1/4   cup plus 2 tablespoons sugar

1    cup heavy cream

10    ounces bittersweet chocolate. melted

■ Bring the milk to a simmer in a medium saucepan. Meanwhile, combine the egg yolks and sugar in a mixing bowl and beat with an electric mixer at medium-high speed until very thick and pale yellow. Add half the warm milk to the egg yolk mixture and whisk until blended. Stir the mixture into the remaining milk and cook over low heat, stirring constantly, until the mixture is thick enough to coat a spoon. Remove from the heat and immediately stir in the cream. Pass the mixture through a strainer into a medium bowl set in an ice bath. Whisk in the melted chocolate and chill. Pour the chilled mixture into an ice cream freezer and freeze according to the manufacturer's instructions.

**MAKES 4 SERVINGS**

## Pomegranate Ice Cream

1   cup orange juice

3/4   cup sugar

1 1/2   cups pomegranate juice

2   cups half-and-half

■ Heat the orange juice in a saucepan over medium-high heat until reduced to 1/2 cup. Add the sugar and stir until dissolved. Add the pomegranate juice and chill. Mix the chilled juices with the half-and-half. Pour the mixture into the container of an ice cream freezer and freeze according to the manufacturer's directions.

**MAKES 4 SERVINGS**

## Dark Chocolate Cheesecake Ice Cream

3   ounces dark chocolate, melted

3   eggs

3/4   cup sugar

2   cups heavy cream

1   cup half-and-half

8   ounces cream cheese, softened

■ Melt the chocolate in a double boiler or in a microwave. Let cool to room temperature. In a blender or food processor, combine the melted chocolate, eggs, sugar, heavy cream, half-and-half, and cream cheese. Process until mixed well. Pour the mixture into the container of an ice cream freezer and freeze according to the manufacturer's instructions.

**MAKES 4 SERVINGS**

### DID YOU KNOW?
The first ice cream parlor in America opened in New York City in 1776.

# Hope Watermelon Festival

**WHERE:** Hope, Arkansas

**WHEN:** Second weekend in August (Thursday through Sunday)

Long before President Bill Clinton put the city of Hope on the national radar screen, watermelons were a calling card for this charming Southern town. Since the mid-1970s, more than 30,000 people each year have come from across the country to participate in such festivities as a seed-spitting contest, a watermelon-eating contest, and the Watermelon Olympics, which include a melon toss and the Watermelon Idol talent contest. Other highlights include an antique car show, a dog show, a baseball card show, arts and crafts, and a 5K run/walk. You also won't want to miss the watermelon weigh-in and auction—some of these summer melons top 200 pounds.

For more information, please visit
*www.hopechamberofcommerce.com.*

### DID YOU KNOW?
The first recorded watermelon harvest occurred nearly 5,000 years ago in Egypt.

## Watermelon Sorbet

2/3  cup sugar

1/2  cup water

2/3  cup light corn syrup

2  tablespoons lemon juice

1/4  of 1 large watermelon, seeded and cut into 1-inch cubes (about 8 cups)

■ In a medium saucepan, combine the sugar, water, and corn syrup. Stir over medium heat until the mixture comes to a boil. Reduce the heat to low and without stirring, simmer for 5 minutes. Stir in the lemon juice; cool to room temperature.

■ Purée the melon cubes, about 2 cups at a time, in a blender or food processor fitted with a metal blade. Stir the puréed mixture into the cooled syrup. Pour into the container of an ice cream freezer. Freeze according to the manufacturer's directions.

**MAKES ABOUT 2 QUARTS**

## Deep-Fried Watermelon

1  watermelon, about 10 pounds

3/4  cup all-purpose flour

2  egg whites, beaten

1/2  cup cornstarch

3  cups vegetable oil
  Confectioners' sugar

■ Cut the watermelon in half and scoop out the pulp. Remove any seeds from the pulp and cut the pulp into diamonds. Coat the watermelon pieces with the flour. Mix the egg whites with the cornstarch and a small amount of water to make a batter.

■ Heat the oil in a deep skillet to about 250 degrees or until small bubbles appear. Dip the watermelon pieces in the batter and add to the oil. Deep fry until the coating becomes firm. Turn off the heat and continue to fry the watermelon until light brown. Remove from the oil and drain on paper towels. Sprinkle with confectioners' sugar and serve.

**MAKES 10 SERVINGS**

**DID YOU KNOW?**
Early explorers used hollowed-out watermelons as canteens.

# Watermelon Waldorf Salad

2   cups cubed watermelon, seeds removed

1/2   cup sliced celery

1/2   cup halved seedless red grapes
    Dash of salt

1/4   cup nonfat coleslaw dressing

2   tablespoons sliced almonds, toasted

■ Mix together the watermelon, celery, and grapes in a large bowl. Just before serving, stir the salt into the coleslaw dressing. Pour the mixture over the fruit and stir until coated. Sprinkle with the almonds.

**MAKES 6 SERVINGS**

# Chicken Salad with Watermelon and Peaches

3   cups chopped cooked chicken

1   cup plain yogurt

1/2   cup mayonnaise

1   teaspoon dried dill leaf or 1 tablespoon snipped fresh dill
    Juice of 1 lemon

Salt and pepper to taste

2   peaches, peeled and diced

2   cups chopped seeded watermelon
    Salad greens for serving

■ Mix together the chicken, yogurt, mayonnaise, dill, and lemon juice in a large bowl. Season with salt and pepper to taste. Just before serving, gently mix in the peaches and watermelon. Serve over salad greens.

**MAKES 4 TO 6 SERVINGS**

# Watermelon Lemonade

6   cups watermelon cubes, seeds removed

1   cup water

1/2   cup sugar

1/2   cup lemon juice

■ Place the watermelon and water in the container of an electric blender. Cover and blend until smooth. Strain through a fine mesh strainer into a pitcher. Stir in the sugar and lemon juice until the sugar dissolves. Refrigerate until chilled, about 1 hour.

**MAKES 6 SERVINGS**

## Watermelon Muffins

1 1/2    cups all-purpose flour

2    teaspoons baking soda

1    teaspoon baking powder
    Pinch of salt

1/8    teaspoon ground cinnamon

6    tablespoons butter, at room
    temperature

2/3    cup sugar

2    eggs

1/2    cup milk

1/2    cup watermelon juice

1/2    cup watermelon pulp

■  Preheat the oven to 350 degrees. Sift the flour, baking soda, baking powder, salt, and cinnamon in a large bowl. In a separate bowl cream the butter and sugar together. Add the eggs. Whip in the milk, watermelon juice, and watermelon pulp. Add the wet mixture to the dry ingredients; blend just to incorporate. Fill greased muffin cups 2/3 full with the batter. Bake for 25 minutes. Transfer to a wire rack to cool.

**MAKES 12 MUFFINS**

**DID YOU KNOW?**

There is a recipe for watermelon rind pickles in the first cookbook ever published in the United States (in 1796).

# Tontitown Grape Festival

**WHERE:** Tontitown, Arkansas

**WHEN:** Third weekend in August (Thursday through Saturday). A children's carnival takes place the two nights before the festival (Tuesday and Wednesday).

Folks have been celebrating the grape in Tontitown for more than 100 years. Spaghetti dinners are served each night to fortify festivalgoers who then go out to enjoy carnival rides, live entertainment, arts and crafts, and a used book sale. There's a run for the grapes in the form of a 5K race, and visitors can enjoy the coronation of Queen Concordia.

For more information, please visit *www.tontitowngrapefestival.com*.

## DID YOU KNOW?

Grapes are classified according to how they will be used. Table grapes are low in acidity and sugar content, and are a standard size, color, and shape. Raisin grapes are low in acidity and high in sugar content, and preferably seedless. Table wine grapes have high acidity and moderate sugar content. Dessert wine and other sweet wine grapes have moderate acidity and high sugar content.

## Grape Salad

*Salad:*

4    pounds green or red seedless grapes, halved

*Dressing:*

8    ounces cream cheese, softened

8    ounces sour cream

1/2   cup sugar

1    teaspoon vanilla extract

*Topping:*

1    cup firmly packed brown sugar

1    cup chopped pecans

■ For the salad, arrange the grapes into a 9 x 13-inch pan.

■ For the dressing, combine the cream cheese, sour cream, sugar, and vanilla in a bowl until smooth. Spread the dressing over the grapes. You can have as many layers as desired.

■ For the topping, combine the brown sugar and pecans together in a small bowl. Sprinkle the topping over the salad. Cover and refrigerate overnight.

**MAKES 12 SERVINGS**

## Chicken Breasts with Grapes

4    large chicken breasts

     Flour for dusting

     Salt and pepper to taste

1/2   plus 1/4 cup butter, divided

1/2   cup diced onion

1    cup white cooking wine

1    cup chicken broth

1/2   pound sliced fresh mushrooms

1    cup white seedless grapes

■ Preheat the oven to 375 degrees. Dust the chicken breasts with flour seasoned with salt and pepper. Heat 1/2 cup of the butter in a skillet and brown the chicken on all sides. Arrange the browned chicken in a single layer in a large baking pan. Add the onion to the pan drippings and cook until soft. Add the cooking wine and chicken broth. Cook until heated through and pour over the chicken. Bake, covered, for 35 minutes.

■ Sauté the mushrooms in the remaining 1/4 cup butter. Remove the chicken from the oven and add the sautéed mushrooms and grapes. Continue baking for 10 minutes more.

**MAKES 4 SERVINGS**

# Grape Jelly

3    pounds ripe seedless Concord grapes, stemmed

1/2    cup water

1    jelly bag or 1-square yard of cheesecloth, several layers thick

7    cups sugar

1/2    (1.75-ounce) box fruit pectin

▨ Crush the grapes thoroughly in a large saucepan. Add the water and bring to a boil. Reduce the heat and simmer, covered, for 10 minutes. Place the jelly bag or cheesecloth inside a colander and place the colander in a large pan. Pour the fruit and liquid in the colander and close the fruit bag or cheesecloth and make a large twist at the top. Squeeze out the juice into a large saucepan. Using a potato masher, press the jelly bag, squeezing out all of the remaining juice from the grapes. Be sure you have 4 cups of juice when finished squeezing. To the measured juice, add the sugar and mix well. Place over high heat and bring to a boil. Stir in the fruit pectin. Bring to a full rolling boil and boil hard for 1 minute, stir-ring constantly. Remove from the heat and skim off the foam with a metal spoon. Pour quickly into glass jars. Cover at once with 1/2 inch of paraffin (melted to seal). Cover with metal or paper lids when completely cool, and screw on the bands.

**MAKES 10 MEDIUM-SIZE JARS**

# Grape Ice Cream

3    cups sugar

3    cups grape juice

3    cups whipping cream

     Juice of 3 lemons

1    quart whole milk (approximately)

▨ Combine the sugar, grape juice, whipping cream, and lemon juice in a large bowl. Chill in the refrigerator for 1 hour. Pour the mixture into a 1-gallon ice cream freezer and fill to the fill-line with milk. Freeze according to the manufacturer's directions.

**MAKES 16 SERVINGS**

---

**DID YOU KNOW?**

The majority of the world's grape crop is used for wine; 27 percent is served as fresh fruit, 2 percent is used as dried fruit, and the remaining 71 percent becomes wine.

# September

# Butter Bean Festival

**WHERE:** Pinson, Alabama
**WHEN:** The Saturday of Labor Day weekend

Most of the festivals featured in this book started as a way to celebrate a local agricultural product. The Butter Bean Festival came about when a group of town leaders in Pinson were sitting around trying to come up with an idea for a festival for their town. One gentleman said they needed to wrap things up because he had a pot of butter beans on the stove waiting for him at home. And that is the genesis of Pinson's Butter Bean Festival. Now more than 25,000 people come on Labor Day weekend to enjoy the butter bean and cornbread cook-offs, 5K and 1-mile runs, a bike road race, a bowling tournament, live music, the Miss Butter Bean Pageant, a motorcycle show, a golf tournament, a tail-waggin' pageant, a softball tournament, and Elvis impersonators.

For more information, please visit *www.butterbeanfestival.com*.

## DID YOU KNOW?

In the South, lima beans are almost always called butter beans, even in markets and restaurants.

## Southern Butter Bean Casserole

1    tablespoon chopped onion

1    tablespoon chopped green bell pepper

1    tablespoon butter

1    (10 3/4-ounce) can tomato soup

1/4  cup water

1    tablespoon brown sugar

1    tablespoon cider vinegar

1    tablespoon dry mustard

2    (16-ounce) cans butter beans, drained

■ Preheat the oven to 375 degrees. Sauté the onion and green pepper in the butter in a large saucepan over medium-high heat. Add the tomato soup, water, brown sugar, vinegar, and dry mustard and cook until heated through. Stir in the butter beans. Pour into a 1-quart casserole dish. Bake for 45 minutes.

**MAKES 8 SERVINGS**

## BBQ Butter Beans

1    (10.7-ounce) can tomato soup

1    cup firmly packed brown sugar

1 3/4 tablespoons dry mustard

1/3  pound uncooked bacon, cut into pieces

1    medium onion, chopped

1    green bell pepper, chopped

3    (16-ounce) cans butter beans, drained

■ Preheat the oven to 350 degrees. Mix the tomato soup, brown sugar, and dry mustard in the bottom of a 2-quart baking dish. Combine the bacon, onion, green pepper, and butter beans in a large bowl and mix well. Spoon into the baking dish and bake for 1 to 1 1/2 hours, or until the onion and bell pepper are tender.

**MAKES 12 SERVINGS**

## Butter Beans

2      tablespoons butter

1/4    cup finely chopped onion

1      pound fresh shelled butter beans

3/4    teaspoon salt

■  In a medium saucepan melt the butter. Sauté the onion in the butter until clear. Add the butter beans and sauté for about 5 minutes, stirring frequently. Add the salt and enough water to cover the beans. Bring to a boil, then reduce the heat to a simmer. Cover and cook for approximately 25 minutes or until the beans are tender, stirring frequently.

**MAKES 6 SERVINGS**

**DID YOU KNOW?**
Butter beans should never be eaten raw because they contain linamarin, which releases a cyanide compound when the seed coat is opened.

# Ayden Collard Festival

**WHERE:** Ayden, North Carolina

**WHEN:** The week following Labor Day (Tuesday through Sunday—a 5-day festival)

The city of Ayden has a rich and diverse history. In the mid-1970s, town leaders decided they wanted to have a festival to bring people to town, and they left it up to the citizens to decide what they wanted to celebrate. Beating out the cucumber and other produce was the mighty collard green. Now thousands of people converge on Ayden each year to enjoy gospel music, a parade, carnival rides, a basketball tournament, line dancers, arts and crafts, horseshoes, a golf tournament, a collard green–eating contest, and all the Collard Queens.

For more information, please visit *www.aydencollardfestival.com*.

---

### DID YOU KNOW?
Ancient Greeks and Romans cultivated collard greens.

## Collard Green Quiche

1    (9-inch) piecrust, unbaked

4    large eggs

1    cup half-and-half

1/3  teaspoon salt

1/3  teaspoon ground black pepper

1/2  teaspoon dried oregano

1/4  cup finely chopped onion

1    cup shredded mild Cheddar cheese, divided

2    cups frozen chopped collard greens, thawed and squeezed dry

1/2  cup chopped mushrooms

1/2  cup chopped green bell pepper

▉ Preheat the oven to 350 degrees. Bake the piecrust for about 8 minutes, and set aside.

▉ In a large bowl, lightly beat the eggs, half-and-half, salt, pepper, oregano, and onion; set aside.

▉ Sprinkle 1/2 cup of the cheese onto the piecrust. Layer the collard greens, mushrooms, and bell pepper in the piecrust. Pour the egg mixture over the vegetables, and sprinkle with the remaining 1/2 cup cheese. Bake for 40 to 50 minutes or until your knife comes out clean when inserted in the center. Let cool for 5 to 10 minutes before serving.

**MAKES 8 SERVINGS**

## Southern-Style Collard Greens

4     pounds collard greens

11/2  quarts water

1     pound ham hocks

1     teaspoon crushed red pepper

1     teaspoon sugar

2     tablespoons butter

▉ Remove the stems from the collard greens and rinse. Soak the greens in salt water for about 1 hour.

▉ Combine the greens and water in a stockpot with the ham hocks, crushed red pepper, sugar, and butter. Bring to a boil. Reduce the heat to low. Cook for 1 hour or until the greens are tender. Add more water if needed.

**MAKES 8 SERVINGS**

# North Carolina Turkey Festival

**WHERE:** Raeford, North Carolina

**WHEN:** Second Saturday in September through the following Saturday (8-day festival)

You can get your fill of turkeys at this North Carolina festival, but luckily Thanksgiving is still far enough out that your appetite will have returned for the big bird by the time late November rolls around. This weeklong festival involves the entire community with such activities as a parade, a dog show, a beach music concert, a car and motorcycle show, and plenty of singing and storytelling. But this festival also brings out the competitor in people, with contests for card players, tennis players, triathletes, and golfers. There's also the big Turkey Bowl Football Game and the turkey cooking contest on the final day of the festival.

For more information, please visit *www.ncturkeyfestival.org*.

---

### DID YOU KNOW?
The heaviest turkey ever raised was 86 pounds, about the size of a large dog.

---

## Fried Turkey

1/4 pound lean salt pork, finely minced

3 garlic cloves, minced

5 to 6 gallons peanut oil, divided

1/2 cup (1 stick) butter

1 teaspoon soy sauce

1/2 teaspoon paprika

Salt and pepper to taste

1 (12- to 15-pound) turkey

■ Combine the salt pork, garlic, and 1 teaspoon of the peanut oil in a heavy skillet over low heat and cook for 30 minutes, or until the drippings have rendered from the salt pork. Turn several times. Add the butter, soy sauce, paprika, and salt and pepper to the skillet. When the butter has melted and become clear, remove the pan from the heat and strain the mixture through cheesecloth or a fine mesh strainer, or process in a blender until no small bits remain. Pour the liquid into a syringe and inject the turkey in several places about 5 inches apart, ensuring that the syringe is pointed in different directions several times for each hole made. Rub the outside of the turkey with any remaining liquid. Put the turkey in a large food-safe plastic bag in the refrigerator overnight. Heat the remaining peanut oil to 340 degrees in a turkey fryer. Deep-fry the turkey for 4 minutes per pound. The turkey will turn a deep brown and will be crisp when done. The temperature in the thickest portion of a thigh should read 175 degrees using an instant read thermometer.

**MAKES 10 SERVINGS**

## Creamed Turkey

3 tablespoons butter

3/4 cup sliced mushrooms

3 tablespoons all-purpose flour

1 1/2 cups milk

1/2 cup hot chicken broth

1 (2-ounce) jar diced pimientos, drained

4 cups diced cooked turkey or chicken

Salt to taste

Ground black or white pepper to taste

■ Melt the butter in a large saucepan over medium-low heat. Sauté the mushrooms until golden and tender. Add the flour; stir until smooth. Slowly add the milk and chicken broth, stirring constantly, until thickened and bubbly. Add the pimientos, turkey, and season with salt and pepper. Cook until heated through, but do not boil. Serve over toast, cornbread, or biscuits.

**MAKES 6 TO 8 SERVINGS**

# Cajun Fried Turkey

2    (10-pound) turkeys or 1 (20-pound) turkey

16   ounces Italian salad dressing

1    tablespoon garlic powder

1    tablespoon onion powder

1    teaspoon celery salt

3    tablespoons Worcestershire sauce

3    tablespoons paprika

1/2  (12-ounce) can beer

4    teaspoons Poultry Magic seasoning

1    teaspoon salt

2    teaspoons black pepper

1 1/2 teaspoons white pepper

2    teaspoons cayenne pepper

4    dashes Tabasco sauce

     Peanut oil for deep-frying

■ Wrap the legs of the turkey with foil. Remove any excess skin and fat from the turkey. In a large bowl combine the salad dressing, garlic powder, onion powder, celery salt, Worcestershire sauce, paprika, beer, Poultry Magic, salt, black pepper, white pepper, cayenne pepper, and Tabasco sauce. Mix well. Pour the mixture into a syringe and inject into the turkey at least 12 hours before frying. Refrigerate.

■ Heat peanut oil to 340 degrees in a turkey fryer. Deep-fry the turkey in the hot oil for 4 minutes per pound.

**MAKES 16 SERVINGS**

## DID YOU KNOW?

In a letter written to his daughter, Ben Franklin suggested that the turkey be the official bird of the United States.

## Hot Brown Sandwiches

● ● ● ● ● ● ● ● ● ● ● ● ● ● ● ● ● ● ● ● ● ● ● ●

| | |
|---|---|
| 2 | tablespoons butter |
| 1/4 | cup all-purpose flour |
| 2 | cups milk |
| 1/4 | cup grated Cheddar cheese |
| 1/4 | cup plus 4 ounces grated Parmesan cheese, divided |
| 3/4 | teaspoon salt |
| 1 | pound cooked turkey, sliced |
| 8 | slices toast |
| 4 | slices tomato |
| 8 | slices bacon, cooked |

■ Melt the butter in a saucepan. Add the flour and stir well. Add the milk, Cheddar cheese, 1/4 cup of the Parmesan cheese, and the salt. Cook, stirring constantly, until thick.

■ Preheat the oven to 425 degrees. In a well-greased baking dish, arrange the turkey slices on the toast and cover with the cheese sauce. Top with the tomato and bacon. Sprinkle evenly with the remaining 4 ounces Parmesan cheese. Bake until bubbly.

**MAKES 8 SERVINGS**

# Berea Spoonbread Festival

**WHERE:** Berea, Kentucky

**WHEN:** Second weekend in September (Friday through Sunday)

You can't get much more Southern than spoonbread. A delicacy for more than three centuries, spoonbread is a pretty good excuse to come to a small Southern town like Berea and enjoy such events as a beauty pageant, carnival rides, a tractor pull, hot-air balloon rides, arts and crafts, live music, a 5K run, clogging, a parade, a spoonbread-eating contest, a motorcycle rally, a car show, a dog show, and a two-man paintball tournament.

For more information, please visit *www.spoonbreadfestival.com*.

## DID YOU KNOW?

The use of sugar in spoonbread or cornbread was not common among old-time Southerners.

## Southern Spoonbread

3 cups milk

1 teaspoon salt

1 teaspoon sugar

1¼ cups cornmeal

3 eggs

1 tablespoon baking powder

2 tablespoons cold water

2 tablespoons butter, softened

■ Preheat the oven to 400 degrees. Heat the milk, salt, and sugar in a large saucepan to a moderate temperature. Remove from the heat. Add the cornmeal to the milk mixture and stir until the mixture resembles mush. Beat the eggs, baking powder, cold water, and butter together in a mixing bowl. Add to the cornmeal mixture. Pour into a 2-quart greased baking dish and bake for 25 to 30 minutes.

**MAKES 6 SERVINGS**

## Rice Spoonbread

1 cup cooked rice

¼ cup cornmeal

1 tablespoon all-purpose flour

1 teaspoon salt

2 tablespoons sugar

1 cup boiling water

2 eggs, separated and beaten

1 cup milk

2 tablespoons butter, melted

■ Preheat the oven to 350 degrees. Combine the rice, cornmeal, flour, salt, and sugar in a bowl. Stir into the boiling water in a large saucepan and cook until thick, stirring constantly. Bring to a boil, and then remove from the heat. Gradually add the beaten egg yolks, milk, and butter. Fold in the beaten egg whites. Bake in a well-greased 2-quart baking dish in a water bath for 40 minutes.

**MAKES 6 SERVINGS**

## Mushroom Spoonbread

1 (10.7-ounce) can condensed cream of mushroom soup

3/4 cup milk

1/2 cup cornmeal

1 tablespoon butter

2 eggs, separated and beaten

1/4 teaspoon salt

■ Preheat the oven to 350 degrees. In a large bowl combine the soup and milk. Stir in the cornmeal. Add the butter, beaten egg yolks, and salt. Mix well. Fold in the stiffly beaten egg whites. Pour into a buttered 1 1/2-quart casserole dish. Bake for 1 hour. Serve at once with butter or gravy.

**MAKES 4 TO 6 SERVINGS**

## Potato Spoonbread

3/4 cup cornmeal

2 teaspoons salt

1 1/2 cups water

2 eggs, lightly beaten

3/4 cup milk

3/4 cup mashed potatoes

1 tablespoon vegetable shortening

■ Preheat the oven to 325 degrees. Combine the cornmeal, salt, and water in a saucepan and bring to a boil for 5 minutes. Remove from the heat. In a bowl combine the eggs, milk, mashed potatoes, and shortening. Add to the saucepan and beat well. Bake in a greased 2-quart baking dish for 40 minutes.

**MAKES 6 SERVINGS**

### DID YOU KNOW?

*Suppone* or *suppawn*, a Native American porridge, is considered by many authorities to be the ancestor of spoonbread.

## Breakfast Spoonbread

1 pound mild sausage

2 onions, chopped

1/4 cup all-purpose flour

1 garlic clove, minced

2 teaspoons sugar

3/4 teaspoon salt

1 teaspoon baking powder

3/4 cup yellow cornmeal

1 egg, beaten

1 1/2 cups milk, divided

■ Preheat the oven to 375 degrees. In a skillet cook the sausage and onions until the sausage is browned. In a large bowl combine the flour, garlic, sugar, salt, baking powder, and cornmeal. Stir in the egg and 1 cup of the milk and mix well. Place the sausage and onions in a 2-quart baking dish. Pour the batter over the mixture. Pour the remaining 1/2 cup milk over the batter and bake for 45 minutes, or until a crust forms. Remove the spoonbread from the oven and serve immediately.

**MAKES 6 SERVINGS**

## Jackson County Spoonbread

1 cup sour cream

1 cup self-rising cornmeal

1/2 cup (1 stick) margarine

2 eggs

2 cups cream-style corn

■ Preheat the oven to 350 degrees. In a large bowl combine the sour cream, cornmeal, margarine, eggs, and corn together. Pour the mixture into a 2-quart greased baking dish and bake for 30 to 40 minutes or until done.

**MAKES 6 SERVINGS**

# Shrimp and Grits: The Wild Georgia Shrimp Festival

**WHERE:** Jekyll Island, Georgia

**WHEN:** The second weekend of September (Friday through Sunday)

One of the only Southern food festivals dedicated to two Southern food favorites: in this case, shrimp and grits. This up-and-coming festival is not only a draw for people who like to cook (there are competitions for both professional and amateur chefs, as well as cooking demonstrations), but also a haven for those eager to enjoy a shrimp-eating contest, music, shrimp boat tours, a golf tournament, a family fun zone, and arts and crafts—all set amid Jekyll Island's beautiful historic district.

For more information, please visit *www.jekyllisland.com/shrimpandgrits*.

## DID YOU KNOW?

Shrimp differ from crabs and lobsters in that they move mainly by swimming rather than crawling.

## Shrimp and Grits with Mushrooms

2    cups water

1    (14-ounce) can chicken broth

3/4    cup half-and-half

3/4    teaspoon salt, divided

1    cup regular grits

3/4    cup shredded Cheddar cheese

1/4    cup grated Parmesan cheese

2    tablespoons butter

1/2    plus 1/3 teaspoon hot sauce, divided

1/4    teaspoon white pepper

4    slices bacon

1    pound medium shrimp, peeled and deveined

1/3    teaspoon black pepper

1/4    cup all-purpose flour

1    cup sliced mushrooms

1/4    cup chopped green onions

2    garlic cloves, minced

1/2    cup low-sodium fat-free chicken broth

2    tablespoons fresh lemon juice
     Lemon wedges for serving

■ Bring the water, 1 can chicken broth, the half-and-half, and 1/2 teaspoon of the salt to a boil in a medium saucepan. Gradually add the grits. Reduce the heat and simmer for 10 minutes or until thickened, stirring occasionally. Add the Cheddar cheese, Parmesan cheese, butter, 1/2 teaspoon of the hot sauce, and the white pepper; mix well. Lower the heat to keep warm.

■ Cook the bacon in a large skillet until crisp. Remove the bacon and drain on paper towels, reserving 1 tablespoon of the drippings in the skillet. Crumble the bacon and set aside.

■ Sprinkle the shrimp with the black pepper and the remaining 1/4 teaspoon salt; dredge in the flour. Sauté the mushrooms in the hot bacon drippings in the skillet for 5 minutes or until tender. Add the green onions and sauté for 2 minutes. Add the shrimp and garlic and sauté for 2 minutes or until the shrimp are lightly browned. Stir in the 1/2 cup chicken broth, the lemon juice, and the remaining 1/3 teaspoon hot sauce and cook for 2 more minutes, stirring to loosen any particles from the bottom of the skillet. Serve the shrimp mixture over the hot cheese grits. Top with the crumbled bacon and serve with lemon wedges.

**MAKES 8 SERVINGS**

# Lecompte Pie Festival

**Lecompte, Louisiana**

*Ron Manville*

Chess Pie (recipe on page 218).

# RC and Moon Pie Festival

**Bell Buckle, Tennessee**

*T. J. Hall*

*Left page:* World's largest Moon Pie.

*Right page, top:* Cutting a Moon Pie decorated as a 50th birthday cake for RC Cola.

*Right page, bottom left:* Display of RC and Moon Pie products.

*Right page, bottom right:* Enjoying a Moon Pie.

*T. J. Hall*

*T. J. Hall*

*T. J. Hall*

# Unicoi County Apple Festival
**Erwin, Tennessee**

*Keeli Parkey, photographer with the* Valley Beautiful Beacon *newspaper*

Fiddle player.

# Butter Bean Festival

**Pinson, Alabama**

*Tori Howell, Shutterbugz Photography*

Cajun food booth belonging
to the butter bean cook-off winner.

# Berea Spoonbread Festival

**Berea, Kentucky**

*Top:* Spoonbread-eating contest.
*Bottom:* Hot-air balloon rides.

Robert Elam

Robert Elam

# Apple Butter Festival

## Berkeley Springs, West Virginia

Jeanne Mozier

Jeanne Mozier

Jeanne Mozier

*Left:* Stirring apple butter in the kettle.

*Top right:* Winners of the youth category of the hog-calling contest.

*Bottom right:* Winners of the beard contest.

*Ron Manville*

Apple-Cranberry Chocolate Cups (recipe on page 222).

# World Chicken Festival

**London, Kentucky**

*Top:* Pie-eating contest.
*Bottom:* World's largest skillet.

*Courtesy of World Chicken Festival*

*Courtesy of World Chicken Festival*

# Suffolk Peanut Festival

## Suffolk, Virginia

*Top:* Ferris wheel.

*Bottom:* Peanut butter sculpture contest.

*Courtesy of Suffolk Festivals, Inc.*

*Courtesy of Suffolk Festivals, Inc.*

# West Virginia Black Walnut Festival

**Spencer, West Viginia**

*Ron Manville*

Black Walnut Cocoa Fudge (recipe on page 235)

# National Shrimp Festival

**Gulf Shores, Alabama**

Ron Wainscott

John Hill

*Top left:* Bowl of shrimp.

*Top right:* Posing for a photo in the shrimp cutout.

*Bottom:* Sand sculpture contest.

Ron Wainscott

# Blairsville Sorghum Festival

**Blairsville, Georgia**

*Top:* Making sorghum.
*Bottom:* Biscuit-eating contest.

# Jack Daniel's® Bar-B-Q Festival

## Lynchburg, Tennessee

*Ron Manville*

Tabasco Jack Wings (recipe on page 261).

# Arkansas Bean Fest and Championship Outhouse Races

## Mountain View, Arkansas

Ed Schuh

Lori Freeze

Ed Schuh

*Top left:* Outhouse races.

*Top right:* Outhouse parade.

*Bottom:* Cooking beans.

# Giant Omelette Celebration

## Abbeville, Louisiana

*Rollman Photography, courtesy of Confrerie d'Abbeville*

Cooking the giant omelette.

# Vardaman Sweet Potato Festival

### Vardaman, Mississippi

*Ron Manville*

Sweet Potato Biscuits (recipe on p. 289).

# Shrimp and Grits

* * * * * * * * * * * * * * * * * * * * * * * * *

*Marinade:*

3   cups white wine

1   teaspoon salt

2   celery ribs, coarsely chopped

1   teaspoon celery seeds

1   garlic clove, minced

1   teaspoon dill seeds

1   bunch fresh basil

2   pounds small shrimp, peeled and deveined

*Grits:*

2¹/₂  cups milk

¹/₂  cup regular grits

¹/₂  cup grated Cheddar cheese

Garlic salt to taste

Salt and pepper to taste

*Shrimp:*

2   large onions, diced

¹/₂  cup olive oil

■ For the marinade, combine the wine, salt, celery, celery seeds, garlic, dill seeds, and basil in a large saucepan and bring to a boil. Cool and chill. Add the shrimp to the marinade and marinate for 4 hours.

■ For the grits, in a large saucepan bring the milk to a boil. Add the grits and cook until soft. Add the cheese, garlic salt, salt, and pepper.

■ For the shrimp, remove the shrimp from the marinade, discarding the marinade. Sauté the shrimp and onions in the olive oil in a skillet. Serve the shrimp over the grits.

**MAKES 6 SERVINGS**

## DID YOU KNOW?

Shrimp and grits is a specialty in the Low Country, which starts just below Myrtle Beach, South Carolina, and continues all the way down to the southernmost part of the Georgia coast.

# The Houston Hot Sauce Festival

**WHERE:** Houston, Texas

**WHEN:** The third weekend in September (Saturday and Sunday)

If you like your food hot and spicy, then you should mark your calendar, book your plane and hotel, and make plans to get down to the Houston Hot Sauce Festival. Yes, they have music, arts and crafts, jewelry, and a kids' zone, but this festival is for the serious chiliheads—folks who like their food hot and spicy. But whether your tastes run mild or wild, you'll find the right foods right here. Join the more than 10,000 people who visit this festival annually to buy and taste salsas, jams and jellies, marinades, barbecue sauces, condiments, spices, dips, and of course, hot sauces.

For more information, please visit *www.houstonhotsauce.com*.

## DID YOU KNOW?

The burning sensation that occurs when hot peppers or sauces hit your mouth is caused by the irritation of trigeminal cells, which can detect pain, pressure, and temperature.

## Kick Butt Cornbread

1    cup sifted all-purpose flour

1/4   cup sugar

4    teaspoons baking powder

3/4   teaspoon salt

1    cup yellow cornmeal

1    cup milk

2    large eggs

1/4   cup vegetable shortening

5    tablespoons salsa

■ Preheat the oven to 425 degrees. Grease a 9 x 9 x 2-inch pan. Sift the flour, sugar, baking powder, and salt into a bowl. Stir in the cornmeal. Add the milk, eggs, and shortening and mix until smooth. Add the salsa and pour the batter into the prepared pan. Bake for 20 to 25 minutes or until the top is golden brown.

**MAKES 8 SERVINGS**

## Pork Chops with Hot Peppers

1/4   cup olive oil

6    semi-boneless pork chops, about 1 inch thick

3    garlic cloves, minced

1    onion, sliced

1    (8-ounce) jar hot peppers, drained

     Water or wine

■ Heat the olive oil in a frying pan large enough to hold all of the pork chops. Brown the pork chops on both sides. Add the garlic, onion, peppers, and enough water or wine to keep the pork from drying. Cover and simmer for 2 to 3 hours or until the meat separates from the bone.

**MAKES 3 TO 4 SERVINGS**

## Texas Hot Chicken Wings

1    (8-ounce) can tomato sauce

1/2   teaspoon garlic powder

1    teaspoon onion powder

5    tablespoons hot sauce

2    tablespoons red pepper flakes

2    tablespoons chopped jalapeño chiles

1    pound chicken wings

■ Preheat the oven to 350 degrees. Combine the tomato sauce, garlic powder, onion powder, hot sauce, red pepper flakes, and jalapeños in a bowl. Dip the wings in the sauce and place on a greased baking sheet. Bake for 20 minutes, basting occasionally with the sauce.

**MAKES 4 SERVINGS**

# Louisiana Sugar Festival

**WHERE:** New Iberia, Louisiana

**WHEN:** Fourth weekend in September (Wednesday through Sunday)

Undoubtedly the sweetest festival in the South, the Louisiana Sugar Festival draws tens of thousands each year with the promise of meeting the new Queen Sugar and other parish queens. Highlights of this New Iberia tradition include the boat parade, a sugar cane exhibit, a garden and flower show, art and photography exhibits, sugar artistry and tasting, fireworks, live music, square dancing, the Sugar Tennis Tournament, and dancing in the street.

For more information, please visit *www.hisugar.org*.

## DID YOU KNOW?

In the late 16th century, a teaspoon of sugar in London cost the equivalent of five dollars.

## Sweet Tea

3    cups water

1    cup sugar

8    to 10 regular-size tea bags

■ Add the water and sugar in a saucepan and bring to a boil; remove from the heat. Add the tea bags and let steep for 20 to 30 minutes. Remove and discard the tea bags. In a 1-gallon pitcher pour in the tea syrup and add enough cold water to fill the pitcher. Stir until well mixed. Serve in tall glasses over ice.

**MAKES 16 SERVINGS**

## Sugary Peanuts

3/4   cup water

1    cup plus 2 tablespoons sugar, divided

1    (8-ounce) can peanuts

■ Preheat the oven to 350 degrees. Combine the water and 1 cup of the sugar into a medium saucepan over medium heat. Cook, stirring, until the sugar dissolves. Add the peanuts. Stir for 5 minutes. Strain the peanuts and spread on a baking sheet. Bake for about 10 minutes. Remove from the oven and sprinkle with the remaining 2 tablespoons sugar. Cool for 10 minutes; remove from the baking sheet.

**MAKES 8 SERVINGS**

## Brown Sugar Brownies

11/3  cups sifted all-purpose flour

1    teaspoon baking powder

1/2   teaspoon salt

1/2   cup (1 stick) butter, softened

1    cup firmly packed light brown sugar

1    egg

1    teaspoon vanilla extract

1/2   cup chopped pecans

■ Preheat the oven to 350 degrees. Lightly grease a 9 x 9 x 13/4-inch pan. Sift the flour with the baking powder and salt; set aside. In a large bowl, mix the butter, brown sugar, egg, and vanilla until smooth. Use a mixer if necessary. Stir in the dry ingredients and pecans until well blended. Spread evenly in the prepared pan. Bake for 25 to 30 minutes, or until the surface springs back when gently pressed with a fingertip. Cool slightly. Cut while still warm.

**MAKES 16 SERVINGS**

# Burnt Sugar Cake

*Burnt Sugar Syrup:*

2/3    cup sugar

2/3    cup boiling water

*Cake:*

1 1/2  cups sugar

1/2    cup vegetable shortening

1      teaspoon vanilla extract

2      eggs

2 1/2  cups cake flour, sifted

3      teaspoons baking powder

1/2    teaspoon salt

3/4    cup cold water

*Seven-Minute Burnt Sugar Frosting:*

2      egg whites

1 1/4  cups sugar

1/4    cup water

       Dash of salt

1      teaspoon vanilla extract

◼ For the burnt sugar syrup, in a heavy skillet melt the sugar over low heat, stirring constantly. When dark brown, remove from the heat. Slowly add the boiling water to the melted sugar. Heat and stir until the sugar dissolves. Bring to a boil and reduce to 1/2 cup. Set aside for use in both the cake and frosting.

◼ For the cake, preheat the oven to 375 degrees. Line two 9 x 1 1/2-inch round cake pans with parchment paper. Gradually add the sugar to the shortening in a mixing bowl, creaming thoroughly. Add the vanilla and mix well. Add the eggs, one at a time, beating for 1 minute after each addition. Sift the cake flour, baking powder, and salt together. Add the dry ingredients to the creamed mixture alternately with the water, a small amount at a time, beating until smooth after each addition. Add 3 tablespoons of the burnt sugar syrup. Beat the batter very well for about 4 or 5 minutes. Pour the batter into the prepared pans. Bake for about 20 minutes. Cool for 10 minutes. Turn the cakes out and cool thoroughly.

■  For the frosting, combine the egg whites, sugar, water, 1/4 cup of the burnt sugar syrup, and the salt in the top of a double boiler. Beat for 1 minute with an electric or rotary beater to blend. Place over boiling water and cook, beating constantly, until the frosting forms stiff peaks, about 7 minutes. Don't overcook. Remove from the boiling water. Add the vanilla. Beat until of spreading consistency, about 2 minutes. Spread the frosting between the layers and on the top and side of the cooled cake.

**MAKES 12 SERVINGS**

## DID YOU KNOW?

Ever since Columbus introduced sugar cane to the West Indies, the region's economy has been based on its cultivation. The climate is perfect for that crop.

# Buckwheat Festival

**WHERE:** Kingwood, West Virginia

**WHEN:** The fourth weekend in September (Thursday through Sunday)

The first Buckwheat Festival in Kingwood was in 1938 and featured all-day horse-trading, sack races, hog calling, and husband calling. The festival is still a big deal today, and attendees can enjoy carnival rides, pageants, a livestock show, a farmer's day parade, road bowling, live music, arts and crafts, fireworks, and a lumberjack show.

For more information, please visit *www.buckwheatfest.com*.

## DID YOU KNOW?

A groat is the small kernel that is revealed when a buckwheat shell is dried and split.

# Buckwheat Pancakes

1    cup sifted all-purpose flour

1/2   teaspoon salt

1    teaspoon baking powder

1    teaspoon baking soda

2    tablespoons sugar

1    cup unsifted buckwheat flour

1    egg, well beaten

1/4   cup (1/2 stick) butter, melted

2    cups buttermilk

■ In a medium bowl, sift the all-purpose flour, salt, baking powder, baking soda, and sugar. Stir in the buckwheat flour. Set aside.

■ In a small bowl, combine the egg, butter, and buttermilk, mixing well. Add to the flour mixture, mixing only until combined (the batter will be lumpy). Meanwhile, slowly heat a griddle until hot. Pour 1/4 cup of the batter onto the hot griddle for each pancake; cook until bubbles form on the surface and the edges become dry. Turn and cook 2 minutes longer, or until nicely browned on the underside. Serve warm with butter and maple syrup.

**MAKES 16 (4-INCH) PANCAKES**

# Buckwheat Banana Muffins

1    cup all-purpose flour

1/2   cup buckwheat flour

1/2   cup whole wheat flour

2    teaspoons baking powder

1    teaspoon baking soda

1/2   teaspoon ground nutmeg

3    medium bananas, very ripe

2    eggs

1/4   cup salad oil

1/4   cup honey

■ Preheat the oven to 375 degrees. In a small bowl combine the all-purpose flour, buckwheat flour, whole wheat flour, baking powder, baking soda, and nutmeg. Slice the bananas into 1-inch chunks. In a food processor or blender, combine the bananas, eggs, oil, and honey; mix until puréed. Pour the banana mixture into the flour mixture; mix lightly just to blend. Spoon the batter into 12 greased or paper-lined muffin cups. Bake for about 20 minutes. Remove from the pan and cool.

**MAKES 12 MUFFINS**

## Apple Buckwheat Pancakes

1 egg
1 cup buttermilk
2 tablespoons oil
1/2 cup unbleached all-purpose flour
1/2 cup buckwheat flour
1 tablespoon sugar
1 teaspoon baking powder
1/2 teaspoon baking soda
1/2 teaspoon salt
1/4 teaspoon nutmeg
1/2 teaspoon ground cinnamon
1 medium apple, chopped

Beat the egg in a large mixing bowl with a rotary beater. In this order add the buttermilk, oil, all-purpose flour, buckwheat flour, sugar, baking powder, baking soda, salt, nutmeg, and cinnamon and beat until smooth. Fold in the apple. Grease a heated griddle with oil if necessary. Pour 1/4 cup of the batter onto the hot skillet for each pancake. Turn when the pancake is puffed and bubbly, and cook on the other side.

**MAKES 8 SMALL PANCAKES**

**DID YOU KNOW?**
Buckwheat is not a grain, but a distant cousin of rhubarb.

# Southern Fried Festival

**WHERE:** Columbia, Tennessee

**WHEN:** Fourth weekend in September (Friday and Saturday)

Whether okra, biscuits, pies, turkeys, or even ice cream, Southerners have found a way to fry it up and make it delicious. And an entire food festival dedicated to Southern-fried food sounds about as decadent as you can get. Between bites, festivalgoers can enjoy live music, a cook-off, a carnival, arts and crafts, antiques, a kazoo parade, a tractor show, and a scarecrow contest.

For more information, please visit *www.southernfriedfest.com*.

## DID YOU KNOW?

Deep-frying is classified as a dry cooking method because no water is used.

# Fried Twinkies

6     Twinkies

4     cups plus 1 tablespoon vegetable oil, divided

1     cup milk

2     tablespoons vinegar

1     cup all-purpose flour

1     teaspoon baking powder

1/2   teaspoon salt

      Popsicle sticks

      Flour for dusting

■ Chill or freeze the Twinkies for several hours or overnight.

■ Heat 4 cups of the oil in a deep fryer to about 375 degrees. In a bowl mix together the milk, vinegar, and the remaining 1 tablespoon oil. In another bowl, blend the flour, baking powder, and salt. Whisk the wet ingredients into the dry ingredients and continue mixing until smooth. Refrigerate the batter while the oil heats. Insert a Popsicle stick lengthwise into each Twinkie, leaving about 2 inches to use as a handle. Dust the Twinkies with flour and dip into the batter. Rotate the Twinkie until the batter covers the entire cake. Place carefully in the hot oil. The Twinkie will float to the top of the oil, so submerge it with a utensil to ensure even browning. Fry for 3 to 4 minutes or until golden. Remove the Twinkies to a paper towel and let drain. Allow the Twinkies to sit for about 5 minutes before serving.

**MAKES 6 SERVINGS**

# Deep-Fried Pickles

2     large egg yolks

1     cup water

1 1/2 cups all-purpose flour

1     (32-ounce) jar whole dill pickles, well drained

      Oil for frying

■ Beat the yolks and water together in a large mixing bowl. Gradually beat in the flour, keeping the batter smooth. Trim the ends off the pickles. Slice the pickles 1/4 inch thick and dry well on paper towels. Heat oil to 375 degrees in a deep skillet. Dip the pickle slices in the batter. Fry in the hot oil until slightly browned. Drain on paper towels and serve at once.

**MAKES 8 SERVINGS**

## Southern-Fried Banana Wonton Wrappers

Canola oil

1 (12-ounce) package wonton wrappers

2 to 3 bananas, sliced

1 (10-ounce) bag mini marshmallows

1 (12-ounce) package mini chocolate chips

Confectioners' sugar to garnish

■ Heat oil to 350 to 375 degrees in a deep skillet. Working with 1 wonton wrapper at a time, place 1 banana slice or 1 marshmallow in the center of the wrapper and sprinkle with a few chocolate chips. Moisten the inside edges of the wonton wrapper with water. Fold two opposite sides together and crimp into a little package. Place several wontons in the hot oil at once, being careful not to overcrowd them. Cook for 1 to 2 minutes or until golden brown. Lift from the oil and place on paper towels to drain. Arrange on a plate and sprinkle with confectioners' sugar.

**MAKES 8 SERVINGS**

## Deep-Fried Cheese

2 eggs

1/2 cup milk

1 cup cornflakes, crushed

1 cup all-purpose flour

2 tablespoons dry mustard

2 tablespoons baking powder

1/4 teaspoon salt

1/2 teaspoon pepper

1/2 cup beer

Oil for frying

10 ounces Monterey Jack cheese, well chilled, cut in strips

■ Beat the eggs and milk together in a medium bowl. Combine the corn flakes, flour, dry mustard, baking powder, salt, and pepper in another bowl. Stir into the egg mixture, blending well. Add enough beer to make the batter the consistency of whipped cream. Heat oil to 375 degrees in a deep skillet. Dip the cold cheese into the batter, coating completely. Deep-fry until golden brown on all sides, about 2 to 3 minutes. Drain well on paper towels.

**MAKES 6 SERVINGS**

## Deep-Fried Ice Cream

| | |
|---|---|
| 1/2 | cup sugar |
| 4 | ounces ground cinnamon |
| 1 | scoop vanilla ice cream |
| 3/4 | cup cornflakes, crushed |
| | Oil for frying |
| 1 | tablespoon honey |
| | Whipped cream |
| | Maraschino cherries |

■ Combine the sugar and cinnamon in a bowl. Roll the ice cream scoop in the cinnamon-sugar mixture, then roll the ice cream in the crushed cornflakes. Make sure the cornflakes stick to the ice cream. Immediately place the ice cream back in the freezer to harden.

■ To deep-fry, heat the oil to 375 degrees. Immerse the coated ice cream in the oil for approximately 5 seconds. Remove the ice cream and allow the oil to drain from the ice cream. Place in a dish. Pour the honey over the ice cream. Serve with whipped cream around the sides, and top with a maraschino cherry.

**MAKES 1 SERVING**

# Irmo Okra Strut

**WHERE:** Irmo, South Carolina

**WHEN:** The last Friday and Saturday in September

For more than 30 years, tens of thousands (we're talking 50,000-plus a year here) have been coming to Irmo to eat and celebrate the okra pod. Visitors, young or old, can have their picture taken with Okraman or visit the kids' zone—Okryland. There's also a street dance, a parade, arts and crafts, carnival rides, musical entertainment, and an okra-eating contest where the first person to eat two pounds of fried okra wins. (They used to use boiled okra, but the end result wasn't always very pretty.)

For more information, please visit *www.irmookrastrut.com*.

## DID YOU KNOW?

Okra is native to tropical regions of Africa and was cultivated in 12th century Egypt.

## Fried Okra

1/2   cup cornmeal

1/3   cup whole wheat flour, sifted

1     teaspoon salt

1/4   teaspoon pepper

1     pound cut okra, fresh or frozen and thawed

1/3   cup vegetable shortening

■ Combine the cornmeal, flour, salt, and pepper in a bowl. Dredge the okra in the dry mixture. Melt the shortening on a hot griddle. Fry the okra for 10 minutes or until golden brown.

**MAKES 6 SERVINGS**

## Okra and Tomatoes

1     cup cut okra

1     medium onion, chopped

1     green bell pepper, chopped

1/4   cup salad oil

3     tomatoes, peeled and quartered

1     tablespoon sugar

1     teaspoon enriched all-purpose flour

1/3   teaspoon salt

1/2   teaspoon pepper

■ Cook the okra in boiling, salted water in a saucepan for 10 minutes; drain. In a large saucepan brown the onion and green pepper in the oil over medium heat. Reduce the heat to low and cook the tomatoes slowly for 5 minutes. Add the okra, sugar, flour, salt, and pepper. Cook over low heat until the vegetables are just tender, stirring as little as possible.

**MAKES 4 SERVINGS**

## Dilled Pickled Okra

3     pounds young okra, washed and drained, stems trimmed short

12    stems of dill

3     cups water

3     cups white vinegar

6     tablespoons salt

■ Pack the okra into clean pint or quart jars. Place a small bunch of dill in each jar. Combine the water, vinegar, and salt in a saucepan and bring to a boil. Fill the jars evenly with the boiling brine. Screw the lids on tight. Process for 5 minutes in a hot water bath. Let stand for at least 3 weeks before using.

**MAKES 12 PINTS**

## Southern Okra Soup with Chicken

2    tablespoons bacon drippings

2    teaspoons minced onion

1/2  cup all-purpose flour

1    teaspoon salt

1    teaspoon black pepper

3    pounds chicken, cut into pieces

2    cups corn, fresh or canned

1    cup sliced okra, fresh or frozen

1    large tomato, chopped

6    cups water

■ Heat the bacon drippings in a large soup pot. Add the onion and stir until heated through. Mix the flour with the salt and pepper. Dredge the chicken pieces in the seasoned flour. Add the chicken pieces to the soup pot, one at a time, browning on all sides. Add the corn and okra; stir. Lower the heat to a simmer. Cover and cook for about 8 minutes, stirring often. Add the tomato and water; simmer for 45 minutes to 1 hour or until the chicken is tender, adding more water if needed. Spoon into large soup bowls with a piece of chicken for each serving.

**MAKES 8 SERVINGS**

## Fried Okra Salad

4    slices bacon

1/4  cup cornmeal

     Salt and pepper to taste

1    pound fresh okra, cut into 1-inch pieces

1    small onion, chopped

1    large tomato, sliced or chopped

■ Fry the bacon in a skillet. Drain on paper towels, reserving the drippings. Combine the cornmeal with salt and pepper to taste in a bowl. Roll the okra in the seasoned cornmeal. Fry the okra in the reserved bacon drippings. Just before the okra is completely cooked, add the onion; drain. Place the okra and onion in a salad bowl. Crumble the bacon and add to the okra. Add the tomato and serve.

**MAKES 6 SERVINGS**

# World Chicken Festival

**WHERE:** London, Kentucky

**WHEN:** The last full weekend in September (Thursday through Sunday)

As the people at the World Chicken Festival like to say, it is a festival filled with "eggsitement." That must be true, as more than a quarter million people come to the home of Kentucky Fried Chicken founder Colonel Harland Sanders every year to celebrate the chicken. Visitors to London also get to see the world's largest skillet and enjoy live music; a huge parade; crowing, strutting, and clucking contests; an egg drop contest; and the redneck games—which include watermelon and pumpkin seed spitting (for distance and accuracy), Spam eating, toilet lid horseshoe, a redneck joke competition, the armpit serenade, bobbing for pig's feet, a burping contest (length of burp and song content), and a corn-shucking competition. There are also plenty of activities for the kids, along with a car show, carnival rides, and the World Chicken Festival cook-off.

For more information, please visit *www.chickenfestival.com*.

## DID YOU KNOW?

The longest recorded flight of a chick is 13 seconds.

## Almond Crunch Chicken Salad

2 (9.75-ounce) cans chicken

1 1/2 cups red grapes, halved

3/4 cup shredded carrots

1/2 cup sliced celery

1 cup Miracle Whip salad dressing

1 tablespoon lemon juice

3/4 cup almonds, slivered

■ In a large bowl combine the chicken, grapes, carrots, celery, Miracle Whip, lemon juice, and almonds. Mix well.

**MAKES 8 SERVINGS**

## Bridget's Melt-in-Your-Mouth Graham Cracker Chicken

1/2 cup oil

1/4 cup milk

2 eggs

1 1/2 tablespoons seasoning salt

1/4 teaspoon black pepper

1 (13.5-ounce) box graham cracker crumbs

3 celery ribs

1 green bell pepper

3 pounds boneless, skinless chicken breasts, cut into strips

■ Preheat the oven to 425 degrees. Pour the oil into a large baking pan and heat in the oven. In a bowl beat together the milk and eggs; set aside. In another bowl combine the seasoning salt, pepper, and graham cracker crumbs. Cut the celery and green pepper into small strips; set aside. Dip the chicken in the egg mixture, then coat with the graham cracker mixture. Add to the baking pan of hot oil. Bake for about 15 minutes or until brown on one side. Remove from the oven, turn over the chicken, placing the celery and green pepper on the bottom of the pan underneath the chicken. Cook an additional 10 to 15 minutes or until the chicken is brown and tender.

**MAKES 8 SERVINGS**

## Sunday Chicken Casserole

1   (3-pound) broiler or fryer chicken

3   tablespoons butter or margarine

1 1/2   cups chopped celery

1/2   medium onion, chopped

8   ounces shredded Cheddar cheese

1   (10.7-ounce) can cream of mushroom soup

3   eggs, slightly beaten

1/2   teaspoon lemon pepper seasoning

1/4   teaspoon black pepper

1   (8-ounce) package herb-seasoned stuffing mix

■ Place the chicken in a Dutch oven. Cover with water and bring to a boil. Cover and reduce the heat. Simmer for 1 hour or until tender. Remove from the heat and drain, reserving 2 cups of broth. When cool enough to handle, bone the chicken and chop the meat into 1/2-inch cubes; set aside.

■ Preheat the oven to 350 degrees. Melt the butter in a large skillet. Add the celery and onion and sauté until tender. Add the reserved broth, cheese, soup, eggs, lemon pepper, and black pepper; mix well. Stir in the chicken. Spoon the mixture into a lightly greased 9 x 13-inch baking pan and sprinkle with the stuffing mix. Bake for 45 minutes.

**MAKES 12 SERVINGS**

## Southern-Fried Chicken

1   (3- to 4-pound) frying chicken

1/2   cup all-purpose flour

1/4   teaspoon baking powder

1/2   teaspoon salt

1/2   teaspoon pepper

1/3   teaspoon paprika

1/2   cup light cream

1   cup oil or vegetable shortening

■ Cut the chicken into pieces; wash and pat dry. Combine the flour, baking powder, salt, pepper, and paprika in a bowl. Dip the pieces of chicken in the cream, then coat as thickly as possible with the seasoned flour. Heat the oil in a skillet to 325 degrees for about 5 minutes, uncovered. Arrange the coated chicken pieces in the skillet. Brown on all sides, about 10 minutes. Cover and reduce the heat to 225 degrees. Fry the chicken for 30 minutes. Remove the cover and fry for an additional 10 minutes.

**MAKES 6 SERVINGS**

# Ethel's Famous Chicken and Dumplings

1    (5-pound) hen

3    cups cold water, divided

1    tablespoon seasoning salt

1    large baking bag

2    (14.5-ounce) cans chicken broth

1/2   cup (1 stick) butter

4    cups all-purpose flour

1/4   teaspoon black pepper

■ Preheat the oven to 350 degrees. Add the hen, 2 cups of the water, and the seasoning salt to the baking bag and bake for 3 1/2 hours. Drain the broth into a large kettle. Set the hen aside to cool.

■ Add the chicken broth and butter to the reserved broth in the kettle. Heat over medium-high heat. While the broth heats, add the flour to a bowl and pat the flour around the side of the bowl. Pour the remaining 1 cup water into the flour and mix until a thick dough is formed. Lay the dough out onto waxed paper and roll out about 1/3 inch thick. Cut into 2-inch squares. Drop the squares into the hot broth and cook for 5 to 8 minutes. Bone the hen and add the meat to the dumplings along with the black pepper and cook for an additional 5 minutes.

**MAKES 12 SERVINGS**

---

**DID YOU KNOW?**

A hen can live up to 20 years, although the average lifespan is 5 to 7 years. Hens lay eggs their entire lives, with production decreasing as they get older.

# North Carolina Muscadine Harvest Festival

**WHERE:** Kenansville, North Carolina

**WHEN:** The last weekend in September (Friday and Saturday)

Southerners have enjoyed the wine from the wild muscadine grape for a very long time. And while wine is still the main end product of the muscadine, Southerners are now using the grape for jams, jellies, muffins, pies, and other delights, as evidenced by the popular recipe contest at the North Carolina Muscadine Harvest Festival. Other activities include shag dancing, arts and crafts, a mechanical bull, live music, farm implement exhibits, and a mobile muscadine lab, which performs chemical analysis for the wine industry. Then there's the cow chip rally, in which you buy a square in a field and if the cow does his cow chip business in your square, you win. (Think bingo but with cow chips.) There are also educational seminars on all things muscadine, as well as plenty of muscadine wine to taste under the North Carolina skies.

For more information, please visit
*www.muscadineharvestfestival.com.*

## DID YOU KNOW?

"Scuppernong" is another name for all muscadine grapes.

# Magnolia Grilled Chicken Breasts

2     or 3 boneless, skinless chicken breasts

2     quarts water

2     tablespoons reduced-sodium salt

1     cup Duplin Wine Cellars Magnolia wine or other muscadine wine, divided

2     tablespoons molasses

1     teaspoon soy sauce, plus additional for rice flavoring

      Dash of garlic salt

2     teaspoons margarine

1     (15.8-ounce) package Boil-in-Bag rice

      Chopped fresh parsley for garnish

      Grape leaves for garnish

■ Soak the chicken breasts in the water seasoned with the salt overnight, in the refrigerator.

■ Remove the chicken breasts from the brine. Marinate the chicken breasts in 1/4 cup of the wine for 25 minutes, turning once. In a small saucepan combine the molasses, 1 teaspoon soy sauce, the garlic salt, and margarine over low heat and cook until the margarine is melted. Pour in the remaining 3/4 cup wine. Stir and cook until reduced over low heat for 20 minutes. Remove the sauce from the heat. Set aside half of the sauce for serving.

■ Prepare the rice according to the package directions adding a splash of soy sauce to the water for seasoning.

■ Preheat a gas grill. Heat well and reduce the flame to medium. Drain the chicken, discarding the marinade. Pat the chicken dry. Brush the chicken breasts on both sides with the sauce and grill, turning and basting every 2 to 3 minutes until done. Do not overcook. Slice the chicken breasts diagonally and serve over of the hot cooked rice. Garnish with parsley and arrange grape leaves around the serving dish.

**MAKES 2 TO 5 SERVINGS**

## Muscadine Trifle

1   (3.4-ounce) package instant vanilla pudding mix

3   cups milk

1   angel food cake, cut into bite-size pieces

1   (21-ounce) can cherry pie filling

l   (29-ounce) can sliced peaches, drained

l   cup muscadine grapes, halved and seeded

1   banana, sliced (optional)

1/2   cup sherry, divided

l   (12-ounce) container frozen whipped topping, thawed

1/2   cup slivered almonds or toasted pecans for garnish

Halved and seeded muscadine grapes for garnish

▪ Combine the pudding mix and milk in a medium bowl and prepare according to the package directions.

▪ Place one-third of the angel food cake in the bottom of a large glass bowl. Add half the vanilla pudding, cherry pie filling, peaches, grapes, and banana, if desired. Add another third of the cake. Sprinkle 1/4 cup of the sherry over the cake. Repeat the layers of pudding, pie filling, peaches, grapes, and banana. Top with the remaining angel food cake. Sprinkle the remaining sherry over the angel food cake. Spread a generous amount of whipped topping on top. Garnish with the almonds or pecans and grapes. Refrigerate 2 hours before serving.

**MAKES 12 SERVINGS**

## Muscadine Muffins

11/2   cups plus 1 tablespoon all-purpose flour, divided

1   teaspoon baking soda

1   teaspoon baking powder

1/2   teaspoon salt

1   cup grape hull preserves

1/2   cup sugar

1/3   cup plus 1 tablespoon butter or margarine, softened and divided

1   egg, lightly beaten

1/3   cup firmly packed brown sugar

1/8   teaspoon ground cinnamon

▪ Preheat the oven to 350 degrees. Combine 11/2 cups of the flour, the baking soda, baking powder, and salt in a bowl and mix well. In a separate bowl combine the preserves, sugar, 1/3 cup of the butter, and the egg in a bowl and mix well. Add to the dry ingredients and mix just until moistened. Fill greased or paper-lined muffin cups 3/4 full with the batter. Mix the brown sugar, the remaining 1 tablespoon flour, and the cinnamon in a bowl. Cut in the remaining 1 tablespoon butter until crumbly. Sprinkle over the tops of the muffins. Bake for 18 to 20 minutes or until the muffins test done. Cool in the pan for 10 minutes. Remove to a wire rack to cool completely.

**MAKES 1 DOZEN MUFFINS**

## DID YOU KNOW?

The muscadine is a wild grape variety native to the southeastern United States.

# October

# Unicoi County Apple Festival

**WHERE:** Erwin, Tennessee

**WHEN:** First weekend in October (Friday and Saturday)

For more than 30 years, Unicoi County has been home to one of the best Southern festivals around. This apple festival has something to offer for the whole family and then some. More than 100,000 people show up every year to enjoy a wide range of entertainment showcased on two stages, a crafts fair featuring over 300 vendors, and a children's area with pony rides, games, inflatable rides, and more. This festival also boasts a slew of beauty pageants, a tennis tournament, all kinds of dancing, and of course, apple cooking contests.

For more information, please visit
*www.unicoicounty.org/applefest.php.*

### DID YOU KNOW?

Approximately 50 percent of the U.S. apple crop is used to make apple juice, applesauce, and dehydrated apple products. The other 50 percent is sold fresh.

## Colossal Caramel Apple Trifle

1    (18.25-ounce) package yellow cake mix

6    cups cold milk

3    (3.4-ounce) packages instant vanilla pudding mix

1    tablespoon apple pie spice

1    (12-ounce) jar caramel ice cream topping

1½  cups chopped pecans, toasted and divided

2    (21-ounce) cans apple pie filling, divided

2    (16-ounce) containers frozen whipped topping, divided

■ Prepare and bake the cake according to the package directions, using two greased 9-inch round baking pans. Cool in the pans for 10 minutes before removing to wire racks to cool completely.

■ In a large bowl, whisk the milk, pudding mix, and apple pie spice for 2 minutes. Let stand for 2 minutes or until soft set. Fit 1 of the cake layers evenly into an 8-quart punch bowl trimming the cake if necessary. Poke holes in the cake with a long wooden skewer. Gradually pour one-third of the caramel topping over the cake. Sprinkle with ½ cup of the pecans and spread with half of the pudding. Spoon 1 can of the pie filling over the pudding. Spread 1 container of the whipped topping over the pudding. Top with the remaining cake layer. Poke holes in the cake and repeat the layers of one-third of the caramel topping, ½ cup pecans, half the pudding, and the remaining 1 can pie filling, ending with the remaining 1 container whipped topping. Drizzle the remaining one-third caramel topping over the whipped topping. Sprinkle with the remaining ½ cup pecans. Refrigerate until serving.

**MAKES 14 SERVINGS**

**DID YOU KNOW?**
Most apples are still picked by hand in the fall.

## Golden Delicious Apple Pie

*Piecrust:*

1     cup all-purpose flour

1/2    teaspoon salt

1/2    cup shredded Cheddar cheese

5     tablespoons cold butter

3     to 4 tablespoons cold milk

*Filling:*

3     tablespoons all-purpose flour

1/2    cup sugar

1/2    teaspoon ground cinnamon

6     cups Golden Delicious apples, peeled and sliced

1     tablespoon lemon juice

*Crumb Topping:*

1/2    cup firmly packed brown sugar

1/2    cup all-purpose flour

1/4    cup (1/2 stick) butter, melted

1     cup coarsely chopped macadamia nuts

■ For the piecrust, mix together the flour, salt, and cheese in a bowl. Cut the butter in with a pastry blender until the mixture resembles coarse crumbs. Sprinkle the mixture with milk, 1 table-spoon at a time, stirring until the mixture holds together and then forms a ball. Roll the dough on a lightly floured board into a 10-inch circle and fit into a 9-inch pie plate.

■ For the filling, preheat the oven to 350 degrees. Mix together the flour, sugar, and cin-namon in a bowl. In a separate bowl toss the apples with the lemon juice, Add the dry mix-ture and toss until the apples are well coated. Spoon the filling into the piecrust.

■ For the topping, combine the brown sugar, flour, butter, and nuts together and sprinkle over the pie. Put the pie into a large brown paper bag. Fold the ends down and fasten with paper clips. Bake for 1 hour.

**MAKES 8 SERVINGS**

## Apple Cake Supreme

*Cake:*

2     cups all-purpose flour

2     teaspoons baking soda

1/2    teaspoon salt

2     teaspoons ground cinnamon

1     teaspoon apple pie spice

3     large eggs

2     cups sugar

3/4    cup vegetable oil

3/4   cup buttermilk

2     teaspoons vanilla extract

2     cups grated apple

1     (8-ounce) can crushed pineapple, drained

1     (3½-ounce) can flaked coconut

1     cup chopped pecans

*Buttermilk Glaze:*

1     cup sugar

1½   teaspoons baking soda

½    cup buttermilk

½    cup (1 stick) butter or margarine

1     tablespoon light corn syrup

1     teaspoon vanilla extract

*Deluxe Cream Cheese Frosting:*

1     (8-ounce) package plus 1 (3-ounce) package cream cheese, softened

3/4   cup (1½ sticks) butter, softened

1     (1-pound) box confectioners' sugar, sifted

1½   teaspoons vanilla extract

1½   cups chopped pecans (optional)

■ For the cake, preheat the oven to 350 degrees. Grease three 9-inch round cake pans and line with waxed paper. Lightly grease and flour the waxed paper and set aside. In a large bowl combine the flour, baking soda, salt, cinnamon, and apple pie spice together. In a separate bowl beat the eggs, sugar, vegetable oil, buttermilk, and vanilla together with a mixer until smooth. Add the flour mixture to the egg mixture and beat until smooth. Fold in the apple, pineapple, coconut, and pecans. Pour the batter evenly into the prepared pans. Bake for 25 to 30 minutes or until a wooden pick inserted into the center comes out clean.

■ For the glaze, in a saucepan bring the sugar, baking soda, buttermilk, butter, and corn syrup to a boil over medium heat. Boil for 4 minutes, stirring constantly until the glaze is golden. Remove from the heat and stir in the vanilla. Cool slightly. Drizzle the warm glaze evenly over the warm cake layers; cool in the pans on wire racks for 15 minutes. Remove from the pans, inverting the layers. Peel off the waxed paper and invert again, glaze side up. Cool completely on wire racks.

■ For the frosting, in a mixing bowl beat the cream cheese and butter at medium speed with an electric mixer until smooth. Gradually add the confectioners' sugar, beating at low speed until light and fluffy. Stir in the vanilla and pecans, if desired. Spread the frosting between the layers and on the top and side of the cake. Chill the cake for several hours before slicing. Store any leftovers in the refrigerator.

**MAKES 12 SERVINGS**

# Spring Hill Country Ham Festival

**WHERE:** Spring Hill, Tennessee
**WHEN:** First Saturday of October

They really do put on the hog each year at the Spring Hill Country Ham Festival. For many Southerners—and this applies to some people who live outside the South, as well—a slice of good country ham in a biscuit is akin to a religious experience. In addition to the delicious country ham, attendees can enjoy live country and bluegrass music, arts and crafts, and a kids' zone where children can be a farmer for a day and learn to milk a cow, gather eggs for breakfast, pick an apple off a tree, build a fire, and cook meat in the wild. This festival also boasts several country ham competitions, a pink pig maze, and a hog-calling contest.

For more information, please visit *www.countryhamfest.com*.

## DID YOU KNOW?

Some say that Andrew Jackson coined the name "redeye gravy" for ham gravy. Jackson, a general at the time, was giving his cook instructions on the meal he wanted. The cook had been drinking the night before and his eyes were red. Jackson told the cook to bring him some country ham with gravy as red as his eyes. From then on, ham gravy has been referred to as "redeye gravy."

## Cheesy Ham and Spinach Bake

2   tablespoons butter or margarine

1/4 cup finely chopped onion

1/2 teaspoon garlic powder

1/2 cup evaporated milk

1/2 cup sour cream

3   ounces cream cheese

1   cup grated Parmesan cheese

1/2 cup grated Monterey Jack cheese

1   cup chopped fresh spinach

1   cup chopped cooked country ham

1   (10-ounce) container refrigerator crescent rolls

■ Preheat the oven to 350 degrees. Very lightly grease a large baking sheet. In a heavy pan or deep skillet over medium-low heat melt the butter. Add the onion and garlic powder. Cook, stirring occasionally until the onion becomes transparent. Add the evaporated milk, sour cream, cream cheese, Parmesan cheese, and Monterey Jack cheese, stirring frequently until the cheeses melt. Remove from the heat and stir in the spinach and country ham.

■ Separate the crescent rolls into triangles. Arrange the triangles on the prepared baking sheet, in a ring shape with the dough points pointing out (like a star) leaving a 2-inch hole in the center. Spoon the filling evenly over the dough being careful not to get any filling in the hole in the center. Wrap the dough points over the filling and tuck them under at the center hole. All of the filling will not be covered. Bake for 25 to 30 minutes or until the dough is baked and the filling is heated through. Serve hot.

**MAKES 8 SERVINGS**

## Great Country Ham

4   (1/3-inch-thick) bone-in country ham steaks

2   tablespoons butter

■ Rinse the steaks with water and pat dry. Heat the butter in a large cast-iron skillet or frying pan over medium-high heat. Cook the steaks for approximately 2 minutes on each side. Remove the steaks from the pan. Reserve the drippings to make Redeye Gravy (page 216).

**MAKES 4 SERVINGS**

## Redeye Gravy

Reserved ham drippings (from Great Country Ham, page 215)

1/2    cup coffee

3    tablespoons brown sugar

2    cups water

■ Combine the reserved drippings, the coffee, brown sugar, and water in a hot skillet. Bring to a boil. Serve over ham, biscuits, or grits.

**MAKES 8 SERVINGS**

## Country Ham Balls

1    pound cooked country ham, ground

1/2    pound bulk pork sausage

1    cup fine dry bread crumbs

1    egg

3/4    cup milk

1    cup firmly packed brown sugar

1/2    cup water

1/2    cup white vinegar

2    teaspoons prepared mustard

■ Preheat the oven to 350 degrees. Combine the ham, sausage, bread crumbs, egg, and milk in a bowl and mix well. Shape the mixture into 1/2-inch balls. Place the balls in a 9 x 13 x 2-inch baking dish. Combine the brown sugar, water, vinegar, and mustard in a saucepan. Stir well. Bring to a boil over medium heat and boil for 1 minute. Pour the sauce over the ham balls. Bake for 45 minutes, basting and turning the ham balls after 25 minutes.

**MAKES 10 APPETIZER-SIZE SERVINGS**

### DID YOU KNOW?

Mold does not affect the quality of a country ham. Like a fine aged cheese, the mold on a country ham indicates proper aging.

# Lecompte Pie Festival

**WHERE:** Lecompte, Louisiana

**WHEN:** First weekend in October (Friday through Sunday)

The Lecompte Pie Festival is about two things really: pie and music. There's a parade, arts and crafts, and all kinds of things for the kids to do, but for the 10,000 or so people who show up here every year, it's really all about the pie. In fact, the festival recommends that all visitors bring their lawn chairs. It's a lot easier to listen to music and eat pie in a lawn chair.

For more information, please visit *www.lecomptepiefestival.com.*

## DID YOU KNOW?

In the 1800s, fruit pie was considered a part of a hearty meal before a hard day's work, and was a common breakfast item.

## Caramel Pie

1¼  cups sugar, divided

¼  cup water

¼  cup all-purpose flour

¾  teaspoon salt, divided

1½  cups milk

3  egg yolks, well beaten

2  tablespoons butter, melted

1  teaspoon vanilla extract

1  (9-inch) piecrust, baked

4  egg whites

¼  teaspoon cream of tartar

¼  cup confectioners' sugar

■ Preheat the oven to 350 degrees. In a heavy skillet heat ½ cup of the sugar until melted and golden brown over low heat. Add the water and cook, stirring until smooth, to make a caramel syrup. Remove from the heat.

■ In a saucepan combine the flour, the remaining ¾ cup sugar, and ½ teaspoon of the salt. Add the milk gradually. Stir in the egg yolks and cook until the mixture starts to thicken, stirring constantly. Stir in the caramel syrup slowly and continue to cook until thick and smooth. Remove from the heat and add the butter and vanilla. Pour the filling into the piecrust.

■ Beat the egg whites, cream of tartar, and the remaining ¼ teaspoon salt in a mixing bowl on high speed until frothy. With the mixer still running, slowly add the confectioners' sugar and beat until the meringue is thick and shiny, about 2 minutes. Spread over the filling and bake for 10 to 15 minutes or until the meringue is browned.

**MAKES 8 SERVINGS**

## Chess Pie

½  cup (1 stick) butter or margarine, melted

1½  cups sugar

3  eggs

1  teaspoon vanilla extract
   Pinch of salt

1½  teaspoons vinegar

1  (9-inch) piecrust, unbaked

■ Preheat the oven to 400 degrees. Combine the butter and sugar in a saucepan and simmer slowly, stirring, for 5 minutes. Remove from the heat and let cool slightly, stirring constantly. Add the eggs, one at a time, beating well after each addition. Add the vanilla, salt, and vinegar; mix well. Pour the filling into the piecrust and bake for 15 minutes. Reduce the heat to 350 degrees and bake for 20 to 30 minutes. Shake the pie gently. The pie is done when the center quivers slightly.

**MAKES 8 SERVINGS**

## Buttermilk Coconut Pie

1 1/2 cups sugar

2 tablespoons all-purpose flour

1/2 cup (1 stick) butter, softened

3 eggs, beaten

1/2 cup buttermilk

1 teaspoon vanilla extract

1/2 cup flaked coconut

1 (9-inch) piecrust, unbaked

Preheat the oven to 350 degrees. In a large mixing bowl combine the sugar, flour, butter, eggs, buttermilk, and vanilla. Beat well until smooth. Fold in the coconut. Pour the mixture into the piecrust, and bake for 45 to 60 minutes. The pie is done when the top is golden and the filling is set in the middle.

**MAKES 8 SERVINGS**

## Southern Pecan Pie

1 cup sugar

3/4 cup (1 1/2 sticks) butter, melted

3 eggs, beaten

3/4 cup light corn syrup

1/4 teaspoon salt

2 teaspoons bourbon

1 teaspoon vanilla extract

2/3 cup chopped pecans

1 (9-inch) piecrust, unbaked

Preheat the oven to 350 degrees. Cream together the sugar and butter in a mixing bowl. Add the eggs, corn syrup, salt, bourbon, and vanilla. Mix until well blended. Spread the pecans in the bottom of the piecrust. Pour the filling over the pecans. Bake for about 45 minutes or until the filling is set.

**MAKES 8 SERVINGS**

# Fudge Pie

4   eggs, beaten

2   squares unsweetened chocolate, melted

1   cup sifted all-purpose flour

2   cups sugar
    Pinch of salt

1   cup (2 sticks) butter, softened

1   teaspoon vanilla extract

1   (9-inch) deep-dish piecrust, unbaked

■  Preheat the oven to 350 degrees. In a large mixing bowl combine the eggs, melted chocolate, flour, sugar, salt, butter, and vanilla and mix until smooth. Pour the mixture into the piecrust. Bake for 30 minutes. Serve warm with vanilla ice cream.

**MAKES 8 SERVINGS**

### DID YOU KNOW?

The first mention of a fruit pie in print occurs in Robert Green's *Arcadia* (1590): "Thy breath is like the steame of apple-pyes."

# Apple Butter Festival

**WHERE:** Berkeley Springs, West Virginia

**WHEN:** Columbus Day weekend (the Saturday and Sunday before the Monday observation of the holiday)

While the celebration of the area apple orchards may be the primary reason Berkeley Springs draws more than 40,000 people each year, it is the festival's myriad activities that keep them coming back year after year. There are, of course, apple butter making demonstrations in the town square, as well as baking contests. But visitors can also enjoy such unique festival activities as a beard and mustache contest, turtle races, and the very popular hog-calling contest. Live music, crafts, an egg toss, and a parade round out the goings-on at this beloved fall festival.

For more information, please visit *www.berkeleysprings.com/apple*.

## DID YOU KNOW?

Apple butter can replace up to three-fourths of the vegetable shortening in most recipes.

## Apple-Cranberry Chocolate Cups

2 1/2   ounces semisweet baking chocolate

2      teaspoons vegetable shortening, divided

2 1/2   ounces white baking chocolate

1/4     cup chopped dried apples

1/4     cup dried cranberries, chopped

1/2     cup boiling water

1/4     teaspoon vanilla extract

1      (8-ounce) package cream cheese, softened

3      tablespoons confectioners' sugar

1      drop red food coloring

1/4     teaspoon grated lemon peel

■ In a microwave melt the semisweet chocolate and 1 teaspoon of the shortening. Brush the mixture evenly on the inside of 12 paper or foil miniature muffin cup liners. Repeat with the white baking chocolate and the remaining 1 teaspoon shortening, brushing the inside of 12 miniature muffin cup liners. Chill until firm, about 25 minutes.

■ Meanwhile, in a bowl combine the apples, cranberries, water, and vanilla. Let stand for 5 minutes. Drain, reserving 2 tablespoons of the liquid. In a mixing bowl combine the cream cheese, confectioners' sugar, food coloring, lemon peel, and the reserved liquid. Beat on medium-low speed for 2 minutes or until smooth. Fold in the apples and cranberries. Cut a small hole in the corner of a pastry or plastic bag; insert a tip. Fill with the apple-cranberry mixture. Pipe into the chocolate cups. Refrigerate for 1 hour until firm. Carefully remove the filling from the liners.

**MAKES 2 DOZEN**

## Homemade Apple Butter

7      pounds apples, peeled, cored, and cut into small pieces

3      pounds brown sugar

1      cup apple cider

2      tablespoons ground cinnamon

■ Preheat the oven to 350 degrees. Combine the apples, brown sugar, cider, and cinnamon in a large, heavy ovenproof pan. Bake for 3 hours, stirring every 1/2 hour. You may also cook the apple butter on the stove over low heat. Pour the apple butter into jars and seal.

**MAKES 6 PINTS**

# Harvest Pumpkin Apple Bread

3   cups all-purpose flour

2   teaspoons ground cinnamon

2   teaspoons baking soda

1 1/2   teaspoons salt

3   cups sugar

1   (15-ounce) can pure pumpkin

4   eggs

1   cup vegetable oil

1/2   cup apple juice or water

1   large baking apple, peeled, cored, and diced

1/4   cup chopped walnuts

■ Preheat the oven to 350 degrees. Grease and flour two 9 x 5-inch loaf pans. Combine the flour, cinnamon, baking soda, and salt in a large bowl. In a separate mixing bowl combine the sugar, pumpkin, eggs, vegetable oil, and apple juice. Beat until just blended. Add the pumpkin mixture to the flour mixture; stir just until moistened. Fold in the apple and nuts. Spoon the batter into the prepared loaf pans. Bake for 65 to 70 minutes or until a wooden pick inserted in the center comes out clean. Cool in the pans on wire racks for 10 minutes; remove the bread from the pans and let cool completely on wire racks.

**MAKES 16 SERVINGS**

# Apple Butter Made with Applesauce

9   cups applesauce

5   cups sugar

1/2   cup cider vinegar

4   teaspoons ground cinnamon

■ Preheat the oven to 325 degrees. Combine the applesauce, sugar, vinegar, and cinnamon in a roasting pan and stir. Cook, uncovered, for 3 to 3 1/2 hours, stirring every 1/2 hour with a wooden spoon. Pour the apple butter into canning jars when finished.

**MAKES 4 PINTS**

# Suffolk Peanut Festival

**WHERE:** Suffolk, Virginia

**WHEN:** Second weekend in October (Thursday through Sunday)

In early October every year, almost a quarter million people come to Suffolk to enjoy a whole bunch of fun activities at the annual Peanut Festival. While some are goober related, all are meant to show visitors a good time. Among the highlights are amusement rides, live music, a demolition derby, truck and tractor pulls, fireworks, helicopter rides, a horseshoe competition, pony rides, bingo, a yo-yo contest, a motorcycle rally, the Gourmet Goober Cook-Off, and a peanut butter sculpture contest.

For more information, please visit *www.suffolkfest.org*.

## DID YOU KNOW?
The world's largest reported peanut was 4 inches long.

# Virginia Peanut Pie

3　large eggs, lightly beaten

1/2　cup granulated sugar

3/4　cup firmly packed light brown sugar

1/2　cup light corn syrup

1/3　teaspoon salt

1　teaspoon vanilla extract

5　tablespoons butter-flavor vegetable shortening (such as Crisco)

1　cup roasted peanuts, chopped

1　(9-inch) piecrust, unbaked

■ Preheat the oven to 350 degrees. Combine the eggs, granulated sugar, brown sugar, corn syrup, salt, vanilla, and shortening in a bowl. Stir in the peanuts. Pour the mixture into the piecrust and bake for 45 minutes or until set. Serve warm or cool.

**MAKES 8 SERVINGS**

# Virginia Peanut Chicken Salad

*Salad Dressing:*

1/4　cup mayonnaise

1/4　cup Miracle Whip salad dressing

1/4　cup sour cream

1　teaspoon curry powder

2　tablespoons brown sugar

*Salad:*

4　cups cubed, cooked chicken

1/2　cup chopped celery

1　(15-ounce) can pineapple bits, undrained

1　large ripe banana, sliced

1 1/2　cups white grapes

1　cup salted Virginia peanuts
　　Coconut for garnish
　　Lettuce leaves for serving

■ For the dressing, combine the mayonnaise, Miracle Whip, sour cream, curry powder, and brown sugar in a bowl. Mix well. Refrigerate overnight.

■ For the salad, combine the chicken, celery, and pineapple with juice in a bowl. Refrigerate overnight.

■ To serve, drain the chicken mixture well. Stir in the banana and grapes. Toss with the salad dressing and add the peanuts. Garnish with coconut and serve on lettuce leaves.

**MAKES 12 SERVINGS**

## Virginia Peanut Goodie Bars

1   cup chocolate chips
1   cup butterscotch chips
1   cup peanut butter
1   cup Virginia peanuts
1/4   cup milk
2   tablespoons vanilla pudding mix
1/2   cup (1 stick) butter
1   pound confectioners' sugar

■ Combine the chocolate chips, butterscotch chips, and peanut butter in the top of a double boiler or in a microwave-safe bowl and cook until melted, stirring until smooth.

■ Line a cookie sheet with waxed paper. Spoon half of the chocolate mixture into the pan, spreading evenly. Refrigerate until set. Stir the peanuts into the remaining chocolate mixture and let stand at room temperature.

■ Combine the milk, pudding mix, and butter in a glass bowl and microwave on high 1 1/2 to 2 minutes or until the mixture boils, stirring once. Stir in the confectioners' sugar and blend well. Spread the mixture over the chilled chocolate layer. Spoon the remaining chocolate-peanut mixture over the top, spreading to cover to the edges. Refrigerate until set, about 2 hours. Lift out of the pan and remove the waxed paper. Cut into squares to the size of your choice. Store in the refrigerator.

MAKES 12 SERVINGS (DEPENDING ON SQUARE SIZE)

## Apple and Peanut Butter Pie

3   cups thinly sliced tart apples
1   (9-inch) piecrust, unbaked
1   tablespoon lemon juice
1/3   cup granulated sugar
1/2   cup all-purpose flour
1/2   cup firmly packed brown sugar
1/4   teaspoon ground cinnamon
1/8   teaspoon nutmeg
1   tablespoon grated lemon peel
5   tablespoons crunchy peanut butter
2   tablespoons butter

■ Preheat the oven to 400 degrees. Arrange the apple slices in the piecrust. Sprinkle with the lemon juice and granulated sugar. In a bowl combine the flour, brown sugar, cinnamon, nutmeg, and lemon peel. Cut the peanut butter and butter into the mixture. Spread over the apples. Bake for 45 to 50 minutes or until the apples are tender.

MAKES 8 SERVINGS

# National Shrimp Festival

**WHERE:** Gulf Shores, Alabama

**WHEN:** Second full weekend of October (Thursday through Sunday)

Every year, 300,000 people congregate on the beautiful beaches of Gulf Shores for one of the South's premiere events, the National Shrimp Festival. Aside from getting their fill of shrimp (if that is even possible), festivalgoers can enjoy both local and nationally known musical entertainment, an incredible fine art and arts and crafts show, a 10K race, and a sand sculpture contest, as well as activities galore for the kids.

For more information, visit *www.nationalshrimpfestival.com*.

## DID YOU KNOW?

The size of a shrimp can range from around 1/2 inch long to almost 12 inches, depending on the species and the location.

## Shrimp Fritters

2   egg yolks

1/2   cup milk

1 1/2   cups sifted all-purpose flour

1   tablespoon baking powder

1/2   teaspoon salt

1/2   teaspoon ground white pepper

1/4   teaspoon paprika

2   teaspoons Worcestershire sauce

1   tablespoon Dijon mustard

2   tablespoons chopped fresh parsley

1/2   cup fresh white bread crumbs

2   tablespoons finely minced cooked onion

2   tablespoons finely minced cooked green bell pepper

1   cup chopped cooked shrimp, cooled

2   egg whites, stiffly beaten

Oil for frying

◼ Beat the egg yolks in a bowl until light. Add the milk, flour, baking powder, salt, white pepper, and paprika. Mix with a few swift strokes. Fold in the Worcestershire sauce, Dijon mustard, parsley, bread crumbs, onion, green pepper, shrimp, and egg whites. Refrigerate for 30 minutes. Heat oil in a deep skillet to 375 degrees. Shape the mixture into golf ball-size balls. Deep-fry the fritters in the oil until golden brown.

**MAKES 8 SERVINGS**

## Southern-Fried Shrimp

3   cups deveined shrimp

2 1/4   teaspoons salt, divided

1/4   teaspoon pepper

1   egg, well beaten

1/2   cup light cream or milk

2/3   cup yellow cornmeal

2/3   cup all-purpose flour

1/2   teaspoon baking powder

Oil for frying

◼ In a large bowl season the shrimp with 2 teaspoons of the salt and the pepper; let stand at room temperature for 15 minutes. In a small mixing bowl combine the egg, cream, cornmeal, flour, baking powder, and the remaining 1/4 teaspoon salt. Mix until well blended and smooth to make a batter. Add to the shrimp. Stir until the shrimp are well coated. Heat oil in a deep-fryer to 375 degrees. Drop the shrimp in the hot oil and cook until light brown.

**MAKES 4 SERVINGS**

# Corn and Shrimp Salad

*Salad:*

6   cups water

1   package shrimp or crab boil

36  medium to large shrimp, peeled and deveined

1½  cups fresh corn kernels

*Dressing:*

1   egg yolk or 2 tablespoons egg substitute

¾   cup olive oil

¾   cup peanut oil

¾   cup red wine vinegar

3   tablespoons Dijon mustard

3   tablespoons minced red onion

2   tablespoons minced fresh parsley

1   tablespoon minced shallot

◼ Combine the water and shrimp boil in a medium saucepan and bring to a boil. Add the shrimp and boil for 1 minute. Turn off the heat and let the shrimp cool in the liquid. Steam the corn kernels for 2 minutes; set aside in the refrigerator.

◼ For the dressing, whisk together the egg yolk, olive oil, peanut oil, vinegar, and Dijon mustard. Stir in the red onion, parsley, and shallot.

◼ Drain the shrimp and place in a serving bowl. Pour the dressing over the shrimp and toss. Cover and refrigerate for 2 hours. When ready to serve, stir the corn in with the shrimp.

**MAKES 6 SERVINGS**

## DID YOU KNOW?
Shrimp can only swim backward.

# Shady Valley Cranberry Festival

**WHERE:** Shady Valley, Tennessee

**WHEN:** Second weekend in October (Friday and Saturday)

While most people don't think about the South when it comes to growing cranberries, people in Shady Valley know that one of the oldest cranberry bogs in the United States is located right in their own town. So in addition to getting to see one of the few bogs below the Mason-Dixon line, visitors to this festival can enjoy a quilt show, canning exhibits, exhibits of Native American relics from the Valley, arts and crafts, live music, carnival rides, and helicopter rides.

For more information, please visit www.johnsoncountychamber.org/JCChamber/events/cranberryfestival.html.

## DID YOU KNOW?

The cranberry got its name because the Pilgrims believed the plant looked like the head of a sandhill crane. It was originally called the "craneberry," but the e was later dropped.

# Cranberry Cobbler

*Filling:*

3   cups fresh cranberries

3/4   cup sugar

2/3   cup chopped pecans

*Crust:*

2   eggs

3/4   cup sugar

3/4   cup all-purpose flour

3/4   cup (1 1/2 sticks) butter or margarine, softened and cut into small pieces

■ For the filling, butter a 10-inch pie plate. Spread the cranberries over the bottom of the plate and sprinkle with the sugar and pecans. Stir together and spread evenly in the pie plate.

■ For the crust, preheat the oven to 325 degrees. Beat the eggs in a bowl until light. Continue beating while gradually adding the sugar and then the flour. Cut the butter into the mixture. When the crust is thoroughly combined and smooth, spread over the filling. Bake for 45 minutes or until the crust browns. Serve hot.

**MAKES 10 SERVINGS**

# Cranberry Jezebel Sauce

1   cup water

1/2   cup granulated sugar

1/2   cup firmly packed light brown sugar

1   (10-ounce) package fresh cranberries

2   tablespoons prepared horseradish, drained

1   tablespoon Dijon mustard

1   (8-ounce) package cream cheese

■ Bring the water, granulated sugar, and brown sugar to a boil. Stir until the sugars have dissolved. Add the cranberries. Return to a boil and cook for 10 minutes. Remove from the heat and stir in the horseradish and Dijon mustard. Chill. Spread over the cream cheese and serve as an appetizer with crackers.

**MAKES 8 SERVINGS**

# Cranberry Fritters

1  cup cranberries

1  cup sugar, divided

1/2  cup water

2  cups all-purpose flour

1  teaspoon baking powder

2  eggs, separated

1/4  cup ice water

1  apple, peeled and diced

Confectioners' sugar for dusting

Raspberry jam

Oil for frying

■  In a saucepan combine the cranberries, 1/4 cup of the sugar, and the water. Cook over high heat until the berries begin to burst. Remove from the heat and chill. Sift together the flour, the remaining 3/4 cup sugar, and the baking powder. Beat the egg yolks with the ice water in a large bowl. Add the dry ingredients, the apple, and chilled cranberries and liquid; mix well. In a separate bowl beat the egg whites until soft peaks form. Fold into the cranberry mixture.

■  In a deep skillet or deep-fat fryer, heat 1 to 2 inches of oil to 350 degrees. For each fritter, drop 2 tablespoons of the batter into the oil. Cook for 1 minute. Turn over and continue frying until golden. Drain the fritters on paper towels. Dust with confectioners' sugar. Serve with raspberry jam.

**MAKES 8 SERVINGS**

# Chocolate-Covered Cranberries

12  ounces milk chocolate chips

2  tablespoons vegetable shortening

12  ounces whole cranberries

■  Melt the chocolate chips and shortening over low heat, stirring frequently until melted. Using a toothpick, dip the cranberries in the chocolate until coated. Place on waxed paper. Refrigerate until firm.

**MAKES 8 SERVINGS**

# West Virginia Black Walnut Festival

**WHERE:** Spencer, West Virginia

**WHEN:** Second weekend of October (Thursday through Sunday)

People are just nuts about the West Virginia Black Walnut Festival. For more than 50 years, tens of thousands of people have come to Spencer to enjoy the numerous foods that can be cooked using black walnuts—and to enjoy activities galore. Among the more popular are the flea market, the quilt show, parades, the nut run, chainsaw artists, arts and crafts, a Civil War exhibit, an ox roast, carnival rides, a gospel sing, livestock sales, a golf scramble, a classic car show, one-room school tours, a majorette competition, live music, and the Black Walnut Bowl football game.

For more information, please visit *www.wvblackwalnutfestival.org.*

## DID YOU KNOW?

Black walnut has been the foremost cabinet wood of North America since colonial times.

## Black Walnut Harvest Cake

4   cups diced fresh apples

2   cups sugar

2   eggs

1   cup salad oil

1   teaspoon vanilla extract

3   cups all-purpose flour

2   teaspoons baking soda

1   teaspoon salt

1   teaspoon ground cinnamon

1   teaspoon nutmeg

1   cup black walnuts, chopped

■ Combine the apples and sugar in a bowl. Let stand for 1 hour.

■ Preheat the oven to 350 degrees. Grease and flour a tube pan. In a mixing bowl beat the eggs. Add the oil and vanilla. Stir in the apple mixture. Sift together the flour, baking soda, salt, cinnamon, and nutmeg. Stir, do not beat, into the apple mixture. Stir in the black walnuts. Pour into the greased and floured tube pan. Bake for 1 hour or until a toothpick inserted in the center comes out clean.

**MAKES 12 SERVINGS**

## Black Walnut Pie

*Pastry:*

1   cup all-purpose flour

1/2   teaspoon salt

1/3   cup vegetable shortening

2   tablespoons water

*Filling:*

1/3   cup butter, melted

2/3   cup sugar

1/2   teaspoon salt

1   cup dark corn syrup

3   eggs

1   cup chopped black walnuts

■ For the pastry, mix the flour and salt together in a bowl. Cut in the shortening with a pastry blender. Sprinkle the water over the mixture. Mix with a fork until all the flour is moistened. Gather the dough together and roll firmly into a ball. Roll the dough into a circle large enough to fit into a 9-inch pie pan.

■ For the filling, preheat the oven to 375 degrees. In a mixing bowl combine the butter and sugar. Add the salt and corn syrup, beating well. Add the eggs one at a time, beating well after each addition. Stir in the black walnuts. Pour into the pastry-lined pie pan. Bake for about 50 minutes or until the filling is set and the pastry is nicely browned. Cool. Serve cold or slightly warm.

**MAKES 8 SERVINGS**

## Black Walnut Cocoa Fudge

| | |
|---|---|
| 3 | cups sugar |
| 1/2 | cup cocoa |
| 1 | cup evaporated milk |
| 1/2 | cup (1 stick) margarine |
| 1 | cup marshmallow crème |
| 1 | teaspoon vanilla extract |
| 1 | cup black walnuts, chopped |

■ Combine the sugar, cocoa, evaporated milk, and margarine in a saucepan. Cook to the soft-ball stage (236 degrees) on a candy thermometer, stirring constantly. Remove from the heat and add the marshmallow crème, vanilla, and walnuts. Pour into 8 x 8 x 2-inch greased pan and cool. Cut into 1-inch squares.

**MAKES 64 PIECES**

## Black Walnut Bon Bons

| | |
|---|---|
| 1 | pound confectioners' sugar |
| 1/3 | cup margarine, softened |
| 1/3 | cup corn syrup |
| 1/2 | teaspoon salt |
| 1/2 | teaspoon vanilla extract |
| 1 | cup chopped black walnuts |
| 1 | (6-ounce) package chocolate chips |
| 1 | (9-ounce) bar chocolate |
| 1 | (2-inch) square paraffin wax |

■ In a 4-quart mixing bowl add the confectioners' sugar, margarine, corn syrup, salt, and vanilla. Mix with your hands until the mixture forms a large ball. Add the walnuts and mix well. Roll the mixture into balls. In the top of a double boiler add the chocolate chips, chocolate bar, and paraffin wax. Stir until melted. Dip each ball into the chocolate mixture. Let cool on a baking sheet.

**MAKES 24 BON BONS**

## Black Walnut Chipped Cookies

1/2  cup (1 stick) butter

1  cup sugar

2  eggs, slightly beaten

1  teaspoon maple flavoring

2 1/2  cups sifted all-purpose flour

2 1/2  teaspoons baking powder

1/2  teaspoon salt

1  cup chopped black walnuts

■ Preheat the oven to 375 degrees. Cream the butter and sugar in a mixing bowl until the mixture is light. Add the eggs and maple flavoring. Mix well. Sift the flour, baking powder, and salt together. Add to the creamed mixture. Mix well. Stir in the chopped walnuts. Drop by table-spoonfuls onto a cookie sheet and flatten with a spoon. Bake in the oven for 10 to 12 minutes.

**MAKES 24 COOKIES**

**DID YOU KNOW?**
The black walnut tree secretes juglone, a natural weed killer that kills many herbaceous plants around the roots of the tree.

# Pumpkin Festival

**WHERE:** Pumpkintown, South Carolina

**WHEN:** Second Saturday in October

Where else but Pumpkintown to celebrate the pumpkin? More than 35,000 people invade Pumpkintown every year. Some come to pick out their Halloween pumpkins, while others come to taste the pumpkin-flavored goodies and to enjoy such other festival activities as a parade, carnival rides, dancing, bluegrass music, arts and crafts, quilts, and what is a highlight for many, the greased pole climb.

For more information, please visit *www.co.pickens.sc.us/tourpickens/festivals.asp.*

## DID YOU KNOW?

The largest pumpkin pie ever created weighed more than 350 pounds and was more than 5 feet in diameter. It took 6 hours to bake and used 80 pounds of cooked pumpkin, 36 pounds of sugar, and 144 eggs.

## Pumpkin Pie

1¼  cups pumpkin purée, canned or fresh

¾  cup sugar

½  teaspoon salt

¼  teaspoon ground ginger

1  teaspoon ground cinnamon

1  teaspoon all-purpose flour

2  eggs, lightly beaten

1  cup evaporated milk

2  tablespoons water

½  teaspoon vanilla extract

1  (9-inch) piecrust, unbaked

■ Preheat the oven to 400 degrees. Combine the pumpkin, sugar, salt, ginger, cinnamon, and flour in a medium mixing bowl. Add the eggs; mix well. Add the evaporated milk, water, and vanilla; mix well. Pour into the piecrust. Bake for 15 minutes. Reduce the heat to 350 degrees and bake for about 35 minutes longer, or until the center is set.

**MAKES 8 SERVINGS**

## Pumpkin Muffins

3  cups self-rising flour

2  cups sugar

2  teaspoons pumpkin pie spice

4  large eggs

½  cup vegetable oil

1  (15-ounce) can pumpkin

1½  cups chopped dates

1  cup chopped pecans, toasted
   Vegetable cooking spray

¼  cup firmly packed brown sugar

■ Preheat the oven to 400 degrees. Stir together the flour, sugar, and pumpkin pie spice in a large bowl. Make a well in the center of the mixture. In a separate bowl stir together the eggs, oil, and pumpkin. Add to the dry ingredients, stirring just until moistened. Stir in the dates and pecans. Line two 12-cup muffin pans with paper liners and coat with cooking spray. Spoon the batter into the cups, filling two-thirds full. Sprinkle evenly with the brown sugar. Bake for 18 to 20 minutes. Remove from the pans immediately and cool on wire racks.

**MAKES 24 MUFFINS**

# Pumpkin Bread Pudding

| | |
|---|---|
| 6 | slices whole wheat bread |
| 3 | eggs, lightly beaten |
| 2 | cups milk |
| 1 | (15-ounce) can pumpkin |
| 1/4 | cup molasses |
| 1/2 | cup sugar |
| 1 | teaspoon vanilla extract |
| 2 | teaspoons ginger |
| 1 1/2 | teaspoons ground cinnamon |
| 1 | teaspoon mace |
| 1/2 | teaspoon nutmeg |
| 1/3 | cup raisins |

■ Preheat the oven to 375 degrees, Tear the bread into small pieces and distribute over the bottom of a 2-quart baking dish. In a large bowl blend together the eggs, milk, pumpkin, molasses, sugar, vanilla, ginger, cinnamon, mace, and nutmeg until smooth. Stir in the raisins. Pour the mixture over the bread. Place the baking dish inside a larger baking pan. Add 1 inch of water to the larger pan. Bake for 70 minutes or until a knife inserted in the center comes out clean. Serve warm or cold.

**MAKES 12 SERVINGS**

# Pumpkin Bread

| | |
|---|---|
| 3 1/2 | cups sifted all-purpose flour |
| 2 | teaspoons baking soda |
| 1 1/3 | teaspoons salt |
| 1 | teaspoon ground cinnamon |
| 1 | teaspoon nutmeg |
| 3 | cups sugar |
| 1 | cup oil |
| 2/3 | cup water |
| 2 | cups canned pumpkin |
| 4 | eggs |

■ Preheat the oven to 350 degrees. Grease and flour 3 loaf pans. Sift together the flour, baking soda, salt, cinnamon, nutmeg, and sugar into a mixing bowl. Make a well in the dry ingredients. In a separate bowl combine the oil, water, pumpkin, and eggs. Pour into the dry ingredients. Mix well until smooth. Divide the batter evenly into the prepared pans. Bake for 1 hour or until done. Cool slightly in the pans, and then turn out onto wire racks to finish cooling.

**MAKES 3 LOAVES**

# Apple and Pumpkin Pie

1      (9-inch) deep-dish piecrust

1/2    cup firmly packed brown sugar

1      tablespoon cornstarch

1      teaspoon ground cinnamon, divided

1/8    plus 1/4 teaspoon salt, divided

1/4    cup water

2      tablespoons butter

2      cups peeled, sliced apples

1      egg, beaten

1      (15-ounce) can pumpkin

1/2    cup granulated sugar

1/2    teaspoon ground ginger

1/8    teaspoon ground cloves

1      (5.3-ounce) can evaporated milk

1      tablespoon lemon juice

■ Preheat the oven to 450 degrees. Bake the unpricked piecrust for 5 minutes. Remove from the oven and set aside. Reduce the oven temperature to 375 degrees.

■ In a medium saucepan, combine the brown sugar, cornstarch, 1/2 teaspoon of the cinnamon, and 1/8 teaspoon of the salt. Stir in the water. Add the butter. Bring to a boil over medium heat, stirring constantly. Stir in the apples. Bring to a boil again. Cover and turn off the heat, leaving the pan on the stove. In a small bowl, beat the egg. Stir in the pumpkin. Add the granulated sugar, ginger, the remaining 1/2 teaspoon cinnamon, the cloves, and the remaining 1/4 teaspoon salt. Mix well. Stir in the evaporated milk.

■ Add the lemon juice to the apples in the saucepan. Spoon the filling into the piecrust. Carefully pour the pumpkin mixture over the apples. Bake for 40 to 45 minutes or until a knife inserted in the center comes out clean. Cool on a wire rack.

**MAKES 8 SERVINGS**

---

**DID YOU KNOW?**
The largest pumpkin ever grown weighed 1,140 pounds.

# World Championship Gumbo Cook-Off

**WHERE:** New Iberia, Louisiana

**WHEN:** Second weekend in October (Saturday and Sunday)

Although the World Championship Gumbo Cook-Off is a two-day event, Day 2 is the part of the festival truly devoted to gumbo. Sure, you'll find plenty of Cajun and Creole food on Saturday with such dishes as jambalaya, boudin, and étouffée. But no gumbo. That is reserved for Sunday when more than 60 teams gather to see who can create that year's best gumbo. After the judges have reached their decision, the lucky crowd of more than 15,000 gets to purchase as many portions as their appetite can handle. It's good that both days have plenty of live bands and Cajun dancing to work off all that food.

For more information, please visit *www.iberiachamber.org*.

## DID YOU KNOW?

Filé, or gumbo filé, is a seasoning made of dried ground sassafras leaves and used in Creole cooking. The Choctaw Indians of Louisiana were the first to use these leaves for flavoring.

## Seafood Gumbo

2 quarts water

2 beef bouillon cubes

1 dried red hot pepper

1 cup chopped ham

3 teaspoons salt, divided

4 teaspoons bacon drippings

1/4 cup all-purpose flour

2 tablespoons vegetable oil

2 1/3 cups chopped okra, fresh or frozen and thawed

1 large onion, chopped

3 garlic cloves, minced

1/2 green bell pepper, chopped

2 celery ribs, chopped

1 (16-ounce) can tomatoes, undrained

1/2 teaspoon dried thyme leaves

2 bay leaves

1/4 cup ketchup

1/2 teaspoon hot pepper sauce

1 tablespoon Worcestershire sauce

1 pound fresh shrimp, peeled, deveined, and halved

1 pound crabmeat, cleaned

1 bunch green onions, chopped

1 tablespoon filé powder

1 (12-ounce) jar oysters, drained

1 cup rice, cooked

■ Combine the water and bouillon cubes in a large kettle. Add the red pepper, ham, and 2 teaspoons of the salt. Bring to a boil over high heat. Reduce the heat to medium. Cover and simmer for 45 minutes.

■ Meanwhile, make a roux by heating the bacon drippings in a skillet over medium heat. Add the flour. Stir until absorbed. Reduce the heat to low and cook for about 25 minutes, stirring constantly, until the flour is browned but not burned. Add the oil and stir to combine. Add the okra, onion, garlic, green pepper, and celery. Sauté until tender. Add the tomatoes with their liquid and cook for 5 minutes. Add the sautéed vegetable mixture to the stock. Stir in the remaining 1 teaspoon salt, the thyme, bay leaves, ketchup, hot pepper sauce, and Worcestershire sauce. Cover and cook slowly for 1 hour. Add the shrimp, crabmeat, and green onions. Cook for 10 minutes. Stir in the filé powder and cook for 15 minutes longer. Add the oysters and cook for 15 more minutes. Before serving remove and discard the bay leaves. Serve over hot cooked rice.

**MAKES 12 SERVINGS**

## Sausage and Chicken Gumbo

1     pound hot smoked sausage, cut into 1/4-inch slices

4     chicken breasts, cut into strips

     Vegetable oil

3/4   cup all-purpose flour

1     cup chopped onion

1/2   cup diced green bell pepper

1/2   cup diced celery

2     quarts hot water

3     garlic cloves, minced

2     bay leaves

2 1/2 teaspoons Creole seasoning

1/2   teaspoon dried thyme

1     teaspoon Worcestershire sauce

1     teaspoon Louisiana hot sauce

     Salt to taste (optional)

     Hot cooked rice

■ Brown the sausage in a Dutch oven over medium heat. Drain on paper towels, reserving the drippings. Brown the chicken in the drippings; drain on paper towels, reserving the drippings. Combine the drippings and enough vegetable oil to measure 1/2 cup. Heat the mixture in the Dutch oven over medium heat until hot. Add the flour to the hot oil. Cook, stirring constantly, until chocolate brown in color. Add the onion, green pepper, and celery. Cook until tender, stirring constantly. Gradually stir in the water and bring to a boil. Return the chicken to the Dutch oven. Add the garlic, bay leaves, Creole seasoning, thyme, Worcestershire sauce, and hot sauce. Simmer, uncovered, for 1 hour. Remove the chicken; set aside to cool. Return the sausage to the Dutch oven and cook, uncovered, for 30 minutes. Add salt, if desired. Add the chicken to the gumbo and heat thoroughly. Remove and discard the bay leaves. Serve over rice.

**MAKES 12 SERVINGS**

## Easy Shrimp Gumbo

3    tablespoons all-purpose flour

3    tablespoons oil

1    onion, finely chopped

1½   quarts water

2    pounds peeled and deveined shrimp

1    teaspoon salt

½    teaspoon black pepper

1    tablespoon filé powder

■ In a large stockpot brown the flour in the oil, stirring constantly. Add the onion and stir until brown. Add the water. Bring to a boil. Add the shrimp, salt, pepper, and filé powder. Reduce the heat and simmer for 30 minutes. Serve over rice.

**MAKES 8 SERVINGS**

### DID YOU KNOW?

There are two types of gumbo: Creole and Cajun. Creole gumbos generally use a lighter-colored, medium-brown roux and may include tomatoes. Cajun gumbos are made with a darker roux and never contain tomatoes.

# Blairsville Sorghum Festival

**WHERE:** Blairsville, Georgia

**WHEN:** Second, third, and fourth weekends in October (Saturday and Sunday)

This festival is so big that it takes three weekends to get all the activities in. Started in the early 1970s, the Blairsville Sorghum Festival kicks off just as farmers from this part of the Blue Ridge Mountains start cutting and stripping the cane they claim makes the best syrup there is. As you might expect to find anywhere you have this much sorghum, you'll also find thousands of biscuits just ready to be covered in syrup, many at the annual biscuit-eating contest. There's also a parade, a square dance, a car show, and contests for rock throwing, pole climbing, log sawing, tobacco spitting, horseshoe throwing, and one to find the oldest person in attendance each day.

For more information, please visit *http://sorghum.blairsville.com/*.

## DID YOU KNOW?

Sorghum is a syrup created from the sorghum cane.

## Sorghum Cookies

2   cups all-purpose flour

2   teaspoons baking soda

1¼  teaspoons ginger

½   teaspoon salt

1   teaspoon ground cinnamon

1   egg

1½  cups sugar, divided

¼   cup sorghum

⅔   cup melted butter

▇ Preheat the oven to 350 degrees. Sift together the flour, baking soda, ginger, salt, and cinnamon in a bowl. In a separate bowl beat the egg. Add 1 cup of the sugar and the sorghum. Mix well. Stir in the butter. Add the sifted dry ingredients and mix well. Shape the dough into 1-inch balls. Dip the balls into water and then roll to cover in the remaining ½ cup sugar. Place the balls on a cookie sheet and bake for 10 to 15 minutes.

**MAKES 24 COOKIES**

## Southern Sorghum Chicken

1   cup all-purpose flour

1   teaspoon salt

⅓   teaspoon pepper

⅔   cup sorghum

6   boneless, skinless chicken breasts

⅔   cup vegetable oil

▇ Preheat the oven to 350 degrees. Mix the flour, salt, and pepper in dish. Pour the sorghum in a separate dish. Dip the chicken breasts in the sorghum and then in the flour mixture. Roll the chicken a second time in the flour and set aside for 10 minutes.

▇ Heat the oil in a large heavy skillet. Fry the chicken just until browned on both sides. Place the chicken in a shallow baking dish and bake for 30 minutes or until tender.

**MAKES 6 SERVINGS**

## Sorghum Pie

5      eggs

1/3    cup sugar

11/3   cups sorghum

1      (9-inch) piecrust, unbaked
       Whipped cream

■ Preheat the oven to 350 degrees. Beat the eggs in a medium mixing bowl until smooth. Add the sugar and sorghum and beat for another minute. Pour the mixture into the piecrust. Bake for 35 to 40 minutes or until a toothpick inserted in the center comes out clean. Cool before serving. Serve with whipped cream.

**MAKES 8 SERVINGS**

## Sorghum Peanut Candy

11/2   cups sorghum

2      cups peanuts

1      teaspoon vanilla extract

1/4    cup melted butter

■ Bring the sorghum to a boil in a saucepan and boil until it forms hard drops when dropped into cold water. Remove from the heat. Stir in the peanuts, vanilla, and butter. Pour the mixture into buttered pans to a depth of 1/2 to 3/4 inch. When cool, cut into serving-size pieces.

**MAKES 8 SERVINGS**

---

**DID YOU KNOW?**

Sorghum is not molasses—molasses is made from sugar cane.

# Gautier Mullet Festival

**WHERE:** Gautier, Mississippi
**WHEN:** Third Saturday in October

The Mullet Festival has nothing to do with that haircut made famous by Billy Ray Cyrus. Here, it's all about the fish. Visit Gautier to celebrate that tasty swimmer and to enjoy live music, fish and wildlife exhibits, arts and crafts, an antique car show, kids' rides, train rides, a cast-net contest, and the ever-popular mullet toss competition.

For more information, please visit *www.gautiermulletfest.com*.

## DID YOU KNOW?

The mullet is credited with saving the area around Niceville, Florida, during the Great Depression. Families were able to use the tasty fish to barter for goods and services in nearby Alabama.

## Fried Mullet

8    mullets, cleaned
2    tablespoons lemon juice
2    teaspoons salt
1/2    teaspoon black pepper
1    cup all-purpose flour
1    cup vegetable oil
     Lemon wedges

■ Sprinkle the fish with lemon juice, salt, and pepper. Coat both sides of the fish evenly with the flour. Heat the oil in a skillet. Add the fish and cook until golden brown, turning twice. Serve each piece of fish with a lemon wedge.

**MAKES 4 SERVINGS**

## Mullet Amandine

2    pounds mullet fillets
2    tablespoons lemon juice
1    teaspoon salt
1/4    teaspoon pepper
1/2    cup all-purpose flour
1/3    cup butter
1/2    cup slivered almonds

■ Sprinkle the fish with the lemon juice, salt, and pepper. Coat the fillets evenly with the flour. Melt the butter in a large skillet. Add the fillets in a single layer. Cook over medium heat for 4 to 5 minutes or until brown. Turn carefully and cook for 4 to 5 minutes longer or until the fish is brown and flakes easily when tested. Drain on absorbent paper and place on a warm serving platter. Sauté the almonds in the skillet until lightly browned. Serve over the fish.

**MAKES 4 SERVINGS**

### DID YOU KNOW?

Because they leap out of the water and skip along the surface, mullets are sometimes referred to as "jumping" mullets or "happy" mullets.

# International Rice Festival

**WHERE:** Crowley, Louisiana

**WHEN:** Third weekend in October (Thursday through Saturday)

More than a quarter million people make the journey to Crowley every year to enjoy all the events at the International Rice Festival. In addition to the musical performances each night, festivalgoers have plenty of other activities to enjoy, including a rice-grading contest, a rice and Creole cookery contest, arts and crafts, a rice-eating contest, parades, a fiddle and accordion contest, a frog derby, rice threshing, a street dance, and the International Rice Queen Pageant.

For more information, please visit *www.ricefestival.com.*

## DID YOU KNOW?

In Burma, a person eats 500 pounds of rice a year. In the United States, the average person eats only 25 pounds of rice each year.

# Red Beans and Rice

| | |
|---|---|
| 1/2 | pound dried red beans |
| 5 | cups water |
| 1/3 | teaspoon dried thyme leaves, crushed |
| 1 | bay leaf |
| 1 | medium green bell pepper, chopped |
| 1 | medium onion, chopped |
| 3 | garlic cloves, minced |
| 1 | tablespoon crushed red pepper |
| 1 | teaspoon salt |
| 1 | pound ham hocks or salt pork |
| 1 | tablespoon ketchup |
| 1 | cup converted rice |

▪ Soak the beans overnight; drain. Combine the beans, water, thyme, bay leaf, green pepper, onion, garlic, red pepper, salt, and ham hocks or salt pork in a Dutch oven. Bring to a boil. Reduce the heat and simmer gently, uncovered, for 1 1/2 to 2 hours or until the beans are tender. Stir in the ketchup. Add more water if the mixture is too thick. In a separate pot, cook the rice according to the package directions. Before serving the beans, remove the ham hocks and discard the bay leaf. Serve the red beans over the hot cooked rice.

**MAKES 5 TO 6 SERVINGS**

# Cajun Rice Salad

| | |
|---|---|
| 1 | cup uncooked white rice |
| 1/3 | cup chopped scallions |
| 1/3 | cup chopped dill pickles |
| 1/3 | cup chopped sweet pickles |
| 1/3 | cup chopped celery |
| 1/3 | cup chopped green bell pepper |
| 1/3 | cup chopped olives with pimientos |
| 3/4 | cup chopped hard-cooked eggs |
| 2 | tablespoons hot sauce |
| 2 | tablespoons prepared yellow mustard |
| 1 | tablespoon olive oil |
| 2 | dashes red wine vinegar |
| 1/2 | cup mayonnaise |
| 1/4 | cup blue cheese salad dressing |
| | Cayenne pepper to taste |

▪ Cook the rice according to the package directions. When cool combine with the scallions, dill pickles, sweet pickles, celery, green pepper, olives, and eggs in a large bowl. In a separate bowl thoroughly mix together the hot sauce, mustard, olive oil, vinegar, mayonnaise, blue cheese dressing, and cayenne pepper. Blend in to the salad and refrigerate overnight.

**MAKES 8 SERVINGS**

# Cajun Dirty Rice

- 8 ounces chicken livers, chopped
- 1/2 cup chopped green bell pepper
- 1/2 cup chopped celery
- 1 large garlic clove, minced
- 1/4 cup (1/2 stick) butter
- 1 package onion soup mix
- 2 cups water
- 1 teaspoon hot pepper sauce
- 1 cup uncooked white rice

In a heavy skillet cook the livers, green pepper, celery, and garlic in the butter over medium heat until the vegetables are tender, stirring often. Stir in the soup mix, water, and hot pepper sauce. Bring to a boil. Stir in the rice. Reduce the heat to low. Cover and simmer for 20 minutes or until the rice is tender.

**MAKES 8 SERVINGS**

## DID YOU KNOW?

There are as many as 40,000 varieties of rice grown on every continent except Antarctica.

# North Carolina Oyster Festival

**WHERE:** Ocean Isle Beach, North Carolina

**WHEN:** Third weekend in October (Saturday and Sunday)

The coastal waters of Brunswick County produce an abundance of oysters, and each year more than 30,000 people come from all over to pay homage to the mighty mollusk. Since 1980, visitors to the North Carolina Oyster Festival have enjoyed live entertainment, a road race, a surfing contest, a kids' area, the North Carolina Oyster Shucking Championships, and an oyster stew cook-off. But even if you don't want to shuck or cook your own, everyone at this festival is welcome and encouraged to eat their fill of oysters.

For more information, please visit
*www.brunswickcountychamber.org.*

## DID YOU KNOW?

The old wives' tale that oysters should only be eaten in months containing an r (meaning the colder weather months), is thought to have originated in the days when oysters were shipped without adequate refrigeration and could easily spoil.

## Oysters Rockefeller Casserole

3   (10-ounce) boxes chopped frozen spinach

1   cup (2 sticks) butter

1/2   teaspoon dried thyme

1/2   cup finely chopped green onions

3/4   cup bread crumbs

2   to 3 dozen oysters, drained

1   tablespoon anise-flavored liqueur (absinthe)

Salt and pepper to taste

■ Preheat the oven to 425 degrees. Cook the spinach according to the package directions. Drain well and set aside. Melt the butter in a large skillet. Add the thyme and green onions and sauté for 2 minutes. Add the bread crumbs and sauté until toasted. Add the oysters and cook until the edges of the oysters begin to curl. Add the liqueur and the cooked spinach to the oyster mixture and mix well. Pour the mixture into a baking dish and bake for 20 to 25 minutes. Season with salt and pepper to taste.

**MAKES 12 SERVINGS**

## Oyster Dressing

Neck and giblets of 1 turkey or chicken

1   (10 1/2-ounce) can cream of chicken soup

1   (10 1/2-ounce) can cream of celery soup

1   large onion, chopped

2   celery ribs, chopped

1   tablespoon poultry mix

4   cups bread crumbs

3   hard-cooked eggs, chopped

1   pint oysters, drained

■ Combine the neck and giblets in a saucepan with enough water to cover. Cook for about 1 hour or until done. Drain, reserving the broth.

■ Preheat the oven to 325 degrees. Cut the lean part of the neck and giblets into very small pieces. Combine the reserved broth, the cream of chicken soup, cream of celery soup, onion, celery, and poultry mix together in a saucepan. Bring to boil. Reduce the heat and simmer for 10 minutes. Add the bread crumbs to a baking dish. Pour the broth mixture over the bread crumbs, reserving 2 cups to make a gravy. Add the eggs and oysters; mix well. Bake for about 30 minutes.

**MAKES 8 SERVINGS**

## Oyster Fritters

4    eggs, separated

1/2    teaspoon salt

1/8    teaspoon pepper

1    tablespoon minced onion (optional)

6    tablespoons all-purpose flour

1    cup oysters, drained and chopped

    Vegetable oil for frying

In a bowl beat the egg whites until stiff. In a separate bowl beat the egg yolks until thick and creamy. Add the salt, pepper, and onion, if desired. Stir in the flour a little at a time. Fold in the oysters and stiffly beaten egg whites. Heat oil in a deep skillet. Drop the batter by spoonfuls into the hot oil and cook until golden brown.

**MAKES 4 SERVINGS**

## Clint's "Oysterpuppies"

1    pint oysters

2    cups House Autry hushpuppy mix (or any hushpuppy mix)

    Pinch of salt

    Pinch of black pepper

1    cup water

    Oil for frying

Drain the oysters, reserving the liquid. Cut the oysters into quarters or halves. Combine the oysters, hushpuppy mix, reserved oyster liquid, salt, and pepper in a large bowl. Add the water to the mixture and stir well. Let stand for 5 minutes. Heat oil in a skillet to 350 to 375 degress. Stir the batter. Using a tablespoon, drop the batter into the hot oil and fry for 3 minutes or until golden brown. Serve with tartar or cocktail sauce.

**MAKES 30 TO 40 OYSTERPUPPIES**

## Oyster Stew

1/3    cup butter

1    pint shelled oysters

5    cups milk

1    cup cream

1 1/2    teaspoons salt

1/2    teaspoon pepper

1    teaspoon paprika

■   Melt the butter in a saucepan over medium heat. Add the oysters and cook for 3 minutes or until the edges of the oysters begin to curl. Add the milk, cream, salt, and pepper. Let heat almost to boiling. Add a sprinkle of paprika to each serving and serve at once.

**MAKES 6 SERVINGS**

## Gammie's Oyster Pie

8    ounces crushed Saltines

1    quart oysters with juice

1    cup (1/2 stick) butter, cut into pats

1    pint half-and-half

    Salt and pepper to taste

■   In a baking dish layer half the Saltines, the oysters with juice, and the remaining Saltines. Top with the pats of butter. Pour the half-and-half over the top and season with salt and pepper. Let sit for 1 hour.

■   Preheat the oven to 350 degrees. Bake for 30 minutes.

**MAKES 8 SERVINGS**

### DID YOU KNOW?

The oyster creates a pearl when foreign matter becomes trapped inside its shell. In response to this irritation, the oyster produces nacre, a substance that coats the foreign material and over time becomes a pearl.

# Arkansas Bean Fest and Championship Outhouse Races

**WHERE:** Mountain View, Arkansas

**WHEN:** The last full weekend in October (Thursday through Saturday)

That's right—outhouse races. But first, there's the Parade of Outhouses. No wonder more than 50,000 people flock to Mountain View to see who wins the revered gold, silver, and bronze potty seat awards. These lucky folks also get to enjoy plenty of beans and cornbread, live music, a beanie weenie dog show, a cornbread cook-off, arts and crafts, children's games, square dancing, and a talent show.

For more information, please visit
*www.yourplaceinthemountains.com.*

## DID YOU KNOW?

Pinto beans are the most widely produced bean in the United States.

## Pinto Bean Casserole

2  pounds ground beef

1  medium onion, chopped

1  medium green bell pepper, chopped

1  (15-ounce) can tomato sauce

1  (16-ounce) can diced tomatoes, undrained

2  cups pinto beans, cooked and drained

1  (7-ounce) package cornbread mix

■ Preheat the oven to 425 degrees. In a large skillet brown the ground beef, onion, and green pepper. Add the tomato sauce, diced tomatoes, and pinto beans. Pour into a 9 x 13-inch baking dish. Prepare the cornbread according to the package directions, but do not bake. Spread the batter over the ingredients in the baking dish. Bake 20 minutes or until the cornbread is golden brown.

**MAKES 12 SERVINGS**

## Pinto Beans

1  pound dried pinto beans

5  cups water

1  medium onion, quartered

1  teaspoon chili powder

1  teaspoon salt

1/2  pound ham hocks or salt pork, cut into cubes

■ Soak the beans overnight; drain. Combine the beans, water, onion, chili powder, salt, and ham hocks or salt pork in a large pot. Bring to a boil; reduce the heat to low. Simmer over low heat for 2 to 2 1/2 hours, or until the beans are very soft. Remove the ham hocks before serving.

**MAKES 8 SERVINGS**

# Pinto Bean Pie

. . . . . . . . . . . . . . . . . . . . . . . . . . .

1/2  cup (1 stick) butter

1  cup firmly packed brown sugar

1  cup granulated sugar

2  eggs

1  cup cooked, mashed pinto beans

1  (9-inch) piecrust, unbaked

Whipped cream or ice cream for serving (optional)

■ Preheat the oven to 350 degrees. Cream together the butter, brown sugar, and granulated sugar in a mixing bowl. Add the eggs. Blend well. Add the pinto beans and mix well. Pour into the piecrust and bake for about 45 minutes. Top with whipped cream or ice cream, if desired.

**MAKES 6 SERVINGS**

**DID YOU KNOW?**
*Pinto* is a Spanish word meaning "painted."

# Jack Daniel's® Bar-B-Q Festival

**WHERE:** Lynchburg, Tennessee
**WHEN:** The last Saturday in October

At the end of October, Jack Daniel's Distillery and the people of Lynchburg play host to more than 60 award-winning barbecue teams. One of the most prestigious barbecue competitions in the world, the Jack Daniel's Bar-B-Q Festival features teams from across the United States and around the world competing in the categories of pork ribs, pork shoulder, beef brisket, and chicken. There's also a Jack Daniel's sauce and dessert competition, for which contestants create recipes containing the hometown product. Teams from outside the United States can be especially creative when entering the Home Cookin' from the Homeland competition—while U.S. teams do the same in the Cook's Choice contest. If that's not enough, there's also a grilling competition. But in addition to all the good barbecue you can eat, you get to enjoy such fun activities as the Country Dog Contest (canines only!), auctions for homemade pies and cakes, and clogging in the Lynchburg town square.

For more information, please visit *www.jackdaniels.com*.

## DID YOU KNOW?

Although Jack Daniel was not the first to operate a distillery, in 1866 in Lynchburg, Tennessee, he was the first to register a distillery with the government. Technically, this makes Jack Daniel's the oldest distillery in the United States.

# Tabasco Jack Wings

*Chicken:*

3/4   cup all-purpose flour

1 1/2   teaspoons salt

1/4   teaspoon black pepper

2   pounds chicken drumettes
Vegetable oil for frying

*Sauce:*

1/2   cup (1 stick) butter

1/2   cup Jack Daniel's Tennessee Whiskey

1/4   cup ketchup

1/3   cup Tabasco sauce, or to taste
Blue cheese dressing for serving
Celery and carrot sticks for serving

■   For the chicken, combine the flour, salt, and pepper in a small bowl. Coat the chicken drumettes with the flour mixture. Heat 2 to 3 inches of oil in a fryer or heavy pot to 375 degrees. Fry the drumettes, a few at a time, until golden brown on all sides and cooked through, about 10 to 15 minutes. Drain on paper towels.

■   For the sauce, combine the butter, whiskey, ketchup, and Tabasco sauce in a small saucepan. Bring to a boil. Dip the cooked wings in the sauce. Serve with blue cheese dressing and celery and carrot sticks.

■   To bake the drumettes, place the chicken in a roasting pan. Brush with melted butter and sprinkle with salt and pepper. Bake in a 450 degree oven until lightly browned and cooked through, about 30 minutes.

**MAKES 8 SERVINGS**

# Jack's Secret Weapon All-Purpose BBQ Glaze

1/2   cup Jack Daniel's Tennessee Whiskey

1/2   cup soy sauce

1/2   cup ketchup

1   cup firmly packed brown sugar

1   teaspoon garlic powder

■   Combine the whiskey, soy sauce, ketchup, brown sugar, and garlic powder in a small saucepan. Simmer until slightly thickened, about 5 minutes.

**MAKES ABOUT 1 1/2 CUPS**

## Sweet, Hot, and Sour Tennessee Whiskey Meatballs

*Meatballs:*

1    pound pork sausage

1    pound ground beef

1/2   cup plain bread crumbs

2    eggs, beaten

1/4   cup milk

1/2   cup finely chopped onion

1/2   teaspoon salt

1/2   teaspoon black pepper

*Sauce:*

1/2   cup apple jelly

1/4   cup spicy brown mustard

1/4   cup Jack Daniel's Tennessee Whiskey

1    teaspoon Worcestershire sauce

     Hot pepper sauce to taste

■   For the meatballs, preheat the oven to 375 degrees. Combine the pork sausage, ground beef, bread crumbs, eggs, milk, onion, salt, and pepper in a large mixing bowl. Mix together well with your hands. Form into 1 1/2-inch balls. Place on an ungreased baking sheet with sides or a jelly-roll pan. Bake for about 30 minutes or until browned and cooked through.

■   For the sauce, combine the apple jelly, mustard, whiskey, Worcestershire sauce, and hot pepper sauce in a large skillet. Stir over medium heat until well blended. Stir in the cooked meatballs. Coat with the sauce and cook for about 5 minutes or until the sauce has thickened slightly. Serve with toothpicks.

**MAKES ABOUT 50 MEATBALLS**

## Jack Daniel's Candied Apples

6    cups peeled and sliced apples

1/4   cup (1 stick) butter

2    to 3 cups sugar

     Jack Daniel's Tennessee Whiskey to taste

■   Combine the apples, butter, and sugar in a large saucepan. Cook over medium heat until the apples are tender. Stir in the whiskey. Cook an additional 5 minutes.

**MAKES 6 TO 8 SERVINGS**

## Tims Ford Tenderloin Tips

1/4    cup (1/2 stick) butter

2    pounds beef tenderloin tips, sliced

     Salt to taste

1    cup sliced mushrooms

1/4    cup chopped onion

1    garlic clove, minced

1/2    cup dry red wine

1/2    cup Jack Daniel's Tennessee Whiskey

1    cup canned crushed tomatoes

2    tablespoons sugar

     Mashed potatoes for serving

■ Melt the butter in a large heavy skillet. Cook the beef quickly until browned. Season with salt. Stir in the mushrooms, onion, and garlic. Simmer for several minutes. Stir in the wine, whiskey, tomatoes, and sugar. Simmer for 30 minutes or until the beef is tender. Serve with mashed potatoes.

**MAKES 4 SERVINGS**

### DID YOU KNOW?

"Sour mash" is not a specific type of whiskey. It simply means that a portion of the previous batch starts the next in order to maintain consistency between the blends. It is quite similar to the process of making sourdough bread.

# Green Tomato Festival

**WHERE:** Juliette, Georgia

**WHEN:** Fourth weekend in October (Saturday through Sunday)

Even though the book and film were set in Alabama, the Southern film classic *Fried Green Tomatoes* was actually filmed on location in tiny Juliette. Fittingly enough, each year a few thousand people come to Juliette and the Whistle Stop Café to enjoy fried green tomatoes, as well as gospel and bluegrass music, arts and crafts, games, and hayrides.

For more information, please visit *www.juliettega.com.*

### DID YOU KNOW?

Although tomatoes are fruits, in 1893 the Supreme Court ruled in the case of *Nix v. Hedden* that tomatoes were to be considered vegetables.

# Fried Green Tomatoes

2   cups all-purpose flour

1   cup cornmeal

1   tablespoon sugar

4   or 5 green tomatoes, sliced 1/2 inch thick

1/4   cup oil or vegetable shortening

Salt and pepper to taste

▓   Mix together the flour, cornmeal, and sugar in a shallow bowl. Dredge the tomatoes in the flour mixture, coating both sides. Heat the oil or shortening in a heavy skillet over medium heat. Add the tomatoes to the hot oil, a few at a time, and fry for about 2 minutes on each side or until golden brown. Remove from the skillet and drain on paper towels. Sprinkle with salt and pepper. Serve hot.

**MAKES 6 SERVINGS**

# Fried Green Tomato BLT

8   slices thick-cut bacon

1/2   cup all-purpose flour

1/4   cup cornmeal

Salt and freshly ground black pepper to taste

1   cup milk

1/4   cup vegetable oil

3   or 4 large green tomatoes, sliced 1/4 inch thick

1/4   cup mayonnaise

8   slices lightly toasted bread

1   large bunch arugula, stems removed, washed and patted dry

▓   Fry the bacon over medium heat until just browned and crispy. Drain on paper towels. Drain the bacon drippings into a cup; set aside. Wipe the skillet with a paper towel. Combine the flour, cornmeal, salt, and pepper in a medium bowl. Add the milk and stir well. Add the oil and reserved bacon drippings to the clean skillet. Place the skillet over medium-high heat. Working in batches, dip the tomato slices in the batter, letting any excess drip back into the bowl. Fry the tomatoes in the hot oil for about 3 minutes per side or until golden brown. Add more oil to the pan if necessary. Drain the tomatoes on paper towels. Spread about 1 1/2 teaspoons of the mayonnaise on one side of each slice of toast. Lay 2 slices of bacon over each of 4 slices of toast. Top each with 2 fried green tomato slices and some of the arugula. Cover with the remaining 4 slices of toast, mayonnaise-side down.

**MAKES 4 SANDWICHES**

## Baked Green Tomatoes

4    large firm green tomatoes

      Salt and pepper to taste

1/2  cup firmly packed brown sugar

3/4  cup coarse buttery cracker crumbs

1/4  cup (1/2 stick) butter, cut into small pieces

■ Preheat the oven to 350 degrees. Cut the tomatoes into 1/2-inch-thick slices. Arrange the tomato slices in a greased baking dish. Season with salt and pepper. Sprinkle each tomato with 1/2 tablespoon brown sugar. Cover the tomatoes with the crumbs and dot with the butter. Bake until the tomatoes are tender but still firm, about 25 to 35 minutes.

**MAKES 6 SERVINGS**

## Hot Green Tomato Pickles

2    quarts quartered green tomatoes

2    cups chopped onions

3/4  cup chopped hot peppers

2    cups sugar

2    tablespoons salt

2    cups white vinegar

1    teaspoon celery seeds

■ Combine the tomatoes, onions, and hot peppers in a large saucepan. In a bowl mix the sugar, salt, vinegar, and celery seeds together. Pour over the tomatoes. Bring to a boil. Remove from the heat immediately. Pour into hot, sterile jars and seal.

**MAKES 6 PINTS**

---

### DID YOU KNOW?

The largest tomato on record weighed seven pounds and was grown in Oklahoma.

# November

# National Peanut Festival

**WHERE:** Dothan, Alabama

**WHEN:** First Friday in November through the following Sunday (10-day festival)

The National Peanut Festival, the largest peanut festival in the United States, is held each year to celebrate the year's harvest and to honor local peanut growers. That said, this festival goes way beyond a celebration of peanuts and is one of the most activity-intensive festivals in the country. In addition to such peanut-related activities as recipe contests, the Little Miss Peanut pageant, and the Miss National Peanut Festival pageant, there are also a marching band contest, a parade, a demolition derby, big-name entertainment, livestock shows, carnival rides, and fireworks. For those looking to come away with a title other than Little Miss Peanut, there are competitions galore, including cake decorating, cheerleading, greased pig, photography, costume, choral, border collie, and all types of livestock.

For more information, please visit *www.nationalpeanutfestival.com*.

## DID YOU KNOW?

On average, Americans eat 3.3 pounds of peanut butter per person, per year. That adds up to more than 700 million pounds, enough to coat the floor of the Grand Canyon.

# Peanut Butter Cake

*Cake:*

| | |
|---|---|
| 5 | eggs, separated |
| 2 | cups sugar |
| 2 | cups all-purpose flour |
| 1 | teaspoon baking soda |
| 1 | cup buttermilk |
| 1 | cup crunchy peanut butter |
| 1/2 | cup (1 stick) butter, melted |
| 1/2 | cup oil |
| 1 | teaspoon vanilla extract |

*Frosting:*

| | |
|---|---|
| 8 | ounces cream cheese, softened |
| 1/2 | cup (1 stick) butter, softened |
| 1 | (1-pound) box confectioners' sugar |
| 1 | teaspoon vanilla extract |
| 1/2 | cup chopped roasted peanuts |

■ For the cake, grease three 9-inch round cake pans. Preheat the oven to 350 degrees. Whip the egg whites until stiff; set aside. Using a mixer at medium speed, combine the egg yolks, sugar, flour, baking soda, buttermilk, peanut butter, melted butter, oil, and vanilla in a large mixing bowl. Fold in the egg whites. Pour the mixture evenly into the prepared pans. Bake for 25 minutes. Cool on wire racks.

■ For the frosting, whip the cream cheese and butter in a mixing bowl until fluffy. Gradually add the confectioners' sugar, vanilla, and peanuts and mix until smooth. Spread the frosting between each layer and on the top and side of the cake.

**MAKES 12 SERVINGS**

# Southern Peanut Butter Pie

| | |
|---|---|
| 2/3 | cup sugar |
| 1/2 | teaspoon salt |
| 1 | cup dark corn syrup |
| 1/3 | cup creamy peanut butter |
| 3 | eggs |
| 1 | cup salted peanuts |
| 1 | (9-inch) piecrust, unbaked |

■ Preheat the oven to 375 degrees. Beat the sugar, salt, corn syrup, peanut butter, and eggs together in a mixing bowl. Stir in the peanuts. Pour the mixture into the piecrust. Bake until the crust is golden brown, about 40 to 50 minutes. The center of the filling may be slightly soft but will become firm as the pie cools. Refrigerate until ready to serve.

**MAKES 8 SERVINGS**

## Peanut Butter Peanut Brittle Cookies

*Peanut Brittle:*

3/4    cup sugar

3/4    cup unroasted peanuts

1/3    cup light corn syrup

1/4    teaspoon salt

1 1/2  teaspoons butter-flavored shortening

3/4    teaspoon vanilla extract

3/4    teaspoon baking soda

*Cookies:*

1/2    cup butter-flavored shortening

1/2    cup granulated sugar

1/2    cup firmly packed light brown sugar

1/2    cup creamy peanut butter

1      tablespoon milk

1      egg

1 1/3  cups all-purpose flour

3/4    teaspoon baking soda

1/2    teaspoon baking powder

1/4    teaspoon salt

*Frosting:*

1 1/2  cups peanut butter chips

■ For the peanut brittle, grease a large baking sheet. Combine the sugar, peanuts, corn syrup, and salt in a 3-quart saucepan. Cook, stirring, over medium-low heat until the temperature reaches 240 degrees on a candy thermometer. Add the shortening and vanilla; cook, stirring, until the temperature reaches 300 degrees. Remove from the heat. Stir in the baking soda. Spread 1/4 inch thick on the baking sheet; cool. Crush enough to measure 1 cup for use in the frosting; set aside.

■ For the cookies, preheat the oven to 375 degrees. Combine the shortening, granulated sugar, brown sugar, peanut butter, and milk in a large mixing bowl. Beat at medium speed of a mixer until blended. Beat in the egg. In a separate bowl combine the flour, baking soda, baking powder, and salt. Gradually add to the sugar mixture, beating at low speed. Shape the dough into 1 1/4-inch balls. Place 3 1/2 inches apart on an ungreased baking sheet. Flatten into 3-inch circles. Bake for 8 to 10 minutes or until brown. Cool 2 minutes on the baking sheet. Remove to a wire rack and cool completely.

■ For the frosting, melt the peanut butter chips in a double boiler over boiling water. Spread the melted chips over half of each cookie. Sprinkle with the reserved 1 cup crushed peanut brittle.

**MAKES ABOUT 24 COOKIES**

## Alabama Peanut Soup

1    cup finely chopped cooked ham

2    cups unsalted, blanched peanuts, chopped fine

1    cup finely chopped green onions (1/2 cup green onion stalks, 1/2 cup green onion tops)

1/2   cup (1 stick) butter

1    cup all-purpose flour

11/2  quarts chicken stock

1    quart beef stock

◼ Sauté the ham, peanuts, and green onion stalks in the butter in a large stockpot. Blend in the flour and cook for 4 minutes, stirring constantly to prevent sticking. Add the chicken and beef stocks and blend with a wire whisk. Cook for 15 minutes, stirring occasionally. Just before serving, add the green onion tops and simmer for 10 minutes.

**MAKES 8 SERVINGS**

## Peanut-Crusted Chicken

1    egg, lightly beaten

2    tablespoons milk

1/2   cup finely ground salted peanuts

1/2   cup cracker meal

2    tablespoons chopped fresh parsley
     Salt and pepper to taste

1    (2- to 3-pound) frying chicken, cut up
     Oil for frying

◼ Combine the egg and milk in a bowl. In a separate bowl combine the peanuts, cracker meal, parsley, and salt and pepper to taste. Dip the chicken pieces in the egg mixture, then dip each piece in the dry mixture. Heat oil in a heavy frying pan. Fry the chicken in the hot oil until each piece is golden brown and tender. Drain and serve hot.

**MAKES 6 SERVINGS**

---

**DID YOU KNOW?**
There are approximately 810 peanuts
in an 18-ounce jar of peanut butter.

# Terlingua International Chili Championship

**WHERE:** Terlingua, Texas
**WHEN:** First Saturday in November

What began in 1967 as an invitational cook-off between two cooks has now become a contest that draws tens of thousands of people to tiny Terlingua (population 700) to watch 300 to 350 of the world's best chili cooks—who compete all year long to obtain a coveted invitation to participate in this International Championship. In the 1990s CASI (Chili Appreciation Society International, Inc.) purchased 320 acres (1/2 square mile) about 4 miles west of the Terlingua ghost town, and the location for this Texas-sized event was standardized. Since then, presentation stages, a permanent judging area, souvenir/beer stands, and a city hall have been built on the property. And while this remains a hard-core cooking event, there's also lots of fun, including live music for all to enjoy.

For more information, please visit *www.krazyflats.com*.

## DID YOU KNOW?

In 1977, the Texas State Legislature introduced a bill designating chili as the official state dish.

# Lady Bug Chili

2 pounds coarse ground beef (chili grind)

1 (14½-ounce) can beef broth

1 (8-ounce) can no-salt tomato sauce

1 whole jalapeño chile

1 whole serrano chile

1 rounded tablespoon onion powder

2 teaspoons garlic powder

3 tablespoons Mexene chili powder, divided

2½ tablespoons light chili powder

2½ tablespoons dark chili powder

3 teaspoons cumin, divided

¼ teaspoon black pepper

¼ teaspoon white pepper

¼ teaspoon cayenne pepper

½ cube beef boullion

½ cube chicken boullion

¼ teaspoon brown sugar

1 (1.4-ounce) package Sazon Goya

½ teaspoon salt

■ In a 4-quart pot brown the ground beef; drain. Add the beef broth, tomato sauce, jalapeño chile, and serrano chile. Bring to a boil. Stir in the onion powder, garlic powder, and 1 tablespoon of the Mexene chili powder. Cover and simmer at a medium boil for 1 hour.

■ Remove the chiles. Squeeze the juice into a small bowl and set aside. Replace the lid and continue at a medium boil for an additional 15 minutes. Stir in the light chili powder, dark chili powder, 2 teaspoons of the cumin, the black pepper, white pepper, cayenne pepper, beef boullion, chicken boullion, brown sugar, and Sazon Goya. Continue to boil, covered, for 30 minutes. Add the reserved chile juice, the remaining 2 tablespoons Mexene chili powder, the remaining 1 teaspoon cumin, and the salt. Cover and simmer for additional 15 minutes. Serve hot.

**MAKES 8 SERVINGS**

# Cin-Chili Chili

2    pounds beef chuck tender, cut into 3/8-inch cubes

1    tablespoon cooking oil

2    tablespoons dark chili powder, divided

2    teaspoons granulated garlic

1    (8-ounce) can tomato sauce

1    (14 1/2-ounce) can beef broth

1    teaspoon chicken bouillon granules

1    teaspoon jalapeño powder

1    tablespoon plus 1 teaspoon onion powder, divided

3    teaspoons garlic powder, divided

1/2  teaspoon red pepper

1 1/2 teaspoons white pepper, divided

16   ounces spring water

2    whole serrano chiles

1/2  plus 1/8 teaspoon salt, divided

1    tablespoon paprika

1    package Sazon Goya or MSG

5    tablespoons medium chili powder

5    tablespoons dark chili powder

2    teaspoons cumin

■ In a 3-quart heavy saucepan combine the beef, oil, 1 tablespoon of the dark chili powder, and the granulated garlic and cook until the beef is browned. Stir in the tomato sauce, beef broth, chicken bouillon granules, jalapeño powder, 1 tablespoon of the onion powder, 2 teaspoons of the garlic powder, the red pepper, 1 teaspoon of the white pepper, the spring water, the remaining 1 tablespoon dark chili powder, the serrano chiles, and 1/2 teaspoon of the salt. Bring to a boil. Reduce the heat and simmer for 1 1/2 hours.

■ In a small bowl combine the paprika, Sazon Goya, the remaining 1 teaspoon onion powder, the remaining 1 teaspoon garlic powder, the remaining 1/2 teaspoon white pepper, and the medium and dark chili powders. Add to the beef mixture. Bring to a boil. Reduce the heat and simmer for 20 minutes. Add additional water or beef broth to create the desired consistency. Remove the serrano chiles when they become soft. Stir in the cumin and the remaining 1/8 teaspoon salt. Simmer for 10 minutes.

**MAKES 8 SERVINGS**

# Horseshoe Chili

. . . . . . . . . . . . . . . . . . . . . . . . . . . . .

2 1/2 pounds lean coarse ground beef or chuck tender, cut into 3/8-inch cubes

1 tablespoon cooking oil

1 teaspoon seasoning salt

1 (8-ounce) can tomato sauce

1 (14 1/2-ounce) can beef broth

6 tablespoons Mexene chili powder, divided

1 1/2 tablespoons onion granules

1 tablespoon paprika

3 1/2 teaspoons garlic granules, divided

1/2 teaspoon salt

1/4 teaspoon black pepper

1/4 teaspoon cayenne pepper

1 beef bouillon cube

1 chicken bouillon cube
    Spring water

3 teaspoons cumin

1/4 teaspoon dark brown sugar

1 package Sazon Goya or 1/2 teaspoon MSG (optional)

1 teaspoon "Original" Louisiana hot sauce

In a 4-quart heavy saucepan add the ground beef, oil, and seasoning salt and cook until the meat is browned. Add the tomato sauce and beef broth and bring to a boil. Reduce the heat and simmer for 30 minutes.

In a small bowl combine 1 tablespoon of the Mexene chili powder, the onion granules, paprika, 2 teaspoons of the garlic granules, the salt, black pepper, and cayenne pepper. Add to the pot. Add the beef and chicken boullion cubes. Continue to simmer for 1 hour. Add spring water if the chili is too thick.

In a small bowl combine the remaining 5 tablespoons Mexene chili powder, the remaining 1 1/2 teaspoons garlic granules, the cumin, brown sugar, Sazon Goya, if desired, and the hot sauce. Add to the pot and simmer for 30 minutes, adding spring water as needed to create desired consistency. Add salt to taste and extra dashes of the hot sauce for additional heat.

**MAKES 8 SERVINGS**

## Sahara Chili

2    pounds coarse ground beef (chili grind)

1    tablespoon cooking oil

1    tablespoon granulated onion

1    (8-ounce) can tomato sauce

1    (14½-ounce) can beef broth

2    tablespoons light chili powder, divided

3    tablespoons dark chili powder, divided

1    teaspoon garlic powder

½    teaspoon salt

3    teaspoons cumin, divided

½    teaspoon cayenne pepper

½    teaspoon black pepper

1    teaspoon chicken granules (or 1 cube chicken bouillon)

1    teaspoon paprika

■ In a large saucepan combine the ground beef, oil, and granulated onion. Cook until the meat is lightly browned. Add the tomato sauce and beef broth and cook for 30 minutes. Stir in 1 tablespoon of the light chili powder, 2 tablespoons of the dark chili powder, the garlic powder, salt, 1½ teaspoons of the cumin, the cayenne pepper, black pepper, and chicken granules. Cook for 1 hour. Stir in the remaining 1 tablespoon light chili powder, the remaining 1 tablespoon dark chili powder, the remaining 1½ teaspoons cumin, and the paprika. Add water if the chili is too thick. Cover and simmer for 30 minutes.

**MAKES 8 SERVINGS**

### DID YOU KNOW?
The use of beans in chili is most common in the South and Midwest.

# Giant Omelette Celebration

**WHERE:** Abbeville, Louisiana

**WHEN:** First full weekend in November (Saturday and Sunday)

How many eggs does it take to make a giant omelette? In historic Abbeville, that number would be 5,000. In addition to partaking of this mother of all omelettes, the 10,000 or more festivalgoers at the Giant Omelette Celebration can also enjoy live entertainment, a tour of homes, a kids' area, an antique implement show, an antique car show, a juried art show, the procession of chefs, and an egg-cracking competition.

For more information, please visit *www.giantomelette.org*.

## DID YOU KNOW?

Ancient Romans are credited with making the first omelettes. Because the dish was sweetened with honey, they called it an *ovemele*, which means "eggs and honey."

## Bacon, Brie, and Grape Omelette

3    eggs

Salt and pepper to taste

1    tablespoon unsalted butter

6    ounces softened Brie, rind removed and cut into pieces

3    slices bacon, crisp-cooked and crumbled

1/3   cup sliced green grapes

■ In a bowl beat the eggs lightly with salt and pepper to taste. In an 8-inch skillet heat the butter over medium-high heat until the foam subsides. Add the eggs and cook, stirring, for 10 seconds. Reduce the heat to medium and continue cooking the eggs until they are just set but still soft and moist. Scatter the Brie over the eggs and sprinkle the bacon and the grapes on top. Fold the omelette over and slide onto a plate.

**MAKES 2 SERVINGS**

## Hash Brown Omelette

3    ounces sharp Cheddar cheese

3    medium potatoes, peeled

1/2   medium onion

1/2   green bell pepper

5    slices bacon

4    eggs

1/4   cup milk

1/3   teaspoon salt

1/3   teaspoon pepper

■ Shred the cheese and set aside. Shred the potatoes, onion, and green pepper and combine in a bowl. In a large skillet fry the bacon until crisp. Crumble the bacon, reserving the drippings. Fry the shredded potatoes, onion, and green pepper in the reserved drippings. Do not stir or turn until the potatoes are crisp on the bottom. Combine the eggs, milk, salt, and pepper in a bowl and mix well. When the potatoes are crisp on both sides, pour the egg mixture over the potatoes. Top with the shredded cheese and crumbled bacon. Remove from the skillet and cut into 6 wedges.

**MAKES 6 SERVINGS**

# Shrimp Omelette

| | |
|---|---|
| 3 | tablespoons butter or cooking oil |
| 2 | garlic cloves, crushed |
| 1 | onion, chopped |
| 2 | ripe tomatoes, chopped |
| 1/4 | pound shrimp, deveined |
| 1/3 | teaspoon salt |
| 1/4 | teaspoon black pepper |
| 4 | eggs |

■ Melt the butter in a large skillet. Sauté the garlic and onion in the butter. Add the tomatoes. Stir in the shrimp and season with salt and pepper. Divide into two portions and set aside.

■ Beat the eggs until fluffy. Pour half the beaten eggs into a greased, heated skillet. Spoon one portion of the shrimp filling over half the omelette and fold. Turn and cook until golden brown on both sides. Remove to a plate and keep warm. Repeat with the remaining half of the eggs and the shrimp filling.

**MAKES 2 SERVINGS**

## DID YOU KNOW?

The Guinness World Record for omelette making is 427 omelettes in 30 minutes.

# Georgia Pecan Festival

**WHERE:** Americus, Georgia
**WHEN:** First Saturday in November

The Georgia Pecan Festival is hosted by the Americus-Sumter County Chamber of Commerce. Among its events are a town parade, musical entertainment, a 5K race, a street dance, arts and crafts, and of course, tons of foods featuring pecans. While in town, be sure to ride the historic Sumter Metric Century train through nearby Plains, home of former president Jimmy Carter. You'll pass by historic Andersonville, home of the United States' POW Memorial. Finish up in Americus while touring past historic Victorian homes, as well as the international headquarters of Habitat for Humanity.

For more information, please visit
*www.americus-sumterchamber.com.*

## DID YOU KNOW?

The pecan is the only major tree nut that grows naturally in North America.

# White Chocolate Pecan Pie

| | |
|---|---|
| 1 | (9-inch) deep-dish piecrust |
| 1/4 | cup (1/2 stick) butter, melted |
| 1/2 | cup sugar |
| 1/2 | cup light corn syrup |
| 3/4 | cup pecans, toasted and chopped |
| 1 | teaspoon vanilla extract |
| 1/4 | teaspoon salt |
| 2 | large eggs, lightly beaten |
| 6 | (1-ounce) premium white chocolate baking squares, chopped and divided |
| 1 | cup pecan halves, toasted |

■ Preheat the oven to 450 degrees. Bake the piecrust for 5 minutes.

■ Reduce the oven temperature to 325 degrees. Combine the butter, sugar, and corn syrup in a saucepan. Cook over low heat, stirring constantly, until the sugar dissolves. Let cool slightly. Add the pecans, vanilla, salt, and eggs. Stir well. Pour the filling into the piecrust. Sprinkle with two-thirds of the white chocolate. Top with the pecan halves. Bake for 50 to 55 minutes or until set. Cover with aluminum foil during the last 10 minutes of baking to prevent excess browning. Let cool on a wire rack.

■ Place the remaining white chocolate in a small heavy-duty zip-top plastic bag; seal the bag. Submerge the bag in hot water until the chocolate melts. Remove the bag from the water. Snip a tiny hole in one corner of the bag; drizzle the white chocolate over the pie.

**MAKES 8 SERVINGS**

# Roasted Pepper Pecans

| | |
|---|---|
| 1 | pound Georgia pecan halves |
| 1 | egg white |
| 1 | tablespoon hot pepper sauce |
| 1 | teaspoon Worcestershire sauce |
| 1 | tablespoon light brown sugar |
| 1/2 | teaspoon coarse salt, or more to taste |

■ Preheat the oven to 300 degrees. In a medium bowl combine the pecan halves with the egg white and stir to coat the pecans. In a small bowl combine the hot pepper sauce, Worcestershire sauce, and brown sugar. Stir well to dissolve the sugar. Spoon over the pecans and stir to combine. Sprinkle with the salt and toss to coat the pecans well. Spread the pecans onto two baking sheets and place in the oven. Bake for about 20 minutes, or until crisp. When cool, store the pecans in airtight tins or plastic bags.

**MAKES 8 SERVINGS**

## Ultimate Chocolate Cookies with Georgia Pecans

| | |
|---|---|
| 2 | ounces unsweetened chocolate |
| 6 | ounces bittersweet chocolate |
| 1/4 | cup plus 2 tablespoons all-purpose flour |
| 1/4 | teaspoon baking powder |
| 1/4 | teaspoon salt |
| 6 | tablespoons (3/4 stick) unsalted butter, at room temperature |
| 3/4 | cup sugar |
| 2 | large eggs |
| 2 | teaspoons vanilla extract |
| 1 | cup semisweet chocolate chips |
| 1 1/2 | cups toasted pecans, coarsely chopped |

■ Preheat the oven to 350 degrees. Place the unsweetened and bittersweet chocolate in a medium heatproof bowl. Place over a pot of simmering water and melt completely. Sift together the flour, baking powder, and salt and set aside.

■ In a mixing bowl cream the butter and sugar using an electric mixer. Add the eggs, then the vanilla and beat on high speed for 2 minutes. Beat in the melted chocolate on low speed until just combined. Fold in the flour mixture with a rubber spatula until just combined. Stir in the chocolate chips and pecans. Using a tablespoon or small ice cream scoop, drop the dough onto a parchment-lined baking sheet, placing 8 cookies on each sheet. Bake for 10 to 11 minutes. Cool on the baking sheets. These ultra-chocolaty cookies are best the day they are made. Leftovers can be wrapped in plastic and stored in an airtight container.

**MAKES 2 TO 3 DOZEN COOKIES**

## Sweet Potato and Georgia Pecan Pone

| | |
|---|---|
| 5 | tablespoons butter, softened and divided |
| 1/3 | cup firmly packed brown sugar |
| 2 | large eggs, at room temperature |
| 1/2 | cup freshly squeezed orange juice |
| 1/2 | teaspoon finely grated orange zest |
| 1 | tablespoon all-purpose flour |
| 3/4 | teaspoon salt |
| 1/2 | teaspoon ground cinnamon |
| 1/2 | teaspoon ground ginger |
| 2 | pounds sweet potatoes, peeled |
| 1 1/4 | cups Georgia pecan halves |
| 1 | tablespoon light corn syrup |

■ Preheat the oven to 350 degrees. In a large bowl with an electric mixer, beat 3 tablespoons of the butter and the brown sugar until light and well blended. Add the eggs and beat until fluffy. Beat in the orange juice and orange zest. Combine the flour, salt, cinnamon, and ginger and stir into the mixture until blended.

■ Coarsely grate the sweet potatoes in a food processor or by hand. Stir into the egg and orange mixture. Melt the remaining 2 tablespoons butter in a 10-inch ovenproof skillet or cast-iron skillet over medium-high heat. Coat the bottom and sides of the skillet with the butter. Spread the sweet potato mixture in the skillet and increase the heat to high, cooking just until the first steam escapes from the middle of the mixture. In a small bowl combine the pecans and corn syrup and coat evenly. Spread the pecans in a single layer on top of the sweet potatoes. Bake on the middle rack of the oven for 40 to 45 minutes or until the center is firm. Cool for at least 15 minutes before serving.

**MAKES 10 SERVINGS**

## Southern-Style Chocolate Pecan Pie

| | |
|---|---|
| 3 | eggs |
| 1 | cup dark corn syrup |
| 3/4 | cup sugar |
| 1/4 | cup (1/2 stick) butter or margarine, melted and cooled |
| 1 1/2 | tablespoons bourbon |
| 1 | cup semisweet chocolate chips |
| 1 | cup coarsely chopped pecans |
| 1 | (9-inch) piecrust, unbaked |

■ Preheat the oven to 350 degrees. Place the eggs in a medium mixing bowl and whisk lightly. Add the corn syrup, sugar, and melted butter. Stir with a wooden spoon to combine well. Stir in the bourbon, chocolate chips, and pecans. Pour the filling into the piecrust. Bake for 45 to 55 minutes, or until a toothpick inserted in the center comes out clean. Cool on a wire rack.

**MAKES 8 SERVINGS**

## Pecan and Cornbread–Crusted Pork Loin

. . . . . . . . . . . . . . . . . . . . . . . . . . . .

3/4   cup pecan halves

2     corn toaster cakes, broken into quarters (or 1¼ cups crumbled cornbread or corn muffins)

2     tablespoons butter

1     tablespoon finely chopped garlic

2     (1-pound) pork tenderloins
      Salt and pepper to taste

3     tablespoons Dijon mustard

◼ Preheat the oven to 400 degrees. In a food processor, combine the pecans and cornbread and process until the pecans are finely chopped. Set aside.

◼ Melt the butter in a medium skillet over moderate heat. Add the garlic and cook until fragrant, about 1 minute. Stir in the pecan mixture to blend with the butter and garlic. Set aside to cool slightly.

◼ Pat the pork dry. Sprinkle with salt and pepper. Place in an oiled shallow baking pan. Spread the mustard thickly over the tenderloins and pat the crumb mixture onto the mustard. Roast the pork in the middle of the oven for 15 minutes. Remove the pork from the oven and tent loosely with foil to prevent the crust from burning. Continue to roast until a thermometer inserted diagonally into the center of the meat registers 158 degrees, about 15 minutes longer. Let the meat stand 10 minutes before slicing.

**MAKES 4 SERVINGS**

### DID YOU KNOW?
*Pecan* is an Algonquian word meaning "a tough nut to crack."

# Georgia Pecan-Crusted French Toast

3   tablespoons butter, divided

3   large eggs, at room temperature

1   cup warm milk

1   teaspoon vanilla extract

1/2   teaspoon ground cinnamon

1/4   teaspoon nutmeg

1/4   teaspoon salt

3/4   cup pecan halves, finely chopped and divided

8   slices challah bread or other dense bread, sliced about 3/4 inch thick

Maple syrup for serving

In a large skillet melt 1 tablespoon of the butter over medium heat. In a bowl beat the eggs, milk, vanilla, cinnamon, nutmeg, and salt until well blended. Sprinkle a heaping tablespoon of the pecans onto a small plate. Dip one slice of bread in the egg mixture to coat both sides, then press one side into the pecans. Repeat with another slice of bread. Cook the slices in the melted butter, pecan-side-down, for about 5 minutes or until lightly browned. Turn and brown the other side. Transfer to a platter. Cover and keep warm in a low oven. Repeat with the remaining bread slices, adding more butter to the skillet as necessary. Serve with maple syrup.

**MAKES 4 SERVINGS**

# Cracklin' Festival

**WHERE:** Port Barre, Louisiana

**WHEN:** Second weekend in November (Thursday through Sunday)

Proof that Southerners don't like to waste food can be found at Port Barre's Cracklin' Festival. Cracklins, that Southern delicacy, draw more than 25,000 people each year—along with the chance to see the Cracklin' Queen beauty pageant, of course. Other highlights of this festival are the parade, arts and crafts, live music, the carnival, and the cracklin' cooking competition.

For more information, please visit
*www.portbarrecracklinfestival.com.*

## DID YOU KNOW?

A cracklin' is a fried piece of pork fat with a small amount of attached skin.

## Cracklins

2    pounds pork skin with fat
     Oil
     Salt and pepper to taste

■ Cut the pork skins and fat into 2-inch squares keeping the pork meat on each square. Place the pork squares in a hot cast-iron pot. Do not overcrowd the pan. Add about 4 inches of oil, making sure all of the pieces are covered with the oil. Cook over high heat until the cracklins (pork squares) are browned and float to the top. Stir constantly to keep the cracklins from sticking and burning. Remove from the grease and drain on paper towels. Sprinkle with salt and pepper while hot. Store in an airtight container.

**MAKES 12 SERVINGS**

## Cracklin' Bread

2     cups cornmeal
1/2   cup all-purpose flour
1/2   teaspoon baking powder
2     tablespoons sugar
2/3   teaspoon salt
1     teaspoon baking soda
2     cups buttermilk
1     egg, beaten
2     cups cracklins

■ Preheat the oven to 400 to 425 degrees. Sift together the cornmeal, flour, baking powder, sugar, salt, and baking soda in a large bowl. Add the buttermilk and egg. Mix well. Stir in the cracklins. Pour the mixture into a greased hot iron skillet and bake for about 30 minutes or until browned.

**MAKES 12 SERVINGS**

---

**DID YOU KNOW?**
Cracklins contain no carbohydrates.

# Vardaman Sweet Potato Festival

**WHERE:** Vardaman, Mississippi

**WHEN:** First Saturday of November through the second Saturday of November (8-day festival)

Since the mid-1970s, people have flocked to Vardaman to celebrate the sweet potato. In addition to the Sweet Potato King and Queen contests for all ages, you can enjoy the recipe contests, a 5K run, a sweet potato pie–eating contest, a sweet potato creatures contest, and an arts and crafts festival. It all winds down on the final night to the Sweet Potato Festival Banquet, featuring musical entertainment, the auctioning of the sweet potato quilt, and awards for the best washed and graded bushel of sweet potatoes.

For more information, please visit
*www.vardamansweetpotatofestival.com.*

## DID YOU KNOW?

Sweet potatoes were the main source of nourishment for Revolutionary War soldiers and early homesteaders.

## Southern Sweet Potato Casserole

*Pecan Sauce:*

1    cup firmly packed brown sugar

1/4   cup light cream

2    tablespoons butter

*Filling:*

2    large sweet potatoes, baked

2    tablespoons butter

1/3   teaspoon salt

6    tablespoons light cream

1    cup pecan halves

■ For the pecan sauce, combine the brown sugar, cream, and butter in a saucepan. Bring to a boil and boil for 2 to 3 minutes. Set aside.

■ For the filling, preheat the oven to 350 degrees. Remove the sweet potato flesh from the skins while still warm and place in a mixing bowl. Season with the butter and salt. Whip the sweet potatoes with an electric mixer while gradually adding enough cream to make a light, fluffy mixture. Spread into a greased 9-inch pie plate. Arrange the pecan halves on top of the sweet potatoes. Top with the pecan sauce. Bake for 20 to 30 minutes or until hot and bubbly.

**MAKES 8 TO 10 SERVINGS**

## Sweet Potato Biscuits

1 1/4  cups all-purpose flour

1    tablespoon baking powder

2    teaspoons brown sugar

1/2   teaspoon salt

1/3   cup vegetable shortening

1    egg

1/2   cup mashed, cooked sweet potatoes

2    tablespoons milk

■ Preheat the oven to 425 degrees. In a large bowl combine the flour, baking powder, brown sugar, salt, shortening, egg, mashed sweet potatoes, and milk. Roll the dough to 1/2-inch thickness. Cut with a round biscuit cutter and place on a baking sheet. Bake for 10 to 12 minutes.

**MAKES 8 BISCUITS**

## Sweet Potato Pie

| | |
|---|---|
| 1/3 | cup butter, softened |
| 1/2 | cup sugar |
| 2 | eggs, beaten |
| 2 | cups cooked, mashed sweet potatoes |
| 3/4 | cup evaporated milk |
| 1 | teaspoon vanilla extract |
| 1/3 | teaspoon salt |
| 1/2 | teaspoon ground cinnamon |
| 1/3 | teaspoon nutmeg |
| 1 | (9-inch) piecrust, unbaked |

■ Preheat the oven to 375 degrees. Cream the butter and sugar together in a mixing bowl. Add the eggs and stir. Add the sweet potatoes and mix well. Stir in the evaporated milk, vanilla, salt, cinnamon, and nutmeg and mix thoroughly. Pour into the piecrust and bake for 40 minutes.

**MAKES 8 SERVINGS**

## Southern Sweet Potato Pone

| | |
|---|---|
| 2 | eggs |
| 1 | cup sugar |
| 1/4 | to 1/2 cup butter, softened |
| 4 | cups grated sweet potatoes |
| 2 | cups scalded milk |
| 1/4 | teaspoon nutmeg, or to taste |
| 1/8 | teaspoon salt |

■ Preheat the oven to 350 degrees. Beat the eggs in a mixing bowl. Add the sugar, butter, sweet potatoes, milk, nutmeg, and salt. Pour into a greased 9-inch baking dish and cook for about 1 hour.

**MAKES 6 SERVINGS**

> ### DID YOU KNOW?
> Sweet potatoes were discovered by Christopher Columbus and his shipmates.

# Chitlin' Strut

First things first. The proper spelling is "chitterlings." And yes, they are pig intestines. But when you're cooking up more than five tons of them for more than 25,000 people in one day, you can call them what you like. In addition to helping you eat like a pig if you want to, the Chitlin' Festival offers visitors the chance to witness one of the South's best "hawg"-calling contests. Other highlights include carnival rides, an antique tractor show, musical entertainment, arts and crafts, and the famous strut contest—so get to gyrating and strut your way to Salley.

For more information, please visit *www.chitlinstrut.com*.

### DID YOU KNOW?
A chitlin' is over three yards long.

# Fried Chitlins

*Chitlins:*

1    (10-pound) frozen bucket chitlins, thawed

1/4  cup salt

1/4  cup crushed red pepper flakes

*Batter:*

2    cups all-purpose flour

1    tablespoon baking powder

1 1/2 tablespoons oil

1    teaspoon salt

1    cup milk

2    eggs, beaten

     Oil for frying

■ For the chitlins, wash the chitlins. Remove the fat and place in a pressure cooker. Fill with enough water to cover. Add the salt and red pepper flakes. Place the lid on the pressure cooker and cook at high pressure, according to the manufacturer's instructions, for 40 minutes. You may also place the chitlins in a large stockpot covered with water and cook for about 5 hours. Check for tenderness by slicing a chitlin with a knife. If the chitlin cuts easily remove from the heat. Cool and drain well. Cut into 5-inch pieces.

■ For the batter, combine the flour, baking powder, oil, salt, milk, and eggs in a mixing bowl. Place the pieces of chitlin in the batter, a few at a time, coating well. Heat oil in a deep skillet to 375 degrees. Deep-fry the chitlins until golden brown.

**MAKES 8 SERVINGS**

# Boiled Chitlins

10   pounds chitlins

6    cups water

1/2  cup vinegar

1    onion, chopped

1    green bell pepper, chopped

     Salt and pepper to taste

■ Wash and clean the linings of the chitlins thoroughly; repeat several times. Place the chitlins in an 8- to 10-quart pot with the water. Add the vinegar, onion, green pepper, and salt and pepper to taste. Bring to a boil over medium heat and cook for about 4 hours, adding water as necessary.

**MAKES 8 SERVINGS**

# White Beans

*This bean dish is traditionally served at Southern chitlin' suppers.*

1 pound dried white beans, picked over and rinsed

5 cups cold water

1/4 teaspoon salt

1/4 teaspoon black pepper

1 medium onion, finely chopped

2 slices smoked bacon

■ In a large stockpot cover the beans with the water and let soak overnight. Drain well in a colander.

■ Return the beans to the stockpot and add enough water to cover. Add the salt, pepper, onion, and bacon to the beans and bring to a boil. Reduce the heat to a simmer and cook for 1 1/2 to 2 hours, until the beans are tender and the liquid thickens.

**MAKES 8 SERVINGS**

# Country Fried Potatoes

*Fried potatoes often appear as an accompaniment to chitlins.*

2 tablespoons butter

2 tablespoons vegetable shortening

4 large potatoes, peeled and chopped

1/3 teaspoon salt

1/3 teaspoon pepper

■ Melt the butter and shortening in a large pan over low heat. Add the potatoes, salt, and pepper. Cook over medium-low heat until a bottom crust forms and is brown. Turn once and cook until brown. Serve hot.

**MAKES 8 SERVINGS**

## DID YOU KNOW?
Chitlins are sometimes used as sausage casings.

# Recipe Credits

*Thank you to the following people and organizations for sharing their recipes for this book:*

## Chocolate Lovers Festival

Triple Chocolate Pound Cake, Susan Pufnock

Toffee Bars, Donna Maddox

Brownie Pudding, Charlotte Axiotis

Chocolate Almond Bark, Patsy Maddox

White Chocolate Party Mix, Joyce Garten

Cookie Brittle, Janice Stenger

## Delray Beach Garlic Festival

Potato-Crusted Diver Sea Scallops, Chef John Hutchinson, J&J Seafood Bar and Grill, Delray Beach, FL

Poached Halibut with Snow Peas, MY 1 Chef, Chef Adam C. Duimstra, Delray Beach, FL

Roasted Duck with Garlic, Oranges, and Grand Marnier, Cugini Grille, Chef Sean Cullinan & Sous Chef James Maugeri, Delray Beach, FL

Applewood-Smoked Bacon and Garlic-Wrapped Jumbo Shrimp, Shore Restaurant & Beach Bar, Executive Chef, Jeff Terentieff, Delray Beach, FL

## Big Squeeze Juice Festival

Claire's Orange Lime Cake, Claire Charles

Orange Squeeze Cake, Janet Whitson

## World Catfish Festival

All recipes courtesy of The Catfish Institute

## Alma Spinach Festival

Spinach Festival Courtesy of the Alma Area Chamber of Commerce

## The Great American Pie Festival

Recipes courtesy of APC Crisco National Pie Championships

Strawberry Cream Delight, Carol Socier

Appealing Apple Caramel Pie, Karen Panosian

Classic Cherry Cherry Bang Bang Pie, Sandy Young

Jammin' Banana Cream Pie, Phyllis Szymanek

### The Ramp Festival

Recipes courtesy of *Follow Your Nose*, the Ramp Festival Cookbook

### North Carolina Pickle Festival

Recipes courtesy of Mt. Olive Pickle Company

### National Cornbread Festival

Special thanks to Linda Carman and Dana Reece

Caribbean Cornbread Crab Cakes, Lanie Smith, Topeka, KS

Chicken Taco Cornbread Wedges with Ranchero Cilantro Drizzle, Jenny Flake, Gilbert, AZ

Monte Cristo Cornbread Skillet Supper, Janice Elder, Charlotte, NC

Alabama Country Supper, Rosemary Johnson, Irondale, AL

Festive Good Luck Cornbread Skillet, Karen Shankles, Knoxville, TN

Sausage Gravy Breakfast Skillet, Ashley Brock, New Albany, OH

Cornbread Supreme, Kay Gay and Helen Hollansworth, Gulf Shores, AL

Pesto Cornbread with Chicken and Sun-Dried Tomato Streusel, Leah Lyon, Ada, OK

White Chicken Chili with Cheddar Hushpuppy Crust, Gaynell Lawson, Maryville, TN

Coastal Carolina Skillet Supper, Victoria McCord, Nashville, TN

### Vidalia Onion Festival

Vidalia and Sausage Casserole, Lori Burkett & Ron O'Neal

Vidalia Casserole in a Jiffy, Annie R. Higgins

Vidalia Brie Surprise, Jan Williams

Vidalia Onion Shrimp Pasta, Sabrina Toole

Sweet Vidalia Pie, Sabrina Toole

### West Tennessee Strawberry Festival

Special thanks to Debbie Brasfield and the Humboldt Chamber of Commerce

Strawberry Crunch, Linda Ziegler

Sassy Berry Salsa, Jennifer Wilson

Strawberry Paradise Surprise, Melissa Swingler

Strawberry Cookies, Janice Shelton

Springtime Strawberry Spinach Salad, Jane Moore

Strawberry Cheese Ball, Ashley Shelton

Strawberry Bread, Sherry Jo Smith

Strawberry Gooey Butter Cookies, Ginger Thomas

Strawberry Jam-N-Cheese Cake, Mary
Mathews

## Poke Salat Festival

Poke and Ham Hot Pocket, Mildred Faulkner
(Granny Nell)

## Ham and Yam Festival

Sweet Potato Hushpuppies, Joyce Lawhorn

Double Praline Raisin and Coconut Yam
Casserole, Sondra Bass

Ham and Swiss Pie, Kathryn Jackson

Yam Blueberry Cream Cheese Pudding Bread,
Donna Barefoot

## Bradley County Pink Tomato Festival

All recipes from *The Bradley County Pink
Tomato Festival 50th Anniversary Cookbook*

Green Tomato Pie, Libby Lyon Stracner

Heavenly Tomato Cake, Jean Frisby

Marinated Carrots, Robin Lipton Lockhart

Cornbread Salad, Brenda Johnson

Open-Faced Tomato Sandwiches, JeNelle
Lipton

Bradley County Caviar, Joel Tolefree

## Louisiana Corn Festival

Pan-Fried Catfish with Crab and Corn
Topping, Beth Douzart, Patricia Newton,
Jenny Lacombe, Denise Hamilton

## RC and Moon Pie Festival

Deep-Fried Moon Pies, Patsy Caldwell

Moon Pie Bread Pudding, Courtesy of Will
Hughes Catering and Market

## Alabama Blueberry Festival

Blueberry Cobbler, Linda Beasley

Blueberry Yum Yum, Sammie Jamieson

Blueberry Pie, Peggy Miller

## Miss Martha's Ice Cream Crankin' Festival

Special thanks to Alison Harris

## Berea Spoonbread Festival

Recipes courtesy of the *Berea Spoon Bread
Festival Spoon Bread Cookbook*, by Sidney
Saylor Farr

## The Houston Hot Sauce Festival

Kick Butt Cornbread, Nancy Howard

### Southern Fried Festival

Southern-Fried Banana Wonton Wrappers, Edie Sutter

### World Chicken Festival

Almond Crunch Chicken Salad, JoAnn Smith

Bridget's Melt-in-Your-Mouth Graham Cracker Chicken, Bridget Surgener

Sunday Chicken Casserole, Penny Robinson

Ethel's Famous Chicken and Dumplings, Ethel Saylor

### North Carolina Muscadine Harvest Festival

Magnolia Grilled Chicken Breasts, Linda Nichols

Muscadine Trifle, Nancy Wilson

Muscadine Muffins, Nancy Wilson

### Unicoi County Apple Festival

Special thanks to Jennifer Helner and the Unicoi Chamber of Commerce

Colossal Caramel Apple Trifle, Genevieve Shelton

Golden Delicious Apple Pie, Genevieve Shelton

Apple Cake Supreme, Betty Jo Day

### Spring Hill Country Ham Festival

Special thanks to Alison Harris

### Apple Butter Festival

Recipes courtesy of The West Virginia University Community Educational Outreach Service of Morgan County (CEOS)

Apple-Cranberry Chocolate Cups, Tama Hiles

Harvest Pumpkin Apple Bread, Tama Hiles

### West Virginia Black Walnut Festival

Black Walnut Pie, Mrs. Verna Ash

Black Walnut Cocoa Fudge, Mrs. Richard G. Lynch

Black Walnut Chipped Cookies, Mrs. Daisy Jones

### North Carolina Oyster Festival

Recipes courtesy of *Saltwater Sensations: The Official Cookbook of the North Carolina Oyster Festival*

Oysters Rockefeller Casserole, Daphne Yarbrough-Jones

Oyster Dressing, Tori Humphrey

Clint's "Oysterpuppies," Clint Humphrey

Gammie's Oyster Pie, Martha F. Benton, Lockwood Folly Realty

## Jack Daniel's Bar-B-Q Festival

Special thanks to Ms. Virginia Bracey and the Lynchburg–Moore County Chamber of Commerce

## Terlingua International Chili Championship

Lady Bug Chili, Dana Plocheck

Cin-Chili Chili, Cindy Reed

Horseshoe Chili, Honey Jones

Sahara Chili, Margaret Nadeau

## Georgia Pecan Festival

Recipes courtesy of the Georgia Pecan Commission

## Chitlin' Strut

Fried Chitlins, Patsy Caldwell

# Index of Cities

# Index of Recipes